THE GREAT NORTHWEST

Preceding pages: At Bandon Beach, Oregon, sea meets shore in a scene of primeval power and beauty.

These pages: In the desert east of Mount Hood, the mighty Columbia rolls quietly between banks of lava.

Following pages: Mount St. Helens, a volcanic cone of noble symmetry, is considered one of the Northwest's most spectacular mountains.

THE GREAT NORTHWEST

The Story of a Land and Its People

By
The Editors of
American West

The Great West Series

AMERICAN WEST PUBLISHING COMPANY

PALO ALTO · CALIFORNIA

Crater Lake—blue jewel of the Cascade Range.

Members of the American West editorial staff
responsible for the creation of this book:

Staff Writers

Bette Roda Anderson   Michael Ames   Donald G. Pike

Editors

Donald E. Bower   Patricia Kollings

Murray Morgan, author and historian, served as special consultant.

Library of Congress Card Number 72-90946   ISBN O-910118-32-9

CONTENTS

FOREWORD

F ROM TIME TO TIME the rectangular cloud that fits lid-like between the Pacific
seaboard and the crest of the Cascade mountains slips away. Then passengers on
the jets descending toward Seattle-Tacoma International Airport may, with one
long look through their plexiglass peerholes, scan the least-known corner of the
continental United States.

To the east, on the enormous sweep of lava plain scoured by ice and rutted by
meltflow, the predominant browns are patterned by the pastels of irrigation.
Directly below, the Cascades poke their jagged edges through the mantle of forest, a
reminder that less than a century ago the crossing of the mountains took not only
time but lives. Spaced along the upthrust ridge, dominating the landscape even
when looked down upon, are the sentinel cones of Baker, Glacier, Rainier, Adams,
St. Helens, and Hood, their serene snowfields giving no hint of the banked fire
within. The forest on the east is a narrow band of fir fading into pine; that to the
west, a spread of fir, cedar, and hemlock spanning a hundred miles to the ocean.

The pattern is simple: a fire-formed plateau to the east, to the west an evergreen
slope, mountains between. But within this simplicity one finds infinite variation
and many surprises.

The sand dunes of the central Oregon Coast are not duplicated elsewhere in the
Northwest; the likes of the cool rain forest of the Hoh on the Olympic Peninsula
cannot be found elsewhere in the world. In the heart of a region notorious for soggi-
ness, the sunburned San Juan Islands have a beauty and aridity almost Aegean.

The land beyond the mountains has a reputation for dryness. A British secret
agent once wrote it off as almost impossible to cross and impossible to redeem, "an
uninterrupted range of desert on which even the wild animals cannot exist." A
century later an American engineer gave similar testimony, "a dead land, bitter
with alkali," a region so hell-like that "even snakes and lizards shun it." Yet engineers and agriculturists have turned it into one of the world's most productive
farm areas.

The story of the Pacific Northwest is largely the history of men's responses to the special challenges—and opportunities—imposed by the lay of the land. The special merit of this book is the emphasis the writers and editors place on the way geology and geography have shaped the area's history and continue to influence its economics and the attitudes of its people. Both illustrations and text indicate the sweep of land and sea, the sense of men and communities as tiny organisms in a vast landscape, the isolation imposed by the mountains and the ocean: beyond all, the remoteness.

Distance shielded northwest America from discovery by Europeans. Two and a half centuries passed between the time when the Spanish reached the west coast of Mexico and the time when they set foot on land north of California. The area lay, meanwhile, on the fringes of European consciousness. Jonathan Swift in *Gulliver's Travels* made it the land of Brobdingnag, a country where everything was on an enormous scale, with natives as tall as a steeple. It became the scene of Juan de Fuca's alleged voyage among Indians rich in gold, silver, and pearls. Its imaginary geography was coursed with the River of the Kings, the River of the West, the Mighty Oregon, to say nothing of the Northwest Passage and the Strait of Anían, all leading to power and wealth.

Even after the emerging technology of the eighteenth century—especially James Lind's discovery of a cure for scurvy and John Harrison's invention of a device for determining longitude at sea—made it possible for mariners to set off for the Pacific Northwest with a better than even chance of getting there, the region remained a place apart, a land "somewhere across the wide Missouri" which appealed to the exceptionally adventurous or ambitious or cantankerous, a lure those attracted could not quite explain.

They came because it was far away. After they arrived, by sail around the Horn, by canoe and horse, or by foot across the plains and mountains, they knew in their bones the distance separating them from the familiar.

Freshness and isolation, the chance to shape a way of life in a land untainted by custom and institution, was much of the area's attraction. But it could be punishment, too. As the white population grew, so did the longing for the familiar. Much of this book deals with the paradoxical struggle of people who had fled the established world to re-establish communication with what they had left behind. They sought rivers that could be run in canoes, passes that could be crossed by wagons, routes and financing for railroads and steamship lines, lanes for telegraph wires and cables. They sought an end to the remoteness their fathers had quested.

The land has been populated, the natural world altered, the distances conquered. Boeing has salesmen in China; Inland Empire farmers subsidize dietitians who show Asians ways to substitute Northwest wheat for rice; Weyerhaeuser has branch offices in Ireland and Indo-China. The land of Brobdingnag has become part of a smaller world. Yet, as the editors show, there remains in the Pacific Northwest a sense of apartness, of special destiny, of northwest America as the place where a man still has opportunity, however remote, however unused, to establish harmony with a beautiful world.

—MURRAY MORGAN

INTRODUCTION

IN THE FAR NORTHWEST CORNER of the United States is a land of uncommon diversity, offering in microcosm a variety of topography, climate, and vegetation nearly as wide-ranging as terra firma can muster. The Pacific Northwest boasts rugged coastline constantly changing under the chisels of wind and water; high mountains complete with live glaciers, and volcanoes that tremble at the edge of activity; broad valleys, deserts, and plateaus—all of which combine to foil easy generalities about the region or its people.

Twenty-five million years ago, when the Cascade Range made its final upward push, the Northwest was divided into east and west. Although successive waves of ice would finally sculpt the peaks and lowlands, and rivers would cut their gorges and valleys, these mountains imparted to the land a schizophrenia of climate and vegetation that persists today and defies treatment of the Northwest as a single region. To the west, receiving moist clouds from the Pacific, are the rain forests of the Olympic Peninsula, the broad and lush valleys of the Puget-Willamette lowlands, and vast forests of the nation's finest virgin timber. To the east, in the rain-shadow of the Cascades, are deserts sustaining little more than sagebrush and jackrabbits, semi-arid plateau lands and meager rivers that disappear into sandy basins. Farther east, the tangled tail of another range, the Northern Rockies, reaches down to further complicate any sense of geographic unity.

The earliest peoples of the Northwest, the Indians, responded to this diversity of the land by developing entirely different cultures: along the coast, amidst plenty, there evolved complicated and stratified societies that traded and gathered excess wealth from shore and sea; inland, where scarcity ruled, wandering bands of hunters and gatherers scraped marginal sustenance from the land. For the Indians of the Northwest, there was no regional unity, no commonality of interests.

Such might have been the case for the white man, too, were it not for the mighty river systems of the Columbia and the Snake, which cut across the entire Northwest tying the region together. Gathering their waters high in the mountains to the east and north, these rivers range across vast stretches of the interior before joining forces for the powerful assault through the Cascades to the sea. Like the winds that whistle east and west through the river gorges trying to equalize the barometric pressure on both sides of the Cascades, man moved back and forth through the river's gateway to bind the inhabitants of the Northwest into a balanced community of commerce. This commerce, fostered by a dearth of easy overland transportation to the eastern United States until late in the nineteenth century, built bonds of habit and interest between the coastal and inland inhabitants—bonds that still unify the Northwest today.

Because of its striking variety of geography and climate, the Northwest frontier offered almost endless opportunities for man to flex his imagination and skills in pursuit of a livelihood—and with the passage of time he would try just about everything. By the end of the eighteenth century, English and American ships were prowling the waters off the Northwest coast in search of furs, and shortly thereafter they moved the operation inland in pursuit of beaver. Later the abundant fishes of the ocean and rivers were caught, processed, and sold with an efficiency that nearly destroyed the industry. Mining excitements brought successive waves of sourdoughs and industrialized mining companies to Idaho, Oregon, and Washington—trailing merchants and overnight towns behind them. Timber, cut first from the accessible coastal forests and later from the high mountains, drew hundreds of hopeful timber barons and mill magnates, and thousands of working stiffs to cut, haul, and mill the lumber. Railroads provided another prospect to thousands, despite the twin obstacles of high capital investment and often non-existant returns. The grazing of cattle and sheep was pursued until Northwest herds surpassed the cattle kingdoms of Wyoming and Montana in numbers. Irrigation in the deserts and plateaus of the Inland Empire brought expectant entrepreneurs and the pioneering skills of thousands to the often marginal lands of the interior, until hundreds of thousands of acres were crosshatched with canals.

But it was not the prospect of life on a frontier or the monomania of empire building that brought most people to the Northwest. Precious few men and women came west to suffer a hard life as pioneers on a wild frontier—rather they came for a better chance at life as they knew it in the East. From the very earliest migrations, along the coastal harbors and the river valleys west of the Cascades, there have risen tidy farms and towns, stable cities, and trading centers reaching for national and world markets. It was the American Dream reflected in miniature, and the foundations it provided helped the entire Northwest to withstand severe economic and social tremors during the years of growth.

To their credit, the people of the Northwest did not simply transplant American civilization—they led the way to political and social reform on a national scale. Most residents still nurture an abiding respect for clean air, clean water, and untrammeled wilderness; and in a nation where Growth Is Good, Oregon is telling prospective settlers to try California instead.

What follows is the story of this region of diversity and often paradox, from the Pacific shore east to the mountains of Idaho and western Montana, from British Columbia south to the California border. It is a stage of heroic proportions, peopled with actors grand and mundane who strove to shape the land and their destinies in the singular mold that is the Pacific Northwest.

PART ONE

A LAND OF CONTRASTS

Brilliant snows on dark volcanic peaks; tall sea-stacks rising from level beaches; the bare Olympic crest towering over the richly upholstered valleys of the rain forest; one of the mightiest rivers on the continent cutting through waterless lava plateaus—every vista in the Pacific Northwest presents contrasts to the eye. Even greater is the diversity of landscape and climate in the region as a whole, from shoreline and lush coastal valleys, across the rugged Cascade ridges and the deserts to the east, all the way to the Northern Rockies.

Mount Rainier above the cloud-capped Cascades.

SAND AND SEACLIFFS

The watery edge—where Pacific waves wash in on crescent beaches and crash white against headland rocks

THE DISTINCTIVE PROFILE of the Pacific Northwest coastline extends almost five hundred air-line miles from the cliffy California border to the inlet waterways of the Strait of Juan de Fuca and the northern fiords of Canada. Along misty coastal highlands, rainfall can be as heavy as anywhere on the continent—up to 115 inches on the lower slopes of the Olympic Mountains. A multitude of rivers—the Rogue, the Umpqua, the Siuslaw, the Willapa, the Chehalis, the Queets, and the Hoh, as well as the venerable Columbia—dispatch the moisture back to the sea.

Land on this ocean edge, like no other coastal highway of the West, is straight, and in some places emphatically growing straighter. Waves crash to shore, transfer their attacking energies directly against shale, sandstone, sometimes against hard volcanic rock, and march toward the interior at a rate, in places, equal to half a foot every year. Suspended matter drifts south with the Japanese (Kuroshio) Current, while longshore currents move sand north and south with the seasons, sometimes blocking inlets and bays, and forming coastal lagoons.

Winter is a good time for beach walking. Fishnet and glass-floats from the Orient may wash ashore on the Olympic seastrip and be left stranded at the high-water mark with other debris: parts of wrecked ships, seashells, agates, driftwood, or perhaps a vertebra from the backbone of a whale.

Life on the ocean side of a beach changes by zones of water depth. In the deep sea, far from reefs, shoals, and shallow places, life is given over to microscopic organisms, both plant and animal, called plankton—

"that which is made to wander." These are the drifters of the sea; at the mercy of the currents, they move with the weakest powers of locomotion. Among their kind are diatoms—single-celled algae—and dinoflagellates—strange creatures that can either make their own food as plants do, or devour other organisms as animals do. Most are only a thousandth of an inch in diameter, yet, they are food for almost every large sea animal.

In the open sea, just beneath the ocean's surface but closer to shore, is the zone of the nektons, where animals with streamlined bodies, backbones, and gills or lungs have the advantage. These fishes, whales, porpoises, seals, sea turtles, and some invertebrates, like shrimp and squid, swim about freely as true vagabonds of the sea. Whales are often seen during their spring and fall migrations along the Washington shoreline. Having no real enemy but man, endowed with leisure time and the ability to swim against the current, many whale species spend summers in the cool water of the Arctic, and winters in the tropics. Among their numbers are the gray, blue, piked, humpback, finback, and sei whales, also the so-called killer whale (or sea wolf), the Baird-beaked, Pacific-beaked, and goosebeak whales, joined by many kinds of dolphins.

Other residents of the cool deep are Pacific halibut, ocean perch, black sea bass, and rock fish, also the mighty salmon, and the smelt.

Close to the water's edge, where sunlight penetrates fully to the ocean floor, some plants and animals lead a stable life with holdfasts attached to rock or other objects. Certain varieties lead two lives—in youth they

The beachwalker on the Olympic Peninsula is dwarfed by monolithic seastacks and vast expanses of sand, sky, and water.

Sandpipers flush, wheel, and scatter as if moved by a common impulse. When disturbed, they dart away with a startled "peet-weet," then alight so suddenly they are almost bowled over by the shock.

are freewheeling cruisers of the currents; in maturity they relinquish their freedom to a permanent anchor. Where surf meets rocky shore barnacles, kelp, oysters, and the like are found; some live near low tide and receive the ever-circulating nutrients of the sea, while others (mussels, rockweed, and the tenacious barnacles) can root so firmly that the splash zone of high tide is no hazard.

Most life is centered, however, in the pools and rocks of low tides, where the anemone, sea cucumber, purple shore crab, Dungeness crab, hermit crab (which has but one large claw), a plumed worm called a "feather duster," purple starfish, sea urchin, brittle star, and sea lemon can find shelter. Between the rocks, in scooplike hollows, are sea snails, limpets, periwinkles, snails, and the ever-adhering barnacles; some may even cling to rocks beneath the kelp and thus remain moist even when the tide is out. Every possible habitat is explored; each pothole, joint, and crack in the rock can be a home for these creatures, yet the better places are often crowded, and the worst can be wastelands. Sand carried by the longshore currents perpetually attacks promon-

tory rocks, and these habitats are shunned by most organisms out of self-preservation. In time, as promontories fall before the waves and the shoreline becomes more linear, these places may also teem with creatures of the tide pool. Onshore, the ubiquitous gull is normally found bickering, dodging other gulls, and looking for food on a sandy beach, though he sometimes heads for the surf when the annual smelt runs begin in May. More reluctant birds wait ashore and let the tide deliver the feast. Pipestem-legged sandpipers pace at surf-edge. Often an entire flock will run along the beach together; if one should turn, the others follow.

WHERE SHORE MEETS SEA is a battlefield—"the primeval meeting-place of the elements of earth and water, a place of compromise and conflict, and eternal change," as Rachel Carson liked to call it. To sample this conflict, to test themselves against the frontier of this sandy and often rocky world have come artists, poets, naturalists, and of late the probing scientists: marine biologists, ecologists, oceanographers, and geologists. Although the reluctant sea is gradually revealing her secrets, dissolving the superstitions and strange lore of her ancient past, the beach is still a place of mystery.

Nearly every beach is young and has the vigor of renewal. Each winter, fierce winds and giant waves sweep everything they can from the high regions of many beaches, depositing their cache just out of view,

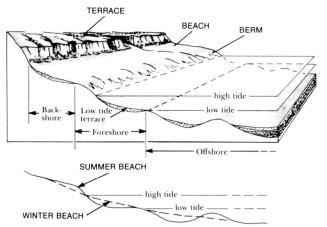

Cross section of a shoreline.

upon the submerged part of the shore. The winter beach is rocky and nearly naked of its sand veneer. Then, six months later, the waves and the winds of summer again rebuild the beach with golden sheets of sand, as though the complete cycle were intended for human amusement and wonder.

Most sands are predominantly quartz, mixed with other, sometimes exotic, minerals, their composition varying according to location. Stooped human forms can be seen walking almost any Oregon or Washington beach, looking for Oregon "jade" and serpentine in the gravel bars of the Rogue and Illinois rivers, or on Gold Beach. Agatized myrtle (and other woods), banded agate stones, jasper, petrified wood, and the fossilized specimens of marine life, which lived up to 25 million years ago, can also be found among the seaside debris. There is material from the interior, too; some southern Washington beaches are entirely gray green, like parched grass, colored with grains of basalt carried seaward by the Columbia and then sowed on the coast.

There are two basic kinds of beaches along this shore —the straight, smooth beach which may curve gently

up to rolling, windswept sand dunes or high bluffs, and the rugged, crescent-shaped beach, bounded by projecting points and headlands. Almost every grain of sand is a recycled product of water and wind erosion and in its lifetime can be reused many times. Sand that lies at the high-water mark—the part of a beach that is dry and difficult to walk on—becomes susceptible to transport by prevailing winds. Waves rarely reach this high in the summer, but wind can easily pick up sand and blow it toward the motherland and the dunes.

Live sand dunes are those that actively move forward; like the nose of a glacier, they cover everything in their path. If left unstabilized by "sand-binding" plants, such as the shore morning glory and the sand strawberry (with its vast network of runners), a marching dune can choke a forest, block an estuary, or even usurp a highway's "right" to eminent domain.

The cusp-shaped beaches of the Quillayute-Ozette (northern) part of the Olympic shoreline give no quarter to sand dunes. Here, at almost the apex of the Olympic Peninsula, cyclone storms prevail against the coast. Wave shock is great; breakers crash against the seacliffs and thunder into coves and caverns, splashing seawater and leaving a spindrift of inert foam as they depart. As the sea erodes the coastline, it leaves offshore pinnacles, known as seastacks, remnants of the former land's edge. They may be found anywhere along the coast of Washington or Oregon. Some are rounded, or flat-topped, with brush or conifers clinging to the rock;

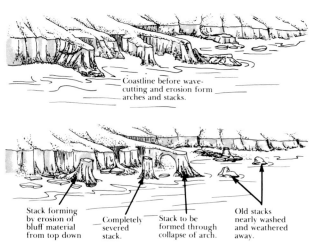

The formation of arches and seastacks by wave-cutting and weathering.

Between Astoria and Newport, the Oregon Coast is extremely varied. Promontories and seastacks flank Cape Foulweather, while just to the south is a smooth, sandy beach.

When the tide is low at Long Beach, Washington, clammers go out. They look for a "dimple" in the sand, dig rapidly with a shovel on the seaward side, finally reach in by hand for their prize.

others are steep-sided, barren, perhaps tapering to a point. Seldom visited because of their isolation, they house the rookeries of many shore and seabirds.

A variety of wave markings remains behind when the receding tide leaves a beach exposed. All beaches have some of these hieroglyphics: swash marks, which record how each wave was succeeded by yet another, perhaps with frequent changes of direction; ripple marks of two varieties—current ripples and oscillatory ripples; and rill marks on higher reaches of the beach, where seawater has tried to seep down through the sand.

No dividing line is drawn between land and sea;

instead, the two must blend, one into the other. About ten feet defines this fuzzy zone, and over that distance each gradual advance and retreat of the tide is marked by litter on the beaches: drifted tree trunks pushed against the rocks; fragments of wood with rounded corners and a satiny smoothness; and chaotic piles of unsorted driftwood, left at the high-tide line near mouths of rivers and large creeks.

Like the beach, the ocean has a pleasing sense of timing and symmetry, as well as an insistence that its dominance over the land be understood.

Waves, not tides, do most of the work of shaping a

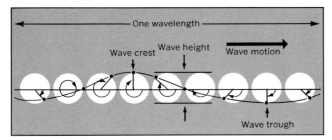

Water particles in a wave at sea move in orbits as the wave passes. Each particle will travel on a circular path that has a diameter equal to the height of the wave. The form of the wave alone advances; the water and any objects that may be suspended in it or floating on it do not. Only in shallows near shore, where the undulating energies of the waves are converted into direct assaults against the land, do the water and debris surge forward.

coastline; their energy comes from the wind far out at sea, in a way not clearly understood, but nonetheless appreciated.

Out of the turmoil of a "running sea" come regular patterns of rounded waves, or swells, often moving outward from more than one part of the ocean; they intersect and some are cancelled, others reinforced, by many wave collisions. It is commonly believed that every seventh wave is larger than the others or more capable of destroying, but this is not true. Instead, the waves approach shore with a constantly varying succession of highs and lows, a fact that befits their random birth.

Watch the flotsam and jetsam bobbing back and forth on each incoming swell and another secret of waves becomes clear: they move only themselves—not a piece of floating driftwood, not even the water very far below their troughs. As a wave passes by, it moves along the surface of the sea. Underneath, the water molecules are moving in a circular orbit, some in a positive direction toward shore, others toward the ocean deep. Mathematicians say the orbit of one water molecule is trochordal, "like a wheel."

As waves move into shallow water from the deep, they change character, from the unassuming swell of open seas to close-packed crests with razor edges. Often a hollow of trapped, compressed air lies tucked under the curl. When such crests meet shore, they outrun the rest of the wave and topple over, or break against the beach. The pattern for the West Coast is one hollow-crested, incoming wave every ten to eighteen seconds—a fairly long period between breakers. With each pulse, pressures of up to tens of thousands of pounds per square foot of seawall can lower the breaking point of rock until, suddenly, cliffwall fragments explode in every direction. To the sea, it is all in a good day's work.

As one turns from the brink of a seacliff, to face each incoming wave, it seems clear that the mighty ocean, and not the land, is the dominant environment of this living earth. And while the rest of the world is arrogantly proud of its haughty mountains, the mysterious sea very slowly creeps inland.

Near Dune City, Oregon, sand has extended into the windbreak at the edge of a forest. Sand-cleared hollows and smooth-shouldered ridges are the work of brisk winds off the Pacific.

CHAPTER 2

THE OLYMPIC RAIN FOREST

A place of cool green twilight that supports
"the greatest weight of living matter, per acre, in the world"

O N THE OCEAN SIDE of Washington's Olympic Peninsula is a forest that has no equal on this continent: a lush rain forest where the burgeoning of life upon life led naturalist Roger Tory Peterson to proclaim it "the greatest weight of living matter, per acre, in the world." The conifers of its upper story average two hundred feet tall, and some rise to three hundred. Below them is a second story of deciduous trees, and lower still a dense understory of shrubs. Every surface that is not already green seems to be swathed in epiphytes—ferns, lichens and mosses—hanging in drapery from the topmost branches, upholstering tree trunks, and laying a carpet on the forest floor.

Classically, the term *rain forest* has been used to refer to tropical jungle, which differs in several respects from the Olympic forest. The tropical climate is oppressively hot, rather than cool and mild. Jungle trees are all broadleaf with slender trunks and thin bark, and woody vines are everywhere; Olympic trees are primarily conifers with wide girths and rough bark, and there are no woody vines, only the rather soft vine maple.

Yet, the similarities between the two types of forest are startling. Both have a pervading air of verdant dampness, for they receive more than one hundred inches of rainfall a year. Both have a profusion of epiphytes that, with the trees, screen out sunlight and create a perpetual green twilight on the forest floor. Above all, there is in both a richness of foliage, a quality of exuberant growth that is the defining characteristic of rain forest.

Of all the trees in the Olympic rain forest, Sitka spruce is the tallest and the most common. Easily identified by bark plates that are loose and flaky, and needles so sharp they can be painful if brushed, the Sitka spruce sends papery-winged seeds cascading and flying far from the fluted boles of the parent. Unlike California's sequoia and giant redwood (which are larger and more massive), spruce has the company of three other mammoth species growing by its side: western hemlock, Douglas-fir, and western redcedar.

Needles of the western hemlock vary in length; the tops of the trees droop slightly, as if to squint at the sunlight that is so rare in the rain forest. Deep in the Quinault Valley, one giant western hemlock stands 125 feet—normally a tree is considered tall at just 100 feet; the girth of this beauty is over eight feet—nearly twice the normal—and in every respect, it is the archetype of its species.

The third grand member of the league of giant trees, the Douglas-fir, is not dominant in the rain forest, as are spruce and hemlock. It is a tree of transition; most Douglas-firs show plainly that their beginning came on soil which was stripped of earlier growth by a river in flood or the sudden slump of a hillside—not uncommon occurrences in western Olympic valleys. But instead of claiming the newfound land for itself and its own seedlings, Douglas fir becomes a living nurselog to the seed of others. Bark furrows, an inch or two deep, shelter hundreds of young hemlock and spruce seedlings. Many will fail to survive, but even if only a few take root, they will eventually grow to overtop the Douglas-fir and perpetuate a timeless balance in the forest.

The rain forest of the Hoh Valley is a complex plant community where all vegetation flourishes to perfection in the abundant moisture.

27

Down trees nurture the seeds of many species. The slowly rotting logs become shaggy with mosses and small sprouts, and form the base for a living colonnade of new trees.

Least common of the rain forest conifers is the western redcedar. Because of its cellular chemistry, redcedar must have acid soil conditions for optimum regeneration; seedbed acid seems to adjust the enzyme balance of the seed, making possible the absorption of water necessary for sprouting. Therefore, large groves of redcedar are found in swamplands near the coast where soil acid is high, but few endure in the well drained rain forest valleys. On the steep Quinault hillsides, red-

cedars attract many a hiker's attention; they grow overlapping, scalelike leaves, rather than needles, and their small, brown cones hang in clusters from branch tips, but the oddest of all is the habit of old-growth cedars—clusters of them may weld their stringy bark together, to live as one unified tree with many distinct treetops.

Below the tallest trees are the bigleaf maples, black cottonwoods, and red alder, then an understory of shrubs and low-growing trees, and at the bottom, close

exceptionally beautiful rain forest of the Hoh, Queets, and Quinault valleys, the ten- to twenty-foot vine maple tangles command more interest than vitriol.

Vine maple grows in just that small amount of sunshine relegated to the forest floor. One who is intently watching the trail amid the oxalis, avoiding vanilla leaf, foamflower, bedstraw, trailing rubus, liverworts, mosses, and ferns, and winding between the nurselogs, will marvel that vine maple can be sensed, without being seen, just by the distinctive soft green light near these clumps.

DRAPED ON THE BRANCHES AND BARK of many giant trees are the life forms which prefer clinging to others—ferns, lichens, and mosses of the rain forest. They appear as the shag rug of the forest floor, as green life on tree trunks (where bark grooves channel the rain and bark roughness provides a steady surface to hold), or as bright swags hanging from tree tops (where light is maximum the year round). All live epiphytically.

The word *epiphyte* means literally "upon a plant," whether the guest lives in the crown of the forest, as 90 percent of them do, or on trunks near the forest floor. The host simply provides a place for the epiphyte; its life is sustained with minerals leached by water trickling down from above, and with nutrients brought by the wind. No parasitic organs are sent into a host's vital tissues, and usually there are no undesirable side effects for either party, though occasionally shade from the epiphyte may disrupt photosynthesis conducted by the host; or an epiphyte may absorb so much rain that the branch it occupies becomes overburdened and breaks.

Selaginella, a relative of clubmoss, is the conspicuous yellow-green "moss" hanging from Olympic bigleaf maples—a preferred host because the rich chemical nutrients leached from its leaves are highly desirable to most epiphytes.

Emerald-green fronds of the licorice fern are almost as easily noticed as selaginella, even though it prefers the high branches. The leathery, desiccation-resistant lichen, on the other hand, are screened from sight by overhead leaves. The licorice fern is sensitive to the drying wind which is common at 250 feet, and it browns and withers even while the forest floor still moulders from the last rain.

to trails, where they can get into the way, vine maples are perversely entangled. Louis Henderson, a pioneer botanist who found his passage undesirably difficult in 1891, described them well: "Cut them out for mules to pass and you find the axe goes through easy, so you think it is as simple as cutting cheese, but start to pull a hunk out of the way, and you find how elastic vine maple is when it rises up and thwacks you!" But today, if one stays to the trails that wind through all the

Born of perpetual snow fields, the Hoh River flows in a valley that once held alpine ice extending to the Pacific.

Many of the plants native to the Olympic rain forest also flourish elsewhere—in the Olympic Mountains, in parts of the Cascades (east of Seattle), and along the foggy, cliff-hung shore from British Columbia to California—but only on the west side of the Olympics do these species reach perfection. In only three valleys, the Hoh, Queets, and Quinault, is the exacting blend of unending saturation, mild temperatures, and gentle topography present to an ideal degree and proportion. Away from these three rivers, or above the critical contour line of one thousand feet, the rain forest is less than prime. Spruce and Douglas-fir predominate with

their nearly equal numbers, and silver fir is conspicuously present; colonnades of trees are less frequent; vine maples grow tall and treelike, and soil and bark show through the green forest mat.

One reason that prime rain forest is restricted to the bottomlands of the three rivers may be the rivers themselves. Each waterway is a juggernaut of logs, debris, and swirling water, shifting constantly within channels on the broad riverbed, along gradients so gradual that in twenty miles, they fall only six hundred feet. The bottomlands are one mile wide, and their walls rise sharply to long ridges that come from central Olympus itself—clearly, these valleys were once chiseled by ice. Furthermore, each of the three spectacular valleys runs toward the southwest, pointing into the eye of most storms, optimizing precipitation, as fog and rain blow in from the ocean and moist, cool air drains down from the peaks.

Each year, 120 to 140 inches of rain drench the Olympic rain forest—some years it is as high as 180 inches, the equivalent of two billion gallons of water for each square mile of forest. This is more rain than will fall in a century of thunderstorms over parts of the Southwest.

When a winter storm is dumping inches of rainfall on the Hoh, Queets, and Quinault valleys, the elk often bed down and doze to wait it out. A hiker seeks shelter in his tent, because not even the great spruce boughs can offer enough protection in a winter downpour.

Precipitation increases with distance up the valley, with the coast actually drier than the rain forest. Kalaloch, on the Pacific, averages 90 inches; at the end of the Hoh Valley, the average is up to 142 inches; and sometimes on Mount Olympus, just thirty miles inland, the yearly rainfall is 200 inches.

For every sunny day over the forest, there are two which are cloudy, depressing summer temperatures and moderating winter's freeze. Clouds act as a reflector, bouncing back more than half of the sun's light into the atmosphere. In the pale gloom on the forest floor, the light available for photosynthesis is only 1 percent of that at the top of the forest canopy. Species growing in this deep shade have had to make some interesting adaptations. Their metabolic rate is slowed; leaves are thinner, so that fewer cells need energy for maintenance; and chloroplasts—the central factories of a

More than a mile above the rain forest is the Bailey Range of Olympic National Park.
Its peaks are the domain of great glaciers, avalanches, and tiny subalpine lakes.

plant's food production—distribute themselves liberally over all top surfaces of the leafy frond.

Wind is reduced by as much as 80 percent in the rain forest, and even the fury of a wind that hits the coast at a hundred miles an hour will only ruffle the tops of the spruce. The trees themselves, the valley wall, and the distance from the sea usually weaken the wind and prevent catastrophe. But occasionally, a gust will roar into the forest from surrounding regions which have been logged, or where there are ranches. Spruces and hemlocks are especially vulnerable if this happens; their roots spread out naturally at the bole, giving the appear-

ance of strength, but they hold the shape of their nurse-log, even after it decays, and penetrate the earth no more deeply than two or three feet. Thus, their grip on the earth and their link to its history appear unexpectedly frail.

But if one counts the years that virgin Sitka spruce have stood in the rain forest, both the current generation and those which preceded it, one goes back through history to before the American Revolution, to before the sailing of Columbus, even to before the Norman Conquest. There is a sense of time and decay in the rain forest, and a sense of regeneration.

CHAPTER 3

LUSH LANDS, FERTILE WATERS

The Willamette Valley and the maze of
Puget Sound waterways—a legacy from the Ice Age

THE PUGET-WILLAMETTE lowland was born some 60 million years ago, when the earth began to sag along a north-south axis from Canada to Oregon. The landscape then would have been totally foreign to the modern eye—no shimmering waterways of Puget Sound that connect safe, inland harbors with the wild, northern sea; no broad, fertile valley of the lazy Willamette, flowing north through Oregon to meet the Columbia. In time, mountains rose on the lowland margins—the Cascades on the east, the Coast Range on the west, interrupted by the Strait of Juan de Fuca. Their uplift helped, at least in part, to construct and accentuate the nearly four-hundred-mile-long valley. Within the lowland are folded and faulted hills, some of which are volcanic rock related to lavas from the Olympic Mountains, Willapa Hills, and Cascade Range.

Admiralty Inlet is the main gateway from the Strait of Juan de Fuca to the inland canals, irregular islands, estuaries, and lakes of the Puget Sound region. Taking the first turn southwest is Hood Canal—a long, narrow arm which brings the sea fifty miles inland to the Olympic Mountains. Somewhat set apart from the other waterways because of its great depth and straight passage, Hood is a canal with only weak tidal currents.

Puget Sound itself is the southeast branch of Admiralty—a busy passageway to Seattle, Tacoma, and other deep-harbor cities. A man-made canal system, linked by Ballard Locks, connects glacially carved Lakes Union and Washington with the sound, adding one more inland channel of transport to the already near-perfect harbor system. When joined by the Rosario, Haro, and Georgia straits, the entire region is a filigree of waterways, islands, and embayments—the Northwest's only all-weather port system.

Some confusion arose on just which waterway was to be the sound. When Captain Vancouver of the British navy first applied the name, he spoke only of a sector from Bainbridge Island south and southwest, but usage has grown so that now all the east branch of Admiralty Inlet bears the same name.

Puget land is smoothly contoured and low-lying—all but the San Juan Islands lies less than five hundred feet above the sound. Between ten thousand and four million years ago, the cooling climate and the increased snowfall in high latitudes and high altitudes spawned immense continental ice sheets in what is now Canada, which slowly spread southward. From the Olympics to the Cascades, the Puget lowland was filled with ice to a point thirty miles south of Olympia. Though only a lobe of the even larger ice mass in British Columbia, the Puget ice sheet reached a depth of one mile over the Bellingham area, and four thousand feet over Seattle. At least four, and perhaps more, such occupations by ice are recorded in the deposits of glacially-carried rock fragments.

Debris from the advance of the earliest Pleistocene ice, the Orting Glaciation, may be found only in the southern part of the glaciated lowland, near the latitude of Tacoma. However, sediments of three younger glacial periods are exposed in the many miles of seacliffs along Puget Sound shores and in the cliffs of Whidbey, Camano, and the San Juan Islands. Though the two

The snowy Olympics overlook Liberty Bay, near Poulsbo, Washington. Safe harbors throughout the Puget Sound region offer residents a watery playground right at their doorsteps.

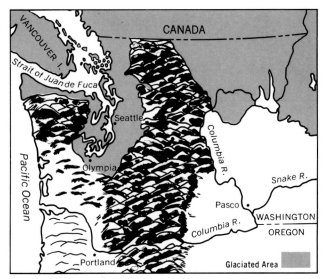

Glaciation in the Northwest: The Puget Lobe extended to south of Olympia as recently as fourteen thousand years ago.

earliest glaciations are beyond the range of radiocarbon dating, geologists equate them with glaciations of the midwestern United States and Europe, some two to three million years ago. The land surface now seen in the Puget lowlands is almost entirely a result of a final glacial advance which began eighteen thousand years ago and is named the Fraser Glaciation. This glaciation not only mantled the lowland, but scoured out the extensive inlets and channels of Puget Sound as well.

Within the Fraser Glaciation there were three periods of advance and retreat. In the first, the Evans Creek period, the ice was of Alpine origin, forming in the Cascade Range and slipping toward the Puget lowland just prior to the advance of continental ice from Canada. Alpine glaciers were also flowing from Olympic mountain valleys. The tongues of ice from the mountains filled valleys which now have only scraped and polished rock, and rubble-strewn floors as reminders of that time. Hundreds of years of warmer climate resulted in a glacial retreat.

Continental ice spread south into the Puget lowland from British Columbia for its final visit in the Vashon period. It crossed the United States–Canadian border around nineteen thousand years ago, reaching Seattle about four thousand years later. Thickening as it flowed south, it inundated much of the northern Cascades

around Mount Baker. Granite boulders carried from Canada by the ice have been discovered as high as 5,700 feet within the Cascades. Ice filled the lowlands to depths greater than a mile. Near Tacoma, the ice thinned to 1,800 feet, and south of Olympia it tapered to its terminus.

From the depth and direction of grooves found on outcrops of hard rock on the San Juan and Lopez islands, and from the elongated, dome-shaped hills, called drumlins, between Everett and Arlington (and several other locations), geologists have determined that the ice sheet split as it passed the Strait of Juan de Fuca. One lobe went west, the other south or southeast, as it banked against the Cascades. The ice extended up major western Cascade valleys. Rivers blocked by the ice formed lakes and river deltas, now dry but still recognizable by their fan shape high on the Cascades. Ice extended across the Snoqualmie River Valley, creating a lake of great size.

When the climate warmed and the Snoqualmie ice dam melted, outlets drained the lake; once again the Snoqualmie River was restored to its valley. However, a river delta that had formed on Tokul Creek diverted the flow to the valley's south side. There the Snoqualmie cut down through the sediments and into a bedrock spur along the wall, and once the rock was notched, the river was trapped in its new course. The spur eroded slowly, but the sediments downstream were quickly removed leaving the now 268-foot Snoqualmie Falls. Over the years Snoqualmie Falls, like Niagara, has retreated up its valley; geologists believe that once headward erosion through bedrock brings the river to the edge of loose valley fill (sediments, again), the river will erode them almost without effort, and the falls will be destroyed.

Ice was present in the Puget lowlands for only about 1,500 years, since Seattle was uncovered about 13,500 years ago. The glacier left in its recessional path sand, gravel, and an unstratified assortment of debris called till. It is usually a compact collection of silt, clay, sand, pebbles, cobbles, and boulders, mixed in a single massive layer, which may be a few feet deep or a hundred. Some of the cobbles and pebbles are faceted and striated, but most have been rounded by streams as they were carried away from the base of the glacier.

At least some of the troughs and adjacent inlets in

NORTHWEST GEOLOGICAL TIME CHART

YEARS AGO (Approximate)	ERA	PERIOD	EPOCH	IMPORTANT EVENTS (Italic type indicates events in the Northwest)
15,000—	Cenozoic	Quaternary	Recent	*Lassen Peak erupts while other Cascade volcanoes slumber.* *Sporadic volcanic activity at Craters of the Moon, Idaho.* *Climate warms and glaciers retreat.*
3,000,000—			Pleistocene	*Northern Washington, Idaho, and Montana are covered one or more times by glacial ice.* *Formation of High Cascade volcanoes; glaciers erode the volcanic peaks and the Cascades.* *Palouse soil begins forming.*
13,000,000—		Tertiary	Pliocene	*A major upheaval in the Cascades (Cascade Orogeny) initiates uplift of the modern range; uplift of the northern Rockies.* *Snake River volcanism is accompanied by subsidence of the Snake River Plain.*
			Miocene	*Eruption of Columbia River basalt; Cascades are partially covered with lava.* *Folding, faulting, and intrusions occur in the middle and southern Cascades.*
25,000,000—			Oligocene	*Vigorous erosion in the northern Cascades and the northern Rockies reduces these ranges to low hills.*
36,000,000—			Eocene	*Eruption of volcanoes in the Cascades and Blue Mountains.*
58,000,000—			Paleocene	*Slow deformation of rock in the Blue Mountains.*
63,000,000—	Mesozoic	Cretaceous		*Retreat of the Pacific Ocean from that part of the continent lying east of the Cascades.* *Major uplift completed in the northern Rockies—metamorphism, faulting, and rise of the batholiths.* *Uplift occurs in the northern Cascades—batholiths are emplaced.* *Pulse of mountain building in the Blue Mountains.*
135,000,000—		Jurassic		*Episodes of volcanism and marine sedimentation in the northern Cascades.* Birds and mammals evolve.
180,000,000—		Triassic		Appearance of the dinosaurs. *Folding, faulting, and metamorphism in the Blue Mountains.*
230,000,000—	Paleozoic	Permian		*Mountain building occurs in the Rockies.*
280,000,000—		Pennsylvanian		Conifer forests appear. Coal swamps form. Reptiles evolve.
310,000,000—		Mississippian		Insects first appear. *Restlessness and early uplift in the Rockies.*
340,000,000—		Devonian		Vertebrates evolve. Fish appear in the seas.
400,000,000—		Silurian		Land plants appear.
430,000,000—		Ordovician		Corals and sea urchins evolve.
500,000,000—		Cambrian		Mollusks and trilobites are dominant life forms.
570,000,000—		Precambrian		*Accumulation begins of many tens of thousands of feet of marine sediment in the Rocky Mountains.*

Where no bridges exist, Puget Sound depends upon ferries. Here one such vessel navigates Wasp Passage in the San Juan Islands, en route between Anacortes and Sidney.

Puget Sound were carved out by this last incursion of Canadian ice, though the origins of all the troughs have been debated since the turn of the century. What tends to support the theory that ice of fifteen thousand years ago supplied the bulldozing power is that the next oldest sediments are deeply eroded, as if they had been overridden by the ice sheet. On Whidbey Island, for example, 250 feet of glacial scouring has been truncated by till from the last glaciation.

In some areas, the ice did extensive excavation, producing the basins of Lake Washington and Lake Sammamish and deepening the sound off Seattle to one thousand feet below sea level. In others it eroded very little, but instead, compacted the land as it passed, exerting pressures up to eight thousand pounds per square inch upon parts of the Seattle area.

The arrival of the Puget lobe was equivalent to creating a mile-high mountain range in the Puget lowland. The rivers flowing from the Cascades to the Pacific Ocean could no longer run north through the lowland but instead were dammed by ice forcing its way into the valleys. As the inevitable lakes filled and rose over the icy barrier, the waters turned south, downhill, and a milky river coursed along the margins of the ice. The waters first collected in a large lake at the southern end of the Puget lobe and eventually overflowed into the Chehalis River. With a discharge then probably several

times that of the modern Columbia, the Chehalis cut a valley that easily accommodates the relatively small river of today.

The climate began to warm 13,500 years ago in the Puget lowland, and as the toe of the ice sheet began to retreat, the ice became thinner. As it shrank to thicknesses of a few hundred feet, it was buoyed up by salt water. Clams and other bottom-dwelling sea molluscs perished beneath debris shed by the drifting and melting ice—clay, sand, and gravel—and remain today as fossils in the sediments of northern Puget Sound. Between Bellingham and the Canadian border, most of the upland topography is shaped from similar deposits of glacial and marine sediments. The Nooksack Valley and Cascade foothills as far as Deming are similarly veneered.

During the very last period of Pleistocene glaciation, the Canadian ice sheet hovered right above the international boundary and crossed over to near Sumas. Streams running off the ice deposited sand and gravel from the border to near Lynden, Washington, and then south to Laurel, where the rubble banked against higher glacial deposits. Small lakes and peat bogs now occupy some of the abandoned channels.

The earth has never been static, a fact particularly evident in the Puget area, where postglacial stream erosion and deposition are modifying the landscape.

Pastoral Whidbey Island, the largest in Puget Sound, has a long shoreline that invites exploration. It was discovered in 1792 by Joseph Whidbey of the Vancouver expedition.

Rivers from both the Olympics and the Cascades discharge silt and sand as they disappear into quieter waters of the sound and its adjacent channels. Deltas thus push seaward, extending the land as some parts of the waterways become filled.

The Skagit River has been building its delta for the past ten thousand years; it has succeeded in surrounding islands with its sediment and annexing their land to its floodplain. This process is occurring on the east sides of Whidbey and Fidalgo, where only a narrow channel preserves their status as islands.

Because most of the sound's channels are affected by ocean tides, not all natural activity in the sound is constructive. The incessant waves breaking against shorelines have left hundreds of miles of beaches, many undercut and rubbly with till, others sharply cut and in retreat landward. Sand is carried back and forth by the waves, pushed onto a beach, and withdrawn as the water runs seaward.

Beaches by the sound are small, sheltered crescents below the shoreline bluffs. They dot the coast discontinuously, giving way to Douglas-fir and cedar grow-

ing out to beachline, or to promontories still resisting the sea's constant attack.

It is a convoluted coastline of 2,167 miles around the Puget shorelands—longer than all the miles of Pacific Northwest coast and knitted tightly together. A large indigenous fish and mollusc population benefits by the environmental variety; deep channels, shoals, thin tidal flats, and beaches offer shelter, an enriched food supply, and mild waters. The cold, nutrient bottom muds from the Strait of Juan de Fuca are churned up and carried to sunlit water layers, where small fish feed and hide among dense algal mats.

In the channels, fertility depends on dissolved and suspended organic matter from incoming fresh-water rivers. The Nooksack, Skokomish, Nisqually, Snohomish, and others build and maintain estuarine tide flats which are at once places of protection and of easy food gathering. The estuaries are transition zones for juvenile fish heading seaward and adults traveling from saline ocean water into the fresh waters that will be their spawning grounds. Chinook, coho, pink, chum, and sockeye salmon swim the waterways and frequent the

Though farms reduce their acreage, thousands of Mima Mounds remain, their origin still a mystery.

tide flats with steelhead and cutthroat trout, and the Dolly Varden. Flats such as the Nisqually Delta also nurture economically important oyster and crab beds, and scallops.

Overhead, scouting herons and grebes search both beaches and flats for their preferred menu items, but competition with clammers and oystermen has turned more than one shorebird inland in search of easier foraging.

Beyond the canals, lakes, marshes, and coastal hills of the Puget lowlands, shrubs, forbs, and grasses form a dense ground cover, while ferns, mosses, and shrubs are common to redcedar slopes and old conifer stands. Wide valleys support an agriculture of extensive grass production and crops like vegetables and berries.

Climate in the sound is mild, partly because the lowlands are sheltered both by the Cascades and by the Olympic Mountains and Coast Range that stand against the intense southwesterly winter storms. Nevertheless, several times each winter cold air builds up on the eastern slopes of the Cascades to sufficient depths that it floods the sound, converges on warm, moist maritime air (brought in by way of the straits), and brings snow

—usually no more than half an inch. The region's infrequent heavy snows are Canadian in origin, resulting from weather systems that move in from the north and pick up moisture over the straits.

Because of the Chehalis Gap and the Olympic Mountains, precipitation decreases markedly from southwest to northeast through the Puget Sound. The gap allows moist winds to enter the southern part of the sound, giving Olympia fifty inches of annual rainfall. The loss of humidity in the air as it passes northward, and the barrier of the mountains also effectively screen out new moisture. Thus Tacoma receives an annual average of around thirty-six inches of rain, and Coupeville only eighteen inches. East of the sound, the Cascade backdrop provides for a second belt of heavy precipitation.

Two seasons dominate the yearly climate pattern; a mild, wet winter—with warming trends due to chinook winds moving off the Cascades—and a cool, dry summer. But even while summer doldrums keep out new precipitation, water remains in good supply, replenished by melting reserves from the Cascades and Olympic snowpacks.

Maritime and continental air masses combine in the Strait of Juan de Fuca to produce startling optical phenomena related to the local climate. Ships have been sighted looming above the horizon in an inverted position, and from viewers out at sea there are reports of bluffs and headlands towering over other objects on the horizon. Vertical distortion seems to be the most commonly observed illusion, and summer afternoons of low wind perpetrate favorable conditions. Warm dry air from the sound, lying over relatively cold ocean air, sets up a pronounced near-surface inversion of air layers; no circulation is possible and thus both air layers stagnate. The mysterious result is that light reflects abnormally off the boundary between the air layers, strongly distorting objects near the water.

SOUTH OF PUGET SOUND, in the valley of the Chehalis and Cowlitz rivers, the land is strewn with sand and gravel of the river-washed flatland. The land is transitional, a space between Puget Sound and the Willamette Valley, with scenery different from either. It is flat and unbroken except for a few hard-rock hills that resist the elements and stand above the gray-brown

The broad, fertile valley that borders the Willamette River near Salem has a climate and geography exceedingly favorable to the needs of man.

valley. With almost no clay among the porous gravels, the water table is deep, and only grasses are hardy enough to grow here in any profusion. These dry lands are called prairies. Occasional stands of Douglas-fir, Oregon white oak, and Scotch broom have invaded in small groups, but they are barely large or dense enough to be called colonies. Above timberline the ground cover blends into a mixture of heather, sedges, shrubs, and low flowering plants.

On some Chehalis-Cowlitz valley prairies perplexing earth features known as the Mima Mounds bead the land. From the air they are closely spaced and arranged in discontinuous rows, but from the ground they appear to be scattered at random. Each mound is a low dome, or heap of gravels and silt, one to seven feet high and from eight to seventy feet in diameter. It is variously told that either the local burrowing pocket gopher, *Thomomys talpoides,* was involved in the mound making, or the mounds are of human construction. But their number seems to rule out either explanation, since between Tenino and Grand Mound, Washington, literally thousands of mounds are visible out in the gravels. Perhaps they originated simply from normal erosion ensuing on frost-heaved blocks of frozen ground.

Farther south the lowland meets and crosses the Columbia River, entering Oregon and the Willamette Valley region. Since no penetrating sea arm gives favorable urban sites to this lowland sector, the Willamette River is the focus for settlement. The towns, closely spaced, are older and more mature than near the sound.

The valley, a flat alluvial plain initially lowered by faults on its east and west edges, was eroded by the Willamette River through relatively nonresistant rock. It is a young valley now, 187 miles long and not more than 20 or 30 miles wide. The old bedrock has been covered with thick sheets of sediment brought down, in part, by valley glaciers, but largely by normal erosion.

The Middle Fork, North Fork, and Salmon Creek flow from headwaters on steep Cascade summits, through rapids, past sand pits, to a meeting near Oakridge, where the rivers join to form the Willamette. It rolls on into Lookout Point Reservoir, then to Eugene and a confluence with the McKenzie River. Once into the rolling valley land, the Willamette weaves an intricate pattern of curving meanders and swings slowly along an indirect path to Portland. With a fall of less than four feet for every mile, there is barely enough drop to keep the waters pushing toward the Columbia, much less to carry a cargo of sediment. Sand and gravel bars form where the river must lighten its load, presenting broadside obstacles which divert the flow into sections, dividing the river into fingers that coalesce and branch, seeking new paths. The slow flow allows trees to invade and crowd aside water, impeding its motion and lengthening the river's course. The river literally ties itself in knots, braiding its channel as it flows.

Because of feeble currents, sandbar obstacles, and encroaching cottonwoods and willows, any sudden burst of runoff used to flood the valley floor, always with spectacular results. Waters would converge from highlands, suddenly lose their speed, build a crest and spread out over the land. Flashy, short-lived floods carried a water volume many times greater than the yearlong average. Inevitably, two dams were built to control flooding on the contrary Willamette: Lookout Point in 1954 and Hills Creek in 1962. These reservoirs protect the hopyards, cornfields, and green carpets of mint upon the floodplain.

Floods have been a part of the Willamette Valley's history since the beginning. Pacific Ocean fluctuations and a changing coastline brought salt water into it many times in the geologic past; in the Pleistocene the valley was a temporary holding basin for waters overflowing glacial Lake Missoula. These floods raged from Montana across northern Idaho and into southeastern Washington, finally spilling into the Willamette Basin. A huge seventeen-mile-long delta at Portland marks the water's escape south; local concentrations of mammoth bones and tusks, and massive boulders in the valley tell that the flood wave hit without warning. High water drained slowly out through a southern gap.

THE PUGET-WILLAMETTE LOWLANDS look precisely as their history would imply. The troughland was formed by slow downward slipping of a weak rock foundation, and the Cascade and Coast ranges rose on the margins. It did not happen rapidly or without interruption; before the lowlands could be even remotely recognizable by present-day standards they passed through millennia of preparation. The three sections became differentiated as glacier sheets moved south from polar regions, then stopped where the Puget territory now ends. And a primordial Willamette River grew old cutting its valley. Just ten thousand years ago the lowlands began to appear as they do today. Puget Sound was a waterway, the prairies of the Chehalis-Cowlitz had formed, and the Willamette had reached its present maturity in a wide valley. Some natural alteration of the landscape continues to occur, though it is almost imperceptible to a casual observer. The northern troughland, once weighted down under ice, has rebounded from the stress and tilted; throughout the trough, periodic adjustments—slumping, weathering, and deposition—are redefining how the land will look on a daily basis, and in the future.

As on beaches around the world, gulls are resident symbols of freedom.

*Throughout the Olympic rain forest life clambers over life in green exuberance.
Here bigleaf maple, clubmoss, and ferns thrive in the Hoh Valley.*

Deep, untrammeled valleys radiate from the Olympic Mountains like spokes from a hub; this one is seen fog-filled from Hurricane Ridge.

Even the crest of Aurora Ridge in the Olympics is heavily upholstered with forest.

43

Tranquil: Gentle dunes near Reedsport, Oregon, border one of the longest, straightest stretches of the Northwest coastline.

Turbulent: Farther north, as at Rialto Beach, Washington, the surf crashes against rocky headlands and boils in captive tidal pools.

From Mount Constitution, the San Juan Islands seem to lie enchanted in the mist, tinted pink by a setting sun. The city of Bellingham and Mount Baker are on the distant horizon.

The ferry from Edmonds to Kingston. The Indians believed Puget Sound and its islands were created by the Great Spirit because he loved beautiful things.

This U-shaped valley of the Napeequa River is scenic testament to alpine glaciation in the Glacier Peak Wilderness Area. Deer, cougar, bobcat, wolverine, and bear roam its dark forests.

47

CHAPTER 4

THE ICE-CARVED CASCADES

Born of lava upon lava, chiseled by glaciers,
and covered today with a dense mantle of forestlands

ONE OF THE IRONIES discovered by early emigrants traveling on the Oregon Trail was that if they survived the Indians, cholera, near-starvation, and fatigue and arrived at The Dalles in Oregon, the worst mountains of their journey still stood in the way of reaching the Willamette Valley. These mountains—the Cascades—are one of the West's great ranges. They rise out of a topographic sag at the north end of the Sierra Nevada and continue through Oregon, Washington, and the southern reach of British Columbia. Never more than one hundred to one hundred fifty miles from the Pacific, the range has a north-south trend, with a border as clearly defined as that of the Sierra Nevada. Though extended, the Cascades are compact and dense. In more than seven hundred miles, there are only three places where inland waters find a way through to the ocean: in the valleys of the Klamath and Pit rivers, and through the Columbia River Gorge.

The usual emigrant route through the Cascades was on the Columbia River, but even if river travel was successful (sometimes it was not), wagons had to be taken apart and reassembled. This cost money and time. An alternate route was first attempted by Samuel K. Barlow, wagon master of an 1845 party, over the south shoulder of Mount Hood. His group gave up at the summit of the route, continuing on without wagons. But Barlow and an associate returned the next year, planning to charge tolls once they finished the route. Even in its completed state, it was roughhewn and difficult; often wagons had to be winched up and down hillsides. Still, it was better than drowning in the Columbia.

Today, motorists have many more choices. Highways penetrate the Cascades on both banks of the Columbia, over the passes in Washington at Snoqualmie, Stevens, and Chinook, and—as the season permits—across the North Cascade Highway; in Oregon through Barlow, Santiam, Willamette, Diamond Lake, and Hayden Mountain passes. Along these routes the traveler can become acquainted with the dark rock and evergreen forest of the Cascades, and their snowcapped volcanic sentinels.

The southern Cascade Range is exclusively of volcanic origin. Geologists have evidence that beneath the lava lies granite which connects the Sierra Nevada with the Klamath Mountains in northwestern California. Though this is the Cascades' lowest region, with much of the countryside below six thousand feet, two High-Cascade peaks, Mount Shasta and Lassen Peak, rise high in the range. From any vantage point one can see conical peaks, domes, lava flows, and other volcanic features. The Cascades are partly forested, but to the east the semiarid climate of the Modoc Plateau supports only scant vegetation.

Stretching northward from the California border, through Oregon, to Snoqualmie Pass are the middle Cascades—broad, rounded mountains, built of lava flows interbedded with sedimentary rocks, subsequently folded, faulted, and uplifted. They are distinguished by the richness of their forests and the energy of their streams. East of the crest is a row of isolated peaks, including Mounts McLoughlin, Thielsen, Three Sisters, Jefferson, Hood, Adams, and Rainier. These volcanic

Carrying the weight of the season, conifers line the ridge from
Denny Mountain's summit, near Snoqualmie Pass, Washington.

Crystalline rocks of the North Cascades have been raised from deep in the earth to challenge the forces of erosion. These peaks lie near Cascade Pass, Washington.

cones and their neighbors are the so-called High Cascades; each is younger than, and tops, the uplift.

North of Snoqualmie Pass the northern Cascades rise in elevation and steepness so dramatically that ridges far to the south seem like foothills by comparison. Springing sharply from the lavas of the Columbia Plateau on the east, these peaks of granitic and metamorphic rocks loom steeply above the Puget lowlands on the west. They seem raised to challenge the elements. Rivers and glaciers responded by creating awesome sculptures: precipitous walls, knife-edged ridges, and alpine lakes.

The Cascades are more than just boisterous streams and exposed rock, more than the home of deer, elk, bear, beaver, mink, badger, weasel, raccoon, and rabbit. Covered with Douglas-fir, sugar pine, hemlock, and cedar, they are also the foundation of a timber industry with yields among the richest of American forest lands. Besides their economic value for lumbering, forests provide the principal vegetative cover protecting the headwaters of Cascade rivers. By securing the watershed against erosion, they keep mountain streams cool and clear, providing a suitable habitat for fish.

All forests are controlled by climate. Pacific winds move inland with their moisture, spilling some 130 inches of annual precipitation upon the seaward slopes of the Coast Range, then slip into the Puget–Willamette lowlands, here yielding only moderate rainfall (40 inches yearly average). As the moist air ascends the Cascade front, rain falls again, increasing its intensity with altitude so that upper summits may receive up to 80 inches a year—much of it as snow. Western slopes are thus the kingdom of the fast-growing, moisture-demanding Douglas-fir. Rainfall expended, the now dry air moves down the eastern slopes and whistles through the tops of a pine forest that can survive on the drier side of the mountains.

Changes in rainfall usually are so sharp on many lower Cascade summits that west-side fir and east-side pine meet with almost no transition zone; in just one half hour's drive across the Snoqualmie or Santiam passes, one completely leaves lofty Douglas stands to enter shorter ponderosa pine forests. But in areas of low rainfall pine is common even on the west. In southern Oregon and northern California, for instance, pine trees have stolen over the crest into the drainages of the Umpqua, Rogue, Klamath, and Sacramento rivers.

Fires, lava flows, and other catastrophes of nature upset the natural balance of a forest to a much more dramatic extent than normal fluctuations of rainfall. They remove ground cover and shade, modify or destroy the soil, and otherwise alter the balances that favor one species over another. Destruction of the forest cover renews the normal competitive and successive processes by which veteran forests have gained eminence.

Once disaster eliminates Douglas-fir, Oregon oak challenges its kingdom. The aggressive oak becomes established easily, but the Cascade growing season is limited by biting cold and deep snow, and the oak grows slowly. In time, new seeds from the pendulous Douglas-fir cones find their way into the nursery, begin competition with oak, and regain their dominance.

The lodgepole pine may be an unrewarded benefactor to the reign of Douglas-fir in the southern Cascades, where rainless lightning storms take massive timber tolls by fire. Small, stony cones hold and protect the lodgepole seed through intense heat, frost, desiccation, and adverse, barren soils. Sprouting when more favorable conditions return, lodgepole pine quickly colonizes the slope, only to be beaten in the end by longer-lived and larger species—Douglas-fir and its cronies, Engelmann spruce, balsam fir, hemlock, white pine, and cedar.

Often, before the lodgepole has a chance to reforest after fire, low brush (or chaparral) may move onto the barren ground, choking out the seedlings. This has happened in the southern Cascades, where the tenacious red and green manzanita can eke out an existence on tortured land with little topsoil and hardly any humus. Other settlers are the sticky laurel and other varieties of ceanothus, currants, and miscellaneous shrubs generally known as snowbrush or buckbrush; they are a valuable game cover and watershed protection.

Generally heavy winter snows, summer drought, and recurring fires will not allow the growth of many hardwood trees, and fall color is limited as the Cascadian summer turns to winter. Some momentary gold is added to somber conifer stands by aspen, ash, cottonwood, tamarack, and sometimes bigleaf maple; but greater brilliance is left to relatively minor members of the forest community—the Douglas maple on eastern slopes and that "poor-relation" kind of tree, the vine maple, on the west. In one burst of red and yellow, the vine maple can make a forest glow with color, a feat that the mighty conifers and even veteran hardwoods cannot challenge.

THE GEOLOGIC EVOLUTION of the Cascades is complex, diverse, deceptive, and in places obscure. The low volcanic mountains in northern California have a relatively simple geologic history, but as one proceeds northward through the middle Cascades to the northern Cascades, that history changes and becomes more complicated. The only events common to both northern and southern ranges have been the Ice Age glaciation of their slopes and the building of the High Cascades.

Though much lava has poured from vents in High-Cascade volcanoes and from lava fields such as those around Mount Adams, Three Sisters, and Lassen Peak, most of the lava that has built the Cascades is of much earlier origin. At the very crest of the southern and middle Cascades are deposits of volcanic ash, light-colored andesite lava, and mudflows that may be as much as 50 million years old. Near Mount Rainier such deposits reach depths of one mile; on the Oregon Cas-

In the middle Cascades the crest is timbered and low, dramatically punctuated by occasional volcanic sentinels, among them Mount Thielsen, right, and the distant Three Sisters.

cades' western flank that thickness is three miles, and in the Cascades of central Washington it is twice that amount. The rock was folded, faulted, and intruded by chambers of cooling magma, called batholiths, which hardened into granite. Later the mountains built during these events were leveled by erosion.

The remnants of these early Cascades nearly disappeared in the floods of Columbia River basalt, between 12 and 20 million years ago. In the gorge of the Columbia River can be seen layers of basalt arched 2,800 feet above their surroundings by the uplift which raised the modern Cascades—the Cascade Orogeny. From the degree of displacement, geologists feel they have some quantitative measure of the uplift, even though the gorge is a low part of the Cascades. Unfortunately, erosion has stripped the Columbia basalt from higher portions of the range, so estimates of the full extent of the mountain building cannot be made. South of Mount Hood there is little satisfying evidence of the Cascade arch; perhaps it lies buried beneath thick sections of recently erupted volcanics, or perhaps the arch never extended farther south than Bend, and the elevation of the southern Cascades results only from accumulated lava and volcanic debris.

Today's High Cascades are not a unique phenomenon. Many older cones poured fire over the land after the Columbia River basalt floods (though few have been identified). Beacon Rock, five miles southwest of Bonneville Dam, and the Wind and Shellrock mountains, fifteen miles to the west, may once have been as imposing as any of the High Cascades of today.

The northern Cascades have been formed by some of the same geologic processes which raised both the Rockies and the Sierra Nevada. More than 250 million years ago the region may have been a lowland, a trough that received cast-off sediments from every mountain in the neighborhood, and from some very far away.

The rocks that remain from those times are marine sediments, dark sandstone, black shale, limestone, and submarine lava flows, which appear in the western foothills of the northern Cascades and the Okanogan River area to the east. There is unmistakable evidence that the ocean once existed where the northern Cascades now rise.

The Cretaceous period, a vast span of 70 million years ending about 60 million years ago, was a time of great change in the ancestral northern Cascades. A mountain uplift began, accompanied by severe folding and faulting of the rock layers and melting and recrystallization of rocks at the core of the range. Numerous batholiths rose from deep in the earth, intruding upon existing rock. Once they were solidified, the batholiths became an integral part of the mountain range.

The forces behind the uplift were so great as to tear apart mountains, forcing huge blocks of the mountain core outward to the margins of the range. One of the greatest of these rock skids, the Shuksan thrust, carried, sheared, and squeezed rocks west. What remains of the fault line itself extends from the vicinity of Mount Baker to the Skykomish River, perhaps even to Easton. A similar but smaller thrust displaced rock eastward six miles from the range. With the rising of the land, the sea retreated.

The northern Cascades of the Cretaceous are not those seen today; by 25 million years ago, they were worn down to gentle hills. It took a new uplift, acting along a single broad arch, and new, revitalized erosion to raise the present rugged, ragged mountains.

Because of its superior resistance to the elements, granite or metamorphic rock is the substance of some of the world's most pinnacled mountains. In the northern Cascades, granite intrusions form Mount Stuart, the Monte Cristo group, the Illabot Range, Dome Peak, and others. Metamorphic peaks include those of the Cascade Pass region, the Pickett Range (north of the Skagit River), Mount Shuksan, and Bonanza Peak—at 10,000 feet the highest of nonvolcanic Cascade peaks.

The varied mountain-building events in the Cascade chain culminated just prior to the Ice Age. The north end of the range was being uplifted and eroded, while its erupting southerly reaches were witnessing the accumulation of lava, ash, and mud. In the past few million years these histories have converged as the final uplift of the modern range, growth of the High Cascade cones, and glacial sculpturing have slowly molded the mountains of today.

Two eastern Cascade valleys serve to illustrate the nature of Cascade glaciation. Methow Valley is Washington's reply to California's Yosemite. The valley walls are steep; the floor is broad and long. The glacier that carved Methow derived in part from alpine ice in the surrounding range and in part from ice that flowed south out of British Columbia over 7,000-foot Harts Pass. The Methow glaciers extended to the present towns of Brewster and Pateros on the Columbia Plateau.

Lake Chelan is a classic example of a glacially carved basin and a testament to the efficiency of glacial erosion. At its zenith, the Chelan glacier stretched from near the Cascade crest to the Columbia River. It had receded well up the valley before the continental ice sheet reached and dammed the valley mouth at Chelan, raising the lake level by hundreds of feet. Water spilled south from the basin and into the Columbia River through Knapp and Navarre coulees, now dry. The valley carved by the Chelan glacier is now occupied by a lake nearly two thousand feet deep.

THESE ARE THE CASCADES. Like the Sierra Nevada and the Rockies, they are a major link in the vast continental mountain chain called the North American Cordillera. The continuing history of volcanism in these lushly forested peaks distinguishes them among American mountain ranges and makes them perhaps the most impressive topographic feature in the great Northwest.

In winter Pacific moisture turns the Cascades around Stevens Pass, Washington, into a skier's paradise.

CHAPTER 5

MOUNTAINS OF FIRE

The High Cascade volcanoes—living reminders of awesome forces that have built this range through the last 50 million years

VOLCANISM is as much a part of the Northwest as Douglas fir, the Columbia River, and the Pacific coastline, and nowhere else in the Northwest are volcanoes more awesome and conspicuous than in the High Cascades. Many volcanic cones, or their remnants, dot the landscape from northern California to the Canadian border; most principal volcanoes lie slightly east or west of the broad Cascade divide, but closely parallel its northerly trend. These peaks are solitary, bearing such names as Lassen, Shasta, Three Sisters, Jefferson, Hood, St. Helens, Adams, Rainier, and Baker; many are ice bound, and two rise well over fourteen thousand feet. Although geologists are uncertain as to their precise ages, the cones formed long after the rise of the surrounding Cascade Range, sometime in the last several million years.

The High Cascades are part of a great "Ring of Fire" encircling the Pacific, which includes such volcanoes as Krakatoa (Indonesia), Fuji (Japan), Cotopaxi (Ecuador), Popocatepetl (Mexico), and others. Modern geology links these volcanoes to the Cascades through the newly respectable theory of continental drift, which explains volcanism and other geological processes on a global scale.

The eruption of a volcano requires a source of molten rock contained within a large chamber that may lie twenty miles or deeper in the earth. This molten rock is called *magma* when below the earth's surface and *lava* when it flows onto the surface.

The eruptive cycle of an existing volcano actually begins while it appears dormant, its tranquil exterior belying the slow but unrelenting changes which have been occurring since the last eruption—a time measured in hundreds, perhaps thousands of years. The magma has been cooling, crystallizing, and driving out its volatile components—primarily water, the major explosive agent of the eruption. Expelled water and dissolved gases migrate to the upper reaches of the magma chamber, filling it with superheated fluid under high pressure. Finally, this pressure becomes too great for the earth to withstand, giving way to an eruption.

As magma nears the earth's surface, water separates and drives ahead of the moving mass. If the vent is blocked, the water—now in the form of steam—accumulates. When the vapors can no longer be confined, the steam, carbon dioxide, nitrogen, and sulfur gases from the magma push outward, explosively clearing the clogged vent. Lava bombs, cinders, and ash—essential ingredients in building the volcanic cone—are propelled out the now active vent by the persistent escape of searing gases. Magma flows, moving along a route of easiest escape, perhaps in an underground tubular conduit used by earlier eruptions or along a fracture or other weakness in the earth's fragile crust.

Magma rises to the surface from ever increasing depths as the lava continues to flow. Almost in a perversion of purpose, the water that gave the eruption its explosive beginnings is necessary to keep the magma fluid. In hell's chemistry, even small amounts of water can lower the melting point of rocks 1000°F or more in the magma chamber. Thus the deeper magma, having lost its water preparing to herald a new eruption, is very

To a mountaineer's eye, the rugged Cascades seem mere foothills at the base of the mighty volcanic peaks—here Mount Adams, seen from Mount Rainier.

viscous. Finally, it becomes so viscous that the lava at the vent can no longer flow; it cools, and again the vent is blocked. Only after the distillation of more water into the upper reaches of the magma chamber is the eruption revitalized.

Nature has multifarious recipes for magma, and not all are right for pyrotechnics. Magma consisting of basalt, rich in iron and calcium minerals, is runny and offers little resistance to the outward rush of volcanic gases. No destructive energies are pent within as the gases escape by a quiet bubbling of emerging lava. Only the viscous magmas are explosive, magmas such as silica-rich andesite, the substance of many High-Cascade volcanoes.

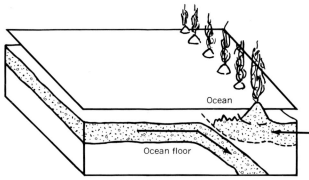

The drifting of the continents at times forces the ocean floor to slip under continental margins. Friction generates heat, which melts rocks and feeds inland volcanoes.

There are four major types of volcanoes: shield, cinder cone, plug dome, and composite. Each one has its representative Northwest landform, but nearly all of the high, magnificent cones of the Cascades are composite volcanoes.

When their lava pours out in quiet eruptions from a central vent, it builds a dome that is much broader than it is high—this is the shield volcano, or the Hawaiian variety, commonly found on the Modoc Plateau. If an eruption is explosive, lava is rendered into fragments of dust, sand, large blocks or bombs, and cinder, usually forming small cones that are steep and almost perfectly symmetrical. The composite volcanoes are formed layer by layer, as lava and explosion fragments settle on the sides of a developing cone.

Plug-dome volcanoes result from the rise of thick, pasty lava that forms a solid mass, blocking the crater between infrequent eruptions. Lassen Peak is the only major Cascade volcano of this type, although many have small domes associated with them.

There are no rules that tell a volcano how to develop, when to be active, when to be dormant, or even that its activity must remain at the summit. Often, as a result of internal pressures or violent activity, a parasitic cone develops on the side of its host, and lava is vented along a new channel. The main magma lines remain intact, but on the shoulder of the cone the weakened crust breaks and lava pours forth through a new vent. These outpourings of lava form satellite cones, such as Echo Rock and Observation Rock on Mount Rainier, and the very prominent Shastina on Shasta.

REMNANTS OF EARLIER VOLCANIC GIANTS are mingled among the present High Cascades. A shield volcano, Mount Newberry, once stood east of the Three Sisters; the outpouring of lava through countless satellite cones on its flank catastrophically collapsed its broad summit to the present cold caldera, five miles across. Mount Tehama, which once stood near where Lassen Peak now rises, had a base fifteen miles across. And Mount Mazama's 11,000-foot summit once stood 5,000 feet above Crater Lake.

For Mount Mazama, the end came seven thousand years ago. Klamath Indian legend recalls that Mount Mazama was the domain of Llao, chief of the world below, who would visit the surface by passing through Mazama's summit crater and be seen as a dark form against the white snow. The chief of the world above was Skell; at times he would stand upon Mount Shasta, one hundred miles to the south. The legend then tells of a war between the gods, a time of great explosions, thunder, burning ash that fell from the sky, and lava that spilled down the mountainside. Flames destroyed the forests and the Klamaths' homes. Seven days of darkness were lit only by the flaming mountains. The battle was climaxed by Mazama's remarkable destruction, as Llao's throne collapsed within itself, sealing shut his door to the surface. Llao was never again to frighten the Indians. As the crater filled with clear water, the lake became serene and beautiful.

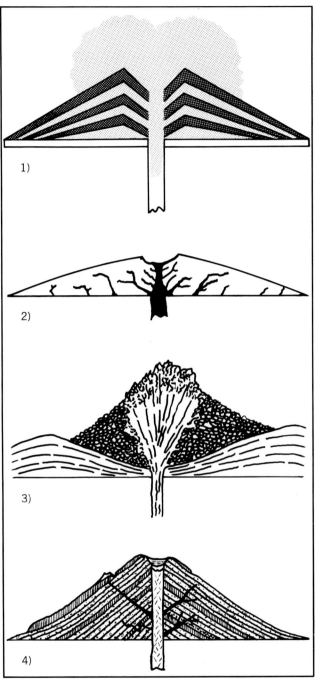

The four major types of volcanic cones

Cinder cone: Formed by the explosive ejection of dust and particles of lava; rarely higher than 1,200 feet.

Shield volcano: A low, broad cone created by thin lavas that flow easily even down gentle slopes.

Plug-dome volcano: A massive dome created by the cooling of lava too thick to flow beyond the vent.

Composite cone: Steep slopes and high summits formed of alternating layers of cinders and lava.

In all respects, the development of Mazama through the millennia had not been unusual. Its rise began hundreds of thousands of years ago; there were times of quiet and cycles of eruption when Mazama developed more and more of its structure. It was quiet through much of the Great Ice Age; glaciers appeared on its slopes and disappeared. But inside, the magma was churning.

Events of Mazama's final eruption probably followed in rapid succession. Increasing stresses likely touched off a series of earthquakes, followed by enormous clouds of exploding gases. Falling ash and embers covered the land and ignited the forests. Pumice was blown from the mountain and carried to the northeast on prevailing winds. Glaciers melted, sending floods of water down the steep mountainside. The summit crater spilled over with frothy material and poured down in a series of glowing avalanches, which came to rest as far as thirty-five miles from the mountain. Large trees fell and were carbonized by the intense heat, then buried deeply under volcanic bombs and debris.

Accompanying the eruptions, great cracks developed beneath the volcano, and as the holocaust continued, molten rock drained out of its magma chamber. Deprived of support, the remainder, Mazama's heavy shell, tumbled inward upon the void. In this way, one of Oregon's highest mountains was transformed into one of the world's deepest lakes.

For the Klamath Indians, the beauty of Crater Lake may have been overshadowed by its fearful legends of birth. Few of the Indians ever trod the game trails which led to this "battleground of the gods," and many believed that only punishment awaited those who looked at the blue water so sacred to the spirits.

Volcanic activity does not usually cease after the cataclysms which form calderas. After the collapse of Mazama, volcanic activity again flared within the caldera, forming the small cone known as Wizard Island and two other cones now hidden by lake water. The rim of Newberry Crater encloses a glittering obsidian flow, and two overlapping cinder cones, all formed after the caldera. The cinder cones separate the placid Paulina and East lakes. Renewed volcanic activity related to Mount Tehama thrust upward the viscous plug-dome lava comprising Lassen Peak, considered a high volcano in its own right.

When burned with atmospheric oxygen and then combined with water vapor, sulfurous volcanic fumes produce highly acrimonious sulfurous and sulfuric acids that can decompose and dissolve rock, accelerating the aging of volcanic rocks. The summit crater of Mount Baker, northernmost of the High Cascades, shows an interesting and less destructive alteration of summit lavas by sulfur compounds. Rising vapors fill most of the crater's porous rock, and crystalline sulfur collects within the many cavities, but rather than decaying vent lavas to rubble, the vapors have frosted much of the lava with a coating of brilliant white opal, giving the summit a porcelainlike appearance.

Mount Baker, northernmost Cascade volcano, has lain dormant for over fifteen thousand years.

O N MANY VOLCANIC SLOPES life is just now reaching equilibrium, with soils maturing and plants and animals learning to live where once the land was sterile. Volcanic soils are among the richest on earth, but they need time to develop. Even after many hundreds of years, most of the Northwest's lava flows retain a fresh look, supporting only lichen and an occasional clump of grass where dust has settled in wind-sheltered niches. Pumice-covered slopes, as on Mount St. Helens, may have such an unstable surface and such complete drainage that trees cannot gain a footing.

There has been ample time for soil formation on most of the Cascade volcanoes; below timberline, often in parklike meadows, alpine fir and mountain hemlock can gain a footing with whitebark pine and Engelmann spruce. At lower elevations trees of the slopes fade to the dominance of nodding western hemlock, white pine, and many species of fir.

The seasons bring distinctive moods to the Cascade volcanoes, and all life takes heed of the changes. Winter is an eight-month affair of heavy snow and sparkling air; trees bend gracefully beneath their heavy burdens and give shelter to many animals. Spring is signaled by the melting of snow, northward flights of ducks and geese, bears' hungry emergence from their winter dens, and deers' migration up the slopes to forage. Birdcalls attract the Cascade hiker, and Clark's nutcrackers, mountain bluebirds, and ravens are commonly seen. Spring also heralds blossoming of forest and meadow.

On Mount Rainier and high in the Cascades, there are two magnificent periods of blooming. June sun brings out Pacific trillium, bunchberry dogwood, three-leaf anemone, and the showy bear grass; mountain parks glow with mountain buttercup, yellow lamb's-tongue, fawnlily (glacier lily), marsh marigold, western pasqueflower, and avalanche fawnlily. Some impatient fawnlilies eagerly push through the snow in July, but August brings the second great display, of lupines, Indian paintbrush, valerian, cinquefoil, American bistort, and many other meadow flowers, which fill the air with a delicate perfume.

Autumn is brooding and unpredictable with its crisp air and bright blue skies interrupted by periodic storms; the mountain roadways that pass near or loop around the great volcanoes are quickly closed by the onset of an early snow. Heaviest precipitation falls on the wind-

When a volcanic cataclysm ripped off the summit of Mount Mazama, it left the volcano's jagged outer walls. Today Crater Lake is a peaceful counterpoint to that violent history.

Ape Cave on Mount St. Helens is a spectacular lava tube two miles long, produced when the shell of the flow cooled and solidified, and the still-molten interior drained away.

ward slopes of the High Cascades, especially between 5,000 and 10,000 feet. Above 6,000 feet, the northern snowfields are perennial, and glaciers may extend below the perennial snowline.

For all their sterile appearance, glaciers can be alive with small creatures. Lowland insects are frequently caught in the updraft currents around mountains and carried onto the summits; they may become trapped in bowl-shaped sun cups, which the sun has burned into the snow. Glacial ice itself might contain the wiggling bodies of thousands of tiny ice worms, which sustain themselves on pollens, spores, dust, and microbes that proliferate as unseen microcolonies upon the snowpack, riding glacial ice to whatever fate may await them.

A glacier can be a plow, a file, or a sled. As a plow, it loosens rock and churns debris already free; as a file, it employs the loose material to rasp and polish solid rock in its pathway; and as a sled, it removes the plowed and filed rock, and any rock that has fallen from valley walls. On Mount Rainier, long glaciers have stripped as much as 2,000 feet from the original cone. Little Tahoma is an ice-carved remnant of that former skin, but it too must fall to vigorous erosion. Its continued destruction was punctuated in 1963 by massive rock-falls, which removed a substantial portion of the sharp, triangular, tooth-shaped projection.

Glaciers are less a result of the cold at high altitude than of an ample moisture supply available from the Pacific, producing more snow in winter months than is melted down in summer. The pressure from each addi-

Winter snows, which belie Mount Hood's fiery roots, do not daunt determined climbers. Immediately below the highest spire is Hood's main vent.

tional season's snowfall converts some bottom snow layers to ice, changing a snow mass into a glacier. The flow builds enormous stresses as bottom layers conform to irregularities of the slope, seeming to move independently of the upper "stories." Huge tension cracks, called crevasses, are the outcome. Often hidden by frail snow bridges, they are a hazard to mountaineers on many Cascade summit climbs. Knowing the risk of traversing crevasses, climbers at Camp Muir on Mount Rainier were once amazed to watch a black bear as he jumped and zigzagged, avoiding the many chasms on Nisqually Glacier.

The inner structure of volcanoes is sometimes exposed by glacial excavation of more youthful lavas. Radial dikes and conduit fillings of North Sister have been bared by Ice Age glaciation. In the same way, the huge Sunset Amphitheater at the head of Puyallup Glacier breaches Rainier's old central plug.

Eruptions in the last few thousand years hold a promise of future activity. North from Newberry Crater is a long fissure where the earth has cracked from internal stresses as lava has pushed upward. Lava from this fissure has changed the course of the Deschutes River and created numerous small cones, among them Lava Butte, formed five to six thousand years ago.

Only centuries ago fresh vents opened on the south slope of South Sister to explode frothy pumice fragments, then to spread thick glassy lavas over the coun-

Fresh-looking lavas, issuing from cones near the North Sister, have spilled all the way to McKenzie Pass, but since the Ice Ages, North and Middle Sisters themselves have been dormant.

tryside; simultaneously, new fissures opened a mile east, pouring out viscous lavas that chilled in steep-sided mounds and flows with tops littered by angular lava blocks and slender shards of obsidian. On these fresh lavas, trees are dramatically absent. Equally young are the black and red cinder cones on North Sister's barren north flank, and the lava streams which issued down from them to McKenzie Pass. A long spill followed White Branch Creek for several miles, overflowing into Linton Creek and forming Linton Lake.

From the summit of McKenzie Pass can be seen the miles of black basaltic wilderness—in one direction seventy square miles of lava from Belknap Crater alone,

in another the basalt tongues and cinder cones of North Sister. The Belknap flows seem frozen to a standstill as they pushed over ice-scraped older lavas.

Mount Shasta's latest eruption, from its central crater, left a veneer of pumice, cinders, lava blocks, and volcanic bombs upon the landscape. This may have occurred as recently as 1786, when an explorer in the area reported an explosive eruption.

Eyewitness accounts by Hudson's Bay Company personnel tell of activity on St. Helens between the mid-1830s and the mid-1850s. The last major eruption of pumice occurred in November, 1842. One French-Canadian witness reported the light from the volcano

Collapse and volcanic refilling of its summit cone have given Mount Rainier a more rounded, broad-shouldered silhouette than other Cascade volcanoes.

The beautiful double cones of Mount Shasta (left) and Shastina rise from a hummocky volcanic lowland; Shasta was joined by its satellite cone when a new vent opened late in its volcanic history.

was so intense that he could find a pin in the grass near his cabin at midnight though the volcano was twenty miles in the distance. Mount St. Helens may be the youngest of the major Cascade cones since its smooth sides show few signs of the glacial erosion evident on other peaks of the High Cascades.

Some ash and considerable steam was erupted from Mount Baker in the early 1840s, and minor amounts of steam still issue from the summit crater. There is little evidence, however, for any significant eruptions in the last few thousand years.

Being the tallest and perhaps most dominating of the High Cascade volcanoes, Mount Rainier has at-

tracted considerable study. Radiocarbon dating procedures conducted on wood samples found buried in pumice and mudflows show that Rainier has erupted at least three times in the last ten thousand years. One series of eruptions about two thousand years ago formed the present summit craters, which contain small steam vents that melt caves in the ice cap.

Observers report that Rainier was in eruption on at least fourteen different occasions between 1820 and 1894. At least one eruption of Mount Rainier between 1820 and 1854 is known to have spread pumice over an area east of Rainier. Captain John Frémont recorded in his journals that Rainier was erupting in November

phenomenon that, in the late 1800s, reports of Hood's eruption were frequent, but examinations of the summit gave proof that no eruption could have occurred within recent times. Mount Hood's cloud plume is by no means unique among high mountains.

In 1914, however, no one could deny the eruption of Lassen Peak. On 30 May several people were looking directly at the volcano when small ash puffs first appeared. No lavas ensued, and the next day a forest ranger investigated the summit; a small crater, twenty-five by forty feet, had formed on the mountain top. Cinders, mud, and rock were scattered about, and ash was found up to one-eighth of a mile away.

In the following year, there were one hundred fifty eruptions, most minor, but many intensely explosive, and by year's end the crater had enlarged to a gaping one thousand-foot hole.

The next May brought the first appearance of glowing lavas; a black mass rose into the crater and spilled down the mountain slopes to form a tongue one thousand feet long. With the winter's accumulation of snow, volcanism on the east slope was taking the form of a devastating mudflow which poured into the valleys of Hat and Lost creeks. Three days later a second mudflow was followed by a *nuée ardente,* a ground-hugging blast of hot gases, charged with dust and rock fragments, felling trees many miles from the summit. This area still lies in devastation.

Activity declined from 1915 to 1917. Though ash and steam eruptions continued to threaten renewed activity, what resulted was only development of new vents and a modification of the old crater walls.

1843, and others reported eruptions in 1820, 1846, and 1854. One or more of these could be related to the pumice eruption. There is no confirming evidence, however, that lava or ash was actually observed in the last half of the nineteenth century; it seems that these reports may have been prompted by sightings of dust rising from large rockfalls and avalanches, by people who wished to see more than was there.

Mount Hood has also undergone imaginary eruptions. On Mount Hood's northern side, in a sheltered summit cirque, clouds frequently collect even on clear days and may rise above the peak in the appearance of steam issuing from the summit. So deceptive was this

GEOLOGISTS are concerned about possible future volcanic activity in the Cascades. Earthquake monitors are taking the pulse rate of major Cascade volcanoes, and aircraft equipped with infrared scanning devices regularly fly over the Cascades. These measurements have not yet shown anything unusual.

In the last few thousand years there have been many outbreaks of volcanism which have produced extensive lava flows, and even in historic times there has been at least minor activity. With time scales as long as millions of years, there is no reason to believe that the present lull is anything more than just that.

CHAPTER 6

THE LAVA PLATEAUS

*Exploring the barren beauty of another kind of landscape,
also poured out from the fiery interior of the earth*

SPARSITY AND SPACIOUSNESS combine in the Northwest's lava plateaus to create a barren land that hides no secrets but its own; it is a land of austere beauty, lacking the apparent complexity to be found in other parts of the Northwest. The interior plateaus include most of the Northwest's lava, their greatest distinction. Having come in vast floods from many elongated fissures, the lavas lie in expansive sheets across the land, in contrast to the spectacular, solitary cones typical of the High Cascades. It is basalt, a fluid lava that spreads quickly and sometimes flowed up to one hundred miles from its origin.

Overlapping lava flows cover almost one hundred thousand square miles from Grand Coulee country to Oregon's desert, from the middle Cascades to the Blue Mountains, and along the Snake River Plain in south-central Idaho. In some areas the lavas are folded or faulted, forming ridges and mountain ranges; elsewhere older rocks protrude through the lava as nonvolcanic mountains. Principal subregions are the Columbia Plateau, the Blue Mountains, the Oregon Desert (known also as either the Great Sandy Desert or the Great Sage Plain), and the Snake River Plain. Some subregions are not part of the standard tour of the Northwest; others are unmistakably scenic attractions.

Southeastern Washington—the Columbia Plateau—is dry, slightly rolling, broken by highlands of the Saddle Mountains, Rattlesnake Hills, and Horse Heaven Hills, and cut by such rivers as the Columbia, Palouse, Umatilla, Snake, and Yakima. From the air, much of the land appears scarred and barren. This is the Chan-

neled Scabland, an intricate pattern of wandering, intersecting channels. The scabland was eroded by high-velocity streams (floods) that resulted from repeated breaking of ice dams upstream. The major floods came down the Clark Fork from glacial Lake Missoula in Montana. The water split into multiple spillways and canyons, or coulees, leaving isolated buttes and mesas like beacons above the devastation. Small coulee lakes, the scattered remnants of the ancient rivers, are easily observed along a highway which travels the Grand Coulee between Dry Falls and Soap Lake. Less accessible than Grand Coulee, Moses Coulee and Dry Coulee are untouched by local irrigation projects and are spectacular illustrations of virgin scabland.

South of Grand Coulee is Washington's Big Bend wheat belt—a treeless but fertile rolling plateau made productive by water from the Grand Coulee irrigation system. An extensive and unique deposit, known as Palouse soil, lies atop the basalt. It is soil formed on loess, a silt deposited by the wind. Most, if not all, was derived from silt (rock flour) carried by the streams of melting glaciers. Some silt has been blown from white bluffs on the Columbia (north of Hanford, Washington), some from the floodplains of the Snake, but most from the nearby Pasco region.

The loess is light-colored and lightweight, darkened on the surface by a rich organic top layer that makes it fertile. It was deposited in places to depths greater than one hundred feet; much of it accumulating before the last glacial advance. Had the Canadian ice sheet dipped south beyond Coulee City, the Palouse country

*Despite its fresh appearances, lava at Craters of the Moon National Monument is surprisingly old
—1,350 years, as chronicled by growth rings in the Triple Twist Tree.*

would not be the fertile wheat producer it is today.

Couched between the rolling hills of Washington's wheat country to the north, a wide and dusty desert to the south, the High Cascades to the west, and Hells Canyon to the east, is the Blue Mountain area, a highland piercing the sea of basalt and one of the most geologically complex parts of the plateau region. Most of its many individual mountain groups (especially the Wallowas) are rugged and extensively glaciated, dotted with high cirques and tarns. Valleys like John Day and Baker are also complex in structure, some resulting from downward folding and some from faults.

In many parts of the Blue Mountains, Columbia River basalt tops the high peaks. Already low hills when lava spread around and over them, the Blue Mountains were submerged by two thousand feet or more of fresh lava. As the hills continued their uplift, basalt became cap rock atop the mountains of sedimentary, metamorphic, and igneous rock. Continuing erosion has since removed portions of the basalt, but extensive areas remain much as when formed, the elevated segments of a lava plateau.

Many Blue-Mountain peaks rise between 9,000 and 10,000 feet—not high by Cascade standards, but high enough to catch and hold snow that nourishes the region's myriad rivers and alpine lakes.

This is ranch country, mainly devoted to the raising of Hereford and Black Angus cattle, and sheep. Valleys are pasture lands that also produce two hay crops every

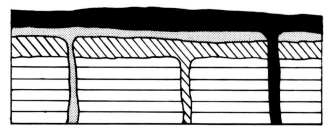
Cross section of a lava plateau reveals numerous layers and long fissure vents hidden by their own lavas.

year. The towns of La Grande, Baker, Durkee, Unity, and John Day, which service ranch needs, are also the gateways to summer and winter resorts—at Anthony Lakes in the Blue Mountains and Wallowa Lake in the Wallowas. Open conifer forests stretch from foothills to timberline and shelter mule deer, elk, and, at Hells Canyon, bighorn sheep newly introduced from the Canadian Rockies.

Most areas of the Blue Mountains are scenic, but few are as geologically important as the John Day Fossil Beds. Situated between the towns of John Day and Condon, Oregon, they consist of several thousand feet of varicolored, nearly pure volcanic ash capped by Columbia River basalt. The lowest bed has been chemically altered to a bright red-brown, and the middle one to green, while the upper stratum remains white, probably its original color. From these beds has come much of the Northwest's storehouse of vertebrate fossils, including ancestors of the modern cat, dog, rabbit, pig, opossum, rodents, and some species presently uncommon in the West—the camel, tapir, rhinoceros, and an extinct vegetarian, cud-chewing hog called the oreodon. All roamed the Northwest about thirty million years ago. In the John Day fossil record has been found a complete evolutionary history of the horse.

Not only do the Blue Mountains contain high summits, but also the deepest canyon in the United States; Hells Canyon on the Snake River, separates the Wallowas of Oregon from the Seven Devils of Idaho. Struggling to survive against the uplifting Blue Mountains, the Snake River has cut a channel almost 6,000 feet deep through basalt and the tougher metamorphic rock greenstone. From the summit of He Devil Peak, seven miles east of Hells Canyon, to river level is a descent of 7,900 feet, whereas from Bright Angel Point,

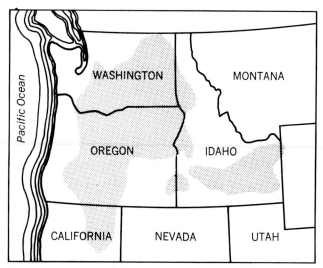
Volcanic plateaus (shaded) were born of fluid lava.

Winter at Dry Falls, where the prehistoric Columbia River plunged four hundred feet from the upper Grand Coulee, thundering like a hundred Niagaras.

equally distant from the Colorado River in Grand Canyon, the descent is only 5,650 feet. Though lacking the vibrant colors of Grand Canyon, the scale of Hells Canyon is spectacular and overwhelming.

Perhaps because Oregonian chambers of commerce have not viewed it as an asset, the Oregon Desert is an area few tourists ever see; yet the desert is as much of a refuge from civilization as the cool mountains. Approximately 180 by 250 miles, or roughly a quarter of the state, the Oregon Desert spans five counties—Deschutes, Crook, Lake, Harney, and Malheur—and has but one major highway. Branching from the main highway are the ranch roads, leading to land where the rainfall never reaches the sea, where the sagebrush plateau is broken by rocky escarpments climbing nearly half a mile. Much wind passes over this land, and its dry handiwork accentuates each rough crack in the earth's surface.

In towns called Blitzen, Plush, Fort Rock and Denio, one hears local lore as expansive as the landscape. It is said that the earliest settlers used the distance for fences, before they discovered the tough old juniper tree. Some old-timers have sworn those gnarled juniper posts had been known to wear out three sets of post holes before the baking sun, wind, and the cold finally made them feeble. Ranchers, service station owners, and other desert proprietors sometimes make a decorative fence around the front of their property with deer horn (never with antelope horn; for some reason, a discarded antelope rack makes such good chewing that it will attract every porcupine for miles around).

The government owns most of the desert—about 70 percent in dry Harney County—particularly the land with no water. For seventy years the land was offered free to homesteaders. Most of those who claimed land left quickly, sometimes before proving up; the hardier eventually sold their title for five to fifty cents an acre.

Life in the desert is surprising and lively, whether

Fertile soil pays dividends to dry-farmers of the Palouse Hills wheatlands, here near Colfax, though light rainfall necessitates alternating crops or letting soil lie fallow.

expressed in the sudden scurry of a sagebrush cotton-tail, the comical mating strut of a sage grouse, the swoop and call from a magpie, the antelope's sudden white flag signal before darting from danger, or even the startling bright burst of color that desert-wise plants save for spring.

Conservation of vital energy is a secret to staying alive in the desert. The perils of imprudence are swift, often as raw as the symbolic skull whitened by a pitiless sun. Ingenious desert plants obey rules of survival gleaned from thousands of years' trial. First, plants must save moisture. The leaves of the Idaho fescue roll inward, as if imitating the needles of the pine; junipers have a form of scale for a leaf, and sagebrush simply resorts to small leaves. Perennials like rabbit brush, in dry years, go dormant, while annuals go to seed quickly in spring, and then die. Seeds have hard, dry exteriors to protect vital tissues inside.

Even when a plant has dwarfed its size, reduced its leaf surface, and shortened its growth period, it has not assured survival against predators. So desert plants make themselves unattractive to animals, including antelope, elk, deer, and rabbits. Some are astringent, some bitter; others—like cacti—have thorns. Wild phlox has dry, leathery leaves; mullein's leaves are wooly; juniper is resinous and sticky as glue. Some species resort to the ultimate and are poisonous.

The Oregon Desert lacks surface water. There are some rivers of respectable size—the Chewaucan, the Silvies, and the Donner and Blitzen—yet little of their water goes any distance. The farther these rivers flow, the smaller they become; finally they evaporate or empty into shallow lakes with no outlets.

In some ways, the apparent aridity is misleading. Under the earth's skin—here composed of two thousand feet of Lake County lava—water is ample. Much of it is hot, and in many parts of Lake and other southwestern counties, hot springs are numerous. Near Paisley, in the Hart Mountain Antelope Refuge, at the base of Steens Mountain, and near Vale are natural hot springs.

From three layers of volcanic ash in the John Day Fossil Beds have come an assortment of plant and animal fossils that suggest eastern Oregon was once warmer and moister than today.

Attempts at drilling wells for drinking water have occasionally and surprisingly yielded man-made geysers when the extreme subterranean heat flashes water to steam at its first chance to escape to the surface.

Another kind of subterranean reservoir waters the Lost Forest, northeast of Christmas Lake, where nine thousand acres of ponderosa pine grow in a region with far too little rain for ponderosa to survive. Fifteen thousand years ago, when climate was moist and interior Oregon shining with huge lakes, ponderosa was abundant, but now the annual rainfall has diminished to a mere ten inches; yet, Lost Forest thrives, supported by a quirk of nature. A surface accumulation of drifting sand covers a lower layer of impervious volcanic debris, and the two layers trap moisture from the limited rainfall. To the roots of the Lost Forest this offers an underground oasis.

Surface water comes and goes with the seasons, and many high desert lakes shrink or dry up altogether during summer months. Even large ones are not im-mune, as was discovered by early settlers at Goose Lake, near the California border. For many years, they wondered about the weathered wagon ruts leading up to the lake shore and continuing from water's edge on the opposite side, for the lake was too deep to ford. Then, one season when the water completely dried up, they found wagon ruts leading across the lake bed.

One need not look very far in the Oregon Desert to find signs of its volcanic history. The glacial scar known as Kiger Gorge in Steens Mountain, near Frenchglen, reveals dozens of successive flows of the dark basalt. The northwest portions of the region in particular display many cinder cones, fresh-looking lava flows, and explosion craters—such as Hole-in-the-Ground—that appear much like bomb craters.

Some of the most beautiful mountains of the Oregon Desert have been caused by gigantic displacements of the land. The earth's thin and brittle crust—much like fractured, uneven winter ice on a lake—is interrupted by fault lines and scarps. Abert Rim, twenty-five miles north of Lakeview, is a scarp which climbs steeply almost three thousand feet above the eastern shore of Abert Lake. Steens Mountain is the result of displacements along two faults. The earth sank on both sides of the central mountain block, and now five thousand feet separate the top of Steens Mountain from the floor of the Alvord Desert.

Hart Mountain was also created by a fault block, but its fame lies in the valley below its three-thousand-foot escarpment, the Hart Mountain Antelope Refuge. The region was selected as a refuge because it includes favorite fawning grounds and has a permanent water supply. About 200 antelope are year-round residents while another 500 are transients, wintering at the Sheldon Antelope Range in Nevada and returning to bear fawns, usually twins, in Oregon. Sharing the refuge are mule deer, a rare group of California bighorn sheep, and in Warner Valley, pelicans.

THE SNAKE RIVER PLAIN, covering much of southern Idaho from Wyoming to Oregon, is Idaho's contribution to the great lava floods of the Northwest.

Though some of the best-known examples of recent volcanism are located in the Cascade Range, Craters of the Moon National Monument on the edge of the Snake River Plain is, for the average visitor, perhaps the best place in the Northwest to view a wide variety of fresh volcanic features.

Most eruptions in Craters of the Moon have occurred along the Great Rift, a series of parallel fractures that run southeast from the Pioneer Mountains for a dozen or more miles. Cinder cones built along or near the rift rise 120 to 800 feet above the plain. Some spilled out lava from cracks in their bases, while around others small spatter cones formed. In some areas low shield-type volcanoes were built, none more than a few tens of feet high. Most eruptions in the monument were quite small in scope and not violent.

While the lava is chiefly basalt, it occurs in two distinctive forms—*pahoehoe* (pah-ho′ay-ho′ay) and *aa* (ah′ah), named for their Hawaiian archetypes. Pahoehoe is almost always a shiny steel blue, ropy and billowy, and sometimes is riddled with caverns. Its wrinkled appearance results when the outer lava, cooler and thus more viscous, is twisted and distorted by the more fluid

Rising beyond Hells Canyon, the 9,000-foot Seven Devils Mountains of Idaho (seen from Hat Point) remain a primitive retreat for the wilderness seeker.

Imnaha River Canyon in the Wallowas, created in the last fifteen million years as the river carved through many cubic miles of basalt.

moving interior. Lava tubes, which occur only in pahoehoe lava, usually form as the main body of the flow cools, restricting active flow to the thickest, hottest part. Eventually the bulk of the flow solidifies and the still-molten lava drains from the interior, leaving a void—the lava tube.

Indian Tunnel is the largest tube within the monument, but many other caves lie along the Great Rift zone. An ancient Indian trail followed the rift connecting the caves, which were once used as temporary shelters or strongholds.

Aa lava is rough and jagged. It flows as a thick mass, and the cool surface crumbles and breaks with the movement of the lava. As pasty chunks separate, they pull with them stringers of lava. These ragged pieces, or "clinkers," ride on the surface; some tumble to the margins, others fall below the flow. When the doughy mass freezes to a halt, the lava flow is a confused mass of angular blocks almost impossible to traverse on foot and most unpleasant for sitting.

One might expect that in a short time the sharp edges of aa lavas might weather away. In Idaho's arid climate, however, weathering is slow, and flows 1,500 years old still look fresh.

Amid so harsh an environment it may seem remarkable there should be any life at all, but along the monument's trails one sees the yellow-pine chipmunk, golden-mantled ground squirrel, chickaree (or red squirrel), and the yellow-bellied marmot foraging and gathering. Mule deer follow their trails throughout the monument, and occasionally a coyote or bobcat comes into view. In the early morning and late afternoon, the rock wren, Clark's nutcracker, and mourning dove can be seen. Midday, swallows and mountain bluebirds search for food with color, dash, and a sense of the acrobatic.

Spring brings out the silvery leaves of the dwarf buckwheat and the pink pompoms, sprinkling color among the cinder slopes. Come June or early July, a magenta hue spreads over wide areas of cinder as dwarf monkey-flowers mat the ground.

Steens Mountain in Oregon was raised as the earth's crust slipped along a fault at its eastern base, creating a dramatic contrast to the flat Alvord Desert.

The usual desert plants—sagebrush, antelope bitter-brush, and rubber rabbit brush—are able to reclaim the younger lava flows. One must look to the cooler, moister north-facing slopes of older cones for the trees—limber pine, aspen, juniper, even Douglas-fir.

Lava tubes are natural refrigerators. In some caves in Craters of the Moon and elsewhere on the Snake River Plain, ice may be found in mid-summer. During winter, the relatively dense cold air sinks into the depths of the caves and freezes water that has drained into the tubes. The warm air of spring and summer does not displace the dense air trapped in the caves. Thus, the ice persists under its blanket of cold air and is replenished when winter comes.

To anyone crossing the Snake River Plain on a sunny summer day, water seems remote. In fact it is not, for beneath the plain lies a vast underground water system, fed by seasonal rains and upstate rivers that quickly disappear into thousands of square miles of fractured basalt. Known as the Snake Plains Aquifer, this underground water system is a tremendous natural resource with a water capacity hundreds of times greater than that of surface reservoirs along the Snake.

The Snake Plains Aquifer is a consequence of ancient battles between rivers of lava and rivers of water for dominance over the land. The Snake Plain is continually sinking, and as it does, the Snake and rivers from the mountainous north have left deposits of gravel, sand, and silt interwoven with many layers of lava from numerous fissures and small shield volcanoes.

Faced with the recurring challenge of the lava flows, some rivers have simply disappeared into the many porous layers of river deposits throughout the lava flows. Such has happened with the Big and the Little Lost rivers, and Birch Creek, which sink into the lava plain northeast of Arco.

The waters which collect in the Snake Plains Aquifer reach the Snake River through gigantic springs in a

Cooled "aa" lava is sharp, angular, and blocky, as in this lava cave at Craters of the Moon.

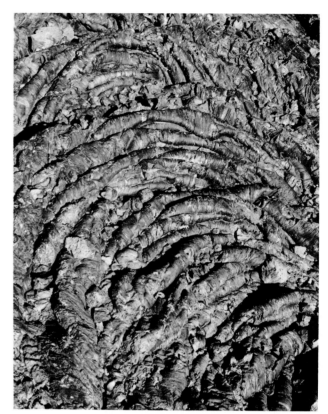

"Pahoehoe" lava has a smooth surface; viscous when hot, it cools into folded, twisted, or ropelike forms.

ninety-four mile stretch of its north bank downstream from Milner Dam. Their contribution to the river flow is considerable. Voluminous Thousand Springs alone pours more water into the Snake River near Hagerman than is carried there by the river itself.

THE GREAT UNIFYING FEATURE of the Northwest's plateau region is the lava flood. Most of the flows spread across the land 10 to 20 million years ago, so long past

that another onslaught of basalt does not seem imminent. However, as in the High Cascades, there are signs that the earth still seethes beneath the lava crust, and there is a possibility, indeed a probability, of renewed activity. To man, seeing through his brief shutter opening in time, the landscape seems immutable, but the character of the plateaus is continually changing as the forces which shaped them—erosion by wind and water, faulting and upheaval, floods and fire—work by the rhythms of slow geologic time.

CHAPTER 7

THE MIGHTY COLUMBIA

From its source high in the Canadian Rockies to its rendezvous with the Pacific, 1,200 miles downstream

IT WAS NAMED for the first ship to enter its waters. It extends 1,200 miles from above Lake Columbia in the Canadian Rockies to a deep-water harbor adjoining the Pacific Ocean. In that length it creates some of the Northwest's most beautiful scenery, much of it upon a lava plateau. Some 259,000 square miles of land lie within its drainage, including nearly all of Idaho, most of Washington and Oregon, the western part of Montana, smaller areas in Wyoming and Nevada, and the northwestern tip of Utah. Gathering strength from scores of tributaries—among them the Kootenai, the Pend Oreille, the Spokane, the Okanogan, the Snake (largest of all), the Deschutes, the Willamette, and the Cowlitz—it meanders in all directions outflanking the mountain barrier between it and the sea. By the time it pours into the Pacific, it has drained one-fourteenth of the continental United States. It is an important salmon river; a river in harness, working for man; a river of many moods, but always beautiful. It is, of course, the Columbia.

Though the existence of a tremendous river in the Northwest had been rumored for centuries—the Spanish calling it by such names as River of the Kings or Río San Roque, the English and Americans postulating a River of the West or the Mighty Oregon—the Columbia's recorded history did not begin until 11 May, 1792, when a young Boston sea captain gathering otter skins for the China market found his way through the tumult of the guardian bar. He named the stream for his ship, the *Columbia Rediviva,* first vessel to carry the American flag around the world. From that crossing of the bar grew the United States claim to the Oregon country.

Meriwether Lewis and William Clark added to American claims of discovery in the area when in 1805 the Corps of Discovery paddled down the Clearwater to the Snake, down the Snake to the Columbia, and down the Columbia to the Pacific. Today busy highways follow the river's course from the Canadian border to Cape Adams and Cape Disappointment, most of the distance remaining in sight of the stream. Along the way are forested mountains, quiet farms shaded by fruit orchards, lacy waterfalls, precipitous cliffs, sandy beaches, overgrown islands, and (as if reflecting a new order of things) works of man—mammoth dams, locks, and bridges.

Melt from the snowfields and glaciers of the Selkirks and other ranges of the Rockies nourishes this great river. For one-sixth of its length it flows between the ranges. In its infancy the river drops only four inches to the mile; the locals call it "The Channel." But at the town of Golden its character changes. The Kicking Horse, carrying water from half a dozen glaciers along the crest of the Canadian Rockies, pours into the Columbia and, doubled in size and strength, it rushes onward with a show of power. At Redgrove Canyon the valley narrows to a gorge one thousand feet across, and the river, sweeping around a sharp curve, generates its first permanent whirlpool, deep and dangerous.

Some thirty miles farther downstream, the Columbia moves gently, almost soundlessly, into a canyon, tilts down a steep slope, and breaks into the disaster area called Surprise Rapids. After twenty rough miles the

Swollen by a spate of tributaries, the Columbia River follows the course it cut long ago through the Cascades. From Crown Point, one can see thirty miles up or down the river.

torrent slows and widens into Kinbasket Lake. Cobalt blue water lies calmly between the ranges, the Selkirks to the west and to the east the Rockies, hill upon hill, peak upon peak, rising to the ice fields below the continental divide.

The calm is deceptive. There were twenty major rapids on the Columbia before the engineers went to work: one-third lay in the twenty-five miles between Kinbasket Lake and the great bend of the river above Boat Encampment; there, after heading toward the Arctic Ocean for its first 230 miles, the river hairpins around the Selkirk escarpment. Held in by the Monashee bulwark, it rushes south by west toward the United States, and the Pacific. It is this change of direction which spared the Columbia the fate of the neglected Mackenzie and made it, as the only navigable gravity route through the Northwest mountains, a river coveted by the maritime nations.

At Revelstoke the Columbia waters enter the long, natural basin of the Upper and Lower Arrow Lakes; they wind through the mountains for a distance of 130 solitary miles.

Below the lakes at the little Doukhobor town of Brilliant, the Columbia is joined by its Canal Flats cradlemate, the Kootenai, which for most of its course flows through Montana and Idaho. Thus augmented, the Columbia races through a valley that rewarded the prospectors of the 1880s, through the smelting town of Trail, and on toward the border. Only one-half mile from the 49th parallel, it joins forces with the Pend Oreille, also known as Clark's Fork. Next to the Snake, the Pend Oreille is the Columbia's most important tributary. Though it carries less water, the Pend Oreille is longer than the Snake, and there was a time when chauvinistic American geographers insisted that its source, near Butte, was the birthplace of the Columbia. Once the combined rivers rushed across the border. Now their movement is sedate, for at the border the Columbia comes under the influence of Grand Coulee Dam. For 151 miles the river is a man-made lake, averaging 4,000 feet in width, 375 in depth, and storing ten million acre feet of water.

In early times the river, on leaving the Okanogan Highlands, may have cut directly to the Columbia Gorge, through which it escaped to the sea. During the Miocene Epoch the valley of low-rolling hills was rent by enormous fissures. Lava welled out and swept across the plain in successive flows that averaged 100 feet in thickness but sometimes exceeded 200 feet. Theoretical calculations put the speed of the fiery waves at twenty-five to thirty miles an hour. Cooling into basalt, the lava cracked like sugary fudge as it shrank, creating the columnar patterns now exposed by erosion. Flow followed flow, the new outpourings sometimes racing across naked rock, at other times—when the pause between flows had been thousands of years—across landscapes sculptured by water flow and softened by vegetation. Trees are found embalmed in basalt.

Molten floods moving up from the southeast met the Columbia, and the river waters probably disappeared into steam. When things cooled down, the drainage flowing out of Canada cut a new channel westward around the northern edge of the intruding basalt. Approaching the rising Cascades, the new Columbia turned south, then, still following the path of least resistance, around or through other highlands, east, south, and again east until it met, almost head on, the westward-flowing Snake. The combined rivers, ponded today in the backwaters of one of the Columbia dams, swing west and take the Columbia's original escape route through the Cascades.

This great curve—in which the Columbia travels nearly three times the air-line distance of 120 miles between its junctures with the Spokane and the Snake—is known as the Big Bend. Its layered surfaces of basalt, scoured and rutted by the bulldozing glaciers of the ice ages and the vanished floods that marked the retreat of the ice caps, are a showplace of geologic architecture.

Even before the Pleistocene ice sheet approached, classic alpine glaciers had formed near the eastern ridge of the Cascades and sculpted deep valleys down the mountainside. A superb example is the basin of Lake Chelan. Ice accumulating in a high mountain valley gouged a U-shaped trough to within three miles of the western reach of the Big Bend. Then the glacier receded, leaving a deep and lovely lake impounded behind the debris the ice had pushed down the mountain.

Such carving by alpine glaciers, however, is but filigree compared to the mighty architecture of subsequent glaciation. Sheets of ice thousands of feet thick pushed down in successive waves from the north and dammed

When it was completed in 1941, Grand Coulee Dam was the largest and most technologically sophisticated hydroelectric system ever devised.

the Columbia near its northern turn around the Big Bend. The river formed a lake, and the lake overflowed across the lava plateau. Where the grade was steep, the cascading water scooped great trenches, now known as *coulees* from the French word "to flow." One of the waterfalls was the equivalent of one hundred Niagaras. When the glaciers retreated and the Columbia dropped back into its old course around the Big Bend, the Grand Coulee—1,000 feet deep, from two to five miles wide, and fifty miles long—was left high and dry, 600 feet above the surface of the Columbia.

The Grand Coulee, arid and barren but obviously carved by water, attracted the attention of explorers, settlers, engineers and promoters. The imagination and technology of man found use for the engineering done by nature. The most massive dam yet built in the Americas—4,300 feet long, 50 feet thick at the top and 550 at the base, containing enough concrete to pave Texas—corked the Columbia below the Grand Coulee. A dozen pumps, each capable of handling 1,600 cubic feet a second, raise the ponded water behind Grand Coulee Dam and pour it into a 1.6-mile feeder canal which empties into the Upper Grand Coulee. The

trough of the coulee is now a reservoir twenty-seven miles long. Water released from the far end of this reservoir is fed into a network of canals and ditches to irrigate hundreds of thousands of acres of rich but previously arid soil.

Conceived as an irrigation project, the Grand Coulee Dam brought so much power to a thinly populated region that foes of the government program suggested the surplus would have to be used to light prairie dog villages. But the power has drawn new customers to the area and transformed what was an extractive economy into one involving sophisticated fabricating plants.

Having impounded the energy of the ocean-seeking water, man has used that power to release the explosive force of the atom. During World War II the government fenced off 440,000 acres of sagebrush desert cradled in the southern arm of the Big Bend. In well-publicized secrecy (everybody knew something was going on; few knew what), 60,000 workers built a line of furnaces which produced the core ingredient of the first atomic bombs. But the process of turning out plutonium has contributed to the pollution of the river, adding radioactivity and, just as dangerous to the ecology, heat.

79

Though the furnaces of the Hanford Atomic Reservation turn some of their waste heat back into electrical energy, the austere towers rising from the dusty haze of the plateau stand beautiful and ominous, symbols of modern man's enigmatic relationship to nature.

Just south of the Hanford Reservation are the tri-cities: Richland, Kennewick, and Pasco. Below them the Columbia, now 928 miles long and carrying as much water as the Missouri, is joined by the Snake, three times longer and far more powerful than the Hudson.

B Y THE TIME they reach this confluence, the waters of the Snake have traveled even farther than those of the Columbia. Both the Snake and its tributary the Lewis rise in Yellowstone Park, near the continental divide. Leaving the park, the parent stream enters flawless Jackson Lake, then sweeps southwest into the completely dry Snake River lava plateau, narrowing through Hells Canyon, then spreading wide near Lewiston as it approaches the Columbia. Emigrants on the Oregon Trail followed the Snake across the hot, dusty lava plateau of southern Idaho, but swung westward toward Oregon as the river prepared to enter America's deepest canyon. At Farewell Bend the travelers took their last look at the Snake; it had been their guide, but the land beside its banks is extremely rugged so many said good riddance. Travelers still follow the river west, and today many population centers of Idaho lie along its route.

Like the Columbia, the Snake is an old river; both were draining their watersheds before the present lava landscape existed. The Snake had a particularly complicated history battling against natural forces which turned aside its flow: lava dams, uplift of mountains, and subsidence of the land. At one early point in the history of the Snake River, its waters may not have had any outlet to the Columbia and thus to the sea. They eventually escaped—either through the southwestern corner of Oregon, or north through Baker and along the drainage of the Grande Ronde River. Pushed east by the Blue Mountain Uplift, the Snake was again entrapped, this time in hard greenstone, and forced to carve Hells Canyon.

Along its 1,036-mile route, the Snake gathers water from 109,000 square miles and pours into the Columbia a volume equal to almost half of what the Columbia carries just above their confluence. Like any river, the Snake varies in volume from year to year, depending on snow and rainfall; it also varies as irrigation needs along its channel change.

Of all the issues involving the Snake River, controversy about irrigation projects burns hottest and longest. Water is most abundant on the Snake near the mouth, where it is also the least needed. On the upper Snake water is scarce, and ranchers and farmers here feel they must flood their fields in the spring and early summer to be ready for the annual summer drought. Irrigation water for the late crop of hay is nearly always in short supply.

Much of the water in the upper Snake region is unrecoverable surface water; Little Lost, Big Lost, and other rivers flowing from the southern Sawtooth range disappear underground into porous lava beds and flow in subsurface channels for many miles. Craters of the Moon National Monument in this region is one of the driest, bleakest lands on earth. So limited is the total inflow to the upper Snake, so massive the use of water during periods of maximum irrigation, that the river sometimes does not flow at all for a short distance below Milner Dam, the final irrigation dam on this section. But just downstream, at Thousand Springs, Lost River emerges and restores the river's normal volume.

In the central Snake region, too, more irrigation water is used than is available, but it is not the Snake that is heavily taxed. About 90 percent comes from the Boise, Payette, Weiser, Owyhee, and Malheur rivers, and only 10 percent from the Snake. The Snake lies several hundred feet below its surrounding upland, and thus the withdrawal of its water would be excessively expensive.

Near Farewell Bend the Snake River is again a major source for irrigation, but need is not great. Much of the land is nonirrigated.

On the Snake, it was irrigation which spurred the construction of dams; eighteen exist along the channel from Jackson Lake to the Columbia, and only two limited stretches of wild water remain. One lies in western Wyoming from the mouth of the Hoback to the Idaho border; the other is downstream from Hells Canyon Dam, where water still flows freely through the haunting black basalt chasm 500 feet deeper than Arizona's Grand Canyon.

Downstream from Hells Canyon the river, still powerful, slows and widens. It was here, at Nez Perce Crossing, that Chief Joseph's band in 1877 was forced to ford the river at flood, en route to exile on a reservation. No lives were lost in the crossing, but many of the horses refused to cross and stampeded back to the old ranges. Their loss added to the weight of bitterness which shortly erupted into massacre and the tragic flight of the tribe toward Canada.

In this same canyon, river pilot W. P. Gray attempted to run lumber with the current in order to save his employer the time and expense of using the overland route. Both Captain Gray and the goods made it.

Between 1850 and 1890 all grain grown north of Hells Canyon was shipped out of the lower Snake region by stern-wheelers such as the *Harvest Queen,* the *Annie Faxon,* and the *Lewiston.* Every three miles along the rough river, there were wharves where these boats loaded. Despite the rapids, most shipping delays were the result of ice floes or low water. In early spring the stern-wheelers would wait ten miles above the mouth of the Snake for the ice jams to pass; that sheltered cove is memorialized today in the name of a nearby dam —Ice Harbor.

Hells Canyon was cut by the Snake River as it pushed seaward against mountains growing up in its path.

T HE SNAKE RIVER does not really end at its confluence with the Columbia; rather, the waters of these two great rivers flow together in one monumental channel. Just south of Pasco, Washington, at Wallula Gap, the Columbia turns west. At one time the river was a torrent slicing through the plateau lavas along what is now the Washington-Oregon border; today hydroelectric plants quiet the river's fury. At one time fifty-pound salmon would fight desperately to surmount the Columbia's many falls; now the falls feared by the *voyageurs* slumber under ponded water. At one time Indians fished for salmon with long-handled nets; now they are mostly gone. The river is greatly changed because it is not free.

While evidence of the river's furious energy lies hidden under reservoirs at The Dalles, and even Columbia Gorge, the gorge itself remains. It is a place of thin, delicate falls trailing like veils across dark cliffs, of misty vistas with volcanoes hanging in the distance; it is also a canyon which even without the thunder of rapids tells of the persistent power of its watery sculptor.

In the western foothills of the Cascades the Columbia meets its final obstruction—Bonneville Dam. Beyond this retaining wall the river is leisurely. Touched by Pacific tides, dotted by islands, the Columbia is no longer a river of the wilderness. Its last 140 miles are epilogue. Wide, muddy, choked with debris, overheated, poisoned by radioactivity and industrial waste, it flows to the sea still beautiful. Seen from the banks, it seems little changed from the time, almost two centuries ago, when Gray's little trading ship explored the bay inside its bar and the *Chatham* of the Vancouver expedition sailed up beyond the Willamette. Nothing that man has done, so far, alters the fact that here in this narrow confine the waters drawn from the great expanse of the Pacific and dropped on much of northwest America, return home.

CHAPTER 8

GLACIER PARK COUNTRY

*The spectacular Northern Rockies of Montana and Idaho—
a vast gallery to display the work of alpine ice*

BETWEEN THE LAVA PLATEAUS of Washington and Idaho, and Montana's eastern plains are a multitude of high mountain ranges known collectively as the Northern Rockies. Tenuously linked by a meandering Continental Divide, most of the ranges lie on a northwest-southeast axis and obey the same directional trend as the Middle and Southern Rockies.

Three basic mountain types emerge from a quagmire of Northern Rockies geology: those developed upon an extensive batholith and satellites to it, those that are upraised blocks of the earth's crust, and those formed as one crustal block moved up and over another. The greatest of the batholiths covers 16,000 square miles of central Idaho. Ancient streams in this region, especially those in the Clearwater and Salmon River area, probably leveled summits to present elevations so that much of the central batholith is disguised as a plateau. The modern generation of rivers by contrast, has cut deep valleys rather than planing off the peaks. The Bitterroot Mountains rise from a margin of the batholith and surmount the plateau.

Faults also controlled mountain growth and valley formation north of the Idaho Batholith, in western Montana and the panhandle of Idaho. Ranges of folded rock are in evidence as well, prominently the Lewis Range—one of the "front" ranges of western Montana. In southwestern Montana mountains arose as great blocks, oriented in a variety of directions about valley basins. Erosion followed the faulting, continuously smoothing the blocks as they rose.

To experience the Northern Rockies, one has to get into the "backcountry"; nowhere in the West is there more isolation than in central Idaho. Distributed over three million acres of wilderness are out-of-the-way regions known as the Selway–Bitterroot Area, Salmon River Breaks, Idaho Primitive Area, and the Sawtooth Primitive Area. Highways touch only the perimeters, except for the few backroads which lead to defunct mines or old homesteads. Anyone wishing to see at close range the ragged peaks, box canyons, or isolated mining towns must plan carefully, for travel is by plane, boat, pack animals, or foot.

The Salmon River and its tributaries slice through parts of central Idaho, and the river trip is still this region's wildest tour. Captain William Clark ventured down the Salmon in 1805, but was halted by white water only fifteen miles from the North Fork; the party turned back, taking a northern route through Lolo Pass.

Sometimes known as the "River of No Return," the Salmon was run for the first time by two partners who floated trappers and prospectors downstream in flatboats steered with long sweeps. Today, rubber rafts and kayaks run all of the forty or more white rapids in the wild Salmon's 220-mile length.

Most mountains of central Idaho are beautiful but threatening and inviolate, so it is all the more welcome to see the Sawtooths, a friendly range (by comparison) that towers above the Sawtooth Valley near Stanley, Idaho. Borah Peak (12,662 ft.) and Hyndman Peak (12,078 ft.)—Idaho's two tallest mountains—lie in their own prominent ranges east of the Sawtooth region and are easily seen from nearby highways. Alp-like Hyndman

St. Mary Lake, lying at the foot of Little Chief and Citadel mountains, is one of many long finger lakes occupying ice-carved valleys in Glacier Park.

83

Peak dominates the Pioneer Mountains while Borah Peak tops the Lost River Range. Wherever there are peaks, there are backpackers, especially in south-central Idaho where high-country tarns yield excellent fishing.

For less isolation than central Idaho there is always Idaho's northern panhandle. Cities stand in the shade of great, dark expanses of forest, so dense with larch, hemlock, and pine they are almost blue-black. Superb scenic highways follow the Kootenai, Clark Fork of the Columbia, Coeur d'Alene, St. Joe, and Spokane rivers. Mountain waters that once drained to only one great Pleistocene lake now flow to many, among them the Priest Lakes (Upper and Lower), the Coeur d'Alene, and the Pend Oreille.

Across the great dividing crest of the northern Rockies, is, in a sense, another world. Idaho and Montana have few ties and much less cultural exchange across their common border than with other neighboring states. Coeur d'Alene and Spokane are almost sister cities, and residents of Pocatello think nothing of the drive to Salt Lake City; but residents of western Montana are steeped in their own cultural heritage.

Where there are cities in western Montana, there are also smelters and mines working the copper, zinc, and lead which are the wealth of this region. Where there are no cities, roads and passes bind extensive recreation areas to the cities. The largest and most magnificent of these retreats is Glacier National Park.

A MAGAZINE REPORTER, early in this century, wrote: "I have not seen all the grand places of the world: but if I were to be asked what one thing in nature had most impressed me I would not say the Canyon of the Yellowstone, beautiful and rich in color though it is, or the Grand Canyon of the Colorado, overwhelming in majesty and inspiring as it is, but I would say that when you stand at the edge of St. Mary Lake and look across and up to the two mountains—one named by the Indians 'Going-to-the-Sun' and the other 'Almost-a-Dog' —you would probably find the one thing on the North American Continent that would inspire you most and make you feel most properly humble." Though perhaps no longer in search of the humbling experience, today's travelers flock to the national parks to enjoy mountain sports and fine sightseeing, and now more of them than ever before are vacationing in Glacier National Park, making this relatively small northern region of Montana one of the busiest sections of the Northern Rockies.

As its name implies, Glacier has been given its present form by alpine ice originating high on the flanks of major peaks, moving slowly down Pleistocene valleys, eventually merging to form a sea of ice at the knees of the Rockies. Though glaciers exist today on many high peaks, the time of their dominance is long past. Mayan-shaped temples of rock have since acquired a new history, held in the legends and records of all the people

The jagged Sawtooth Mountains have formed on an edge of a great body of granite—the Idaho Batholith. Geologists have discovered evidence that the same rock lies under the Sawtooth Valley.

who have seen Glacier: the Indians, explorers, miners, scientists, and tourists. Each has seen different meanings in the mountains.

Most people first encounter the park from Going-to-the-Sun Highway, named for the mountain, which in turn commemorates an Indian legend. The principal hero of Blackfoot mythology is a semisupernatural being called Napi ("Old Man"). He created the rocks, rivers, forests, prairie, and all animals; he gave man the breath of life, then taught him the arts of hunting and agriculture. Napi lived in the sun, and when his work on

earth was done, he returned to his home by way of a great and noble mountain—Going-to-the-Sun. The legend says that after Napi's disappearance his chosen people looked up to see a field of snow near the peak's summit, and it was shaped like the old chief's profile; some said it was Napi, watching over those in the valley.

Earliest exploration of Glacier came in the 1700s by French trappers of the Hudson's Bay Company, followed much later by an abortive exploration by Meriwether Lewis in 1806. A year later St. Louis trappers began vying with the Blackfeet for fur and buffalo

Pend Oreille is Idaho's largest lake. Fishermen know its Kamloops trout and its landlocked salmon, called the "kokanee"; picnickers and campers know its small islands and fiordlike bays.

hides, with Indian hostility largely preventing exploration. Then in 1834 Father Peter John De Smet, accompanied by Hugh Monroe, a friend of the Blackfeet, penetrated Glacier and named St. Mary Lakes. After 1850 organized parties knowing established routes of approach began to enter the mountains, beginning a period of discovery which continued to 1900.

George Bird Grinnell came in the eighties, beginning his many explorations of the region. He was the first white man to discover a great natural rift in the mountain mass, a route often used by early tribes to cross the Rockies—to Gunsight Lake, over the pass above it, down a dangerous drop to the bottom of a compound cirque, then southwest to the Flathead River.

Like earlier explorers, Grinnell named many of the features along his route of travel, among them Blackfoot Glacier, once the largest ice mass in the park but now shrunken and broken into several small glaciers; Mount Jackson; Blackfoot Mountain; and Baring Falls, where heavy-boned water ouzels nest beside the tumbling water, often diving into the icy stream to walk submerged, hunting for food.

The early 1890s brought prospectors dazzled with tales of rich strikes and lured by the yellow, red, and green tint of the mountains. One obstacle alone seemed to stand in the way of wealth—the land belonged to the Blackfeet. In 1895, for the consideration of $1,500,000, tribal members signed a treaty deeding Indian land in

Glacier's peaks of ancient limestone, shale, and quartz sandstone have sheer, beautiful faces and strong vertical joints.

Glacier to the government; this action signaled the start of Glacier's biggest mining boom. Crowds of miners staked out claims, and the town of Altyn sprang up near Swiftcurrent Lake. Everyone was looking for copper ore, which had been discovered to the west near the heads of Mineral and Quartz creeks. Though few were finding any ore in the east, the vein was thought to extend through the dividing range and to crop out in the Many Glaciers section.

A similar frenzy over gold, silver, copper, and oil was brewing near St. Mary, as prospectors began burrowing like gophers all over those hillsides. However, only small quantities of anything valuable were ever shipped out of Glacier, and that was done frequently for display. Hopes did not pan out, for the lonely peaks proved too poor for the miners. They left their empty tunnels, slag heaps, and rusty equipment and the mining booms collapsed.

The park's first dirt road, from Lake McDonald to Kintla Lake, was built when there was oil fever in McDonald Valley, but once Glacier became national property in 1910, secondary highways were discouraged. Thus the long lonely road to Kintla Lake (which borders the park's northwestern margin) was anomalous, as were cabins of homesteaders within the public domain. In winter, snow drifts and twenty-below temperatures proved to the homesteaders that the mountains were too rugged for civilization, and like the miners, they abandoned the effort. Glacier was left to the scientist and the tourist.

A 1917 report by the National Park Service stressed heavily the construction of one highway between St. Mary Lake and Lake McDonald. By 1925, two survey parties began work on Going-to-the-Sun Highway, one on each side of the divide. As originally planned, the west-side route was to wind in switchbacks up the Logan Creek Valley, but an architect named Vint changed all that. After making a study in the field, Vint ferreted out the present grade, which makes just one switchback in the entire climb to Logan Pass and in places is literally hung to the Garden Wall. The road was built under difficult and hazardous circumstances, much of it through or beside solid rock.

Glacier's mountains belong to the Lewis Range and display a structure which is unique in the Northwest and the Rockies. Created by an "overthrust," mobile rock layers apparently slid up onto other layers that were stationary, producing a fifteen- to thirty-five-mile skid of rock upon rock. Thus, there are no foothills east of the Montana front range; the mountains seem to have been cast full-grown upon the plains. One old warrior, called Chief Mountain, now stands detached from other peaks near the northeastern boundary of Glacier, where the Lewis Overthrust can be clearly seen. The Plains Indians became familiar with this peak and used it as a landmark, because its form was distinguishable far out on the prairie.

As the mountains of Glacier rose, they pushed up many fossilized elements of their own prehistory. Exposed by a roadcut near the one switchback of Going-to-the-Sun Highway are rosettes of primitive plant life, like cross sections of cabbages. One-half billion years ago they were colonies of algae—single-celled organisms that survive even in the present. One would have to go a mile deep into the Grand Canyon to see rock as old as this, yet here it lies at the edge of the highway.

Though Glacier National Park is one of the outstanding wilderness regions of the park system, Going-to-the-Sun Highway makes sight-seeing from the road an unusually exciting experience. Active waterfalls, glacier-fed lakes, and redcedar forests usher the way to the summit pass (6,664 ft.), and if rain has just fallen or clouds are forming, Glacier's highest peaks disappear into the clouds. One understands why the Indians believed Glacier to be the dwelling place of great spirits. Sperry Glacier, the Garden Wall, Logan Pass, Weeping Wall, Baring Creek Falls, St. Mary Lake, Triple Divide Peak, and other remarkable vistas may be seen from the highway; many more await the tourist who is also a hiker. More than one thousand miles of trail crisscross the park, and solitude waits just beyond the trail head.

Whether on a trail in Glacier, or in central Idaho's Primitive Area, or high above Upper Priest Lake, one realizes that this land is immense and unusually varied. Other peaks may reach to summits higher than the Northern Rockies, but few, not even the highest Cascades, have been so spectacularly styled by the ice on their shoulders or the rivers at their feet. Whereas low regions are often muted by ice and water, the Northern Rockies have been honed to an outstanding brilliance.

To Blackfoot Indians the pyramid peaks of Glacier Park were the domain of great spirits.
This is Mount Reynolds near Logan Pass, with beargrass in the foreground.

*At Multnomah Falls this Oregon stream splashes 620 feet in two leaps on its brief,
four-mile journey from its source in the Cascades to the Columbia.*

**Mount Rainier, king of the Cascade Range (seen here from Tipsoo Lake), is made doubly impressive
by one of the largest single-peak glacial systems in the "lower forty-eight."**

Mount Hood, rising out of one of the lowest parts of the Cascade Range, towers to 11,235 feet under perpetual snow.

Overleaf: Leaving new ski tracks in the snow and being the first to view a freshly frosted peak are winter delights of the North Cascades.

*Parched Coyote Valley, like most of the
Oregon Desert, has no permanent rivers.*

*At Palouse Falls State Park, Washington,
erosion has terraced the basalt plateau.*

95

Beauty Bay, Lake Coeur d'Alene, in the Idaho Panhandle—where mountains, water, and sunshine can be enjoyed close to city limits.

The Snake River plunges 212 feet over Shoshone Falls, near Twin Falls, Idaho. In summer the flow is diminished by irrigation.

A peaceful stretch of the Salmon River above Rhett Bar, Idaho. In its wilder reaches the Salmon—the "River of No Return"—is a favorite of white-water runners.

Stunning rhododendrons freely spread their color at the knees of Mount Hood, taking full sun in the cool summer of the Cascade highlands.

Foxglove.

Bunchberry.

Indian thistle.

Oregon grape.

Vine maple.

Fireweed.

Western anemones.

Prickly pear.

Fern.

Wild strawberry.

Skunk cabbage.

Ptarmigan.

Canada goose.

Sea lions.

Brown trout.

Mallards.

Ochre stars and green anemones.

Hawks owl.

Bobcat.

Mule deer.

Mountain goat.

Black bear.

Coyote.

Raccoon.

Badger.

Roosevelt elk.

PART TWO

BEFORE THE WHITE MAN

For the Indians the Northwest was not a hostile wilderness to be discovered and subdued but a Mother Earth of life-giving ocean and rivers, fertile valleys, and homes from which to thank and appease the supernatural. From the sea-going Indians of the coast to the wandering hunters and gatherers of the interior plateaus, they lived in close harmony with the land, finding life to be a constant search for compromise with nature and for survival.

The "Medicine Mask Dance," by Paul Kane.

CHAPTER 9

INDIANS OF THE COAST

The spenders, the savers, and the traders—three major native cultures of the bountiful Northwest shore

FEW PLACES ON EARTH have blessed primitive men with as great bounty as once existed along the northwest coast of North America. The sea and river mouths there provided Indians with year-round abundance in return for a few months' labor. Out of this richness grew some of the most advanced hunting-and-gathering societies the world has ever known—an extraordinary complex of cultures that extended along the Pacific Coast all the way from southern Alaska to northern California.

The three major branches of Northwest Indian culture shared a common element of wealth, but they differed sharply in how they responded to it. The Nootkas and Kwakiutls of the British Columbia coast were spenders, using their abundant leisure to feast, and to distribute their bounty with a prodigality and protocol reminiscent of Renaissance courts. The Yuroks, Karoks, and Hupas of northern California were hoarders, displaying their possessions but not giving them away. The Chinooks along the Columbia River were traders, middlemen in the native economy.

How long these peoples had lived on their generous shore before the white men came is lost in the shadows of prehistory. Archaeologists have found evidence of human habitation here at least 12,000 years ago, but they have turned up little firm evidence of modern tribes' origins. Native folklore, and finds indicating a migration down the Skeena River then north and south along the coast, suggest that they migrated from inland regions in comparatively recent times.

As the Northwest Indians, group by group, had replaced older residents of the coast sometime in the past, so would they too be replaced. In the mere two hundred years since the first white man landed, the red man's culture that had been developing over hundreds, perhaps thousands, of years has all but vanished. Populations are decimated. The riches from the sea seem paltry beside twentieth-century affluence. Cultural identity itself is nearly lost between the enticements and encroachments of white society. About all that remain are artifacts, legends, and a few die-hard customs like the potlatch; yet, in these one can still glimpse the glory that was Northwest Indian culture.

THE NOOTKAS, like most of the coastal peoples, were children of the sea. They knew the rituals and techniques for skimming what they needed from a Pacific that teemed with primeval plenty. In early spring, when schools of herring ran thick, they would comb the sea with rakes, depositing the fish in their canoes on the follow-through. (Similar rakes were used by the Nootkas and other tribes for candlefish, a kind of oily smelt which, when dried, could be lit and used as candles.) The Nootkas caught halibut, too, and dogfish, a type of shark whose oil was used for trade and its skin for sandpapering canoes.

Giant kelp beds along the coast were important to the Indians in a variety of ways. Cured kelp stems made strong fishing lines, and the bulbs were convenient containers for whale oil. In summer, when sea otter pups napped on the kelp beds, Indian hunters would kidnap

When Captain James Cook explored the Pacific shore of Vancouver Island in 1778, he found a thriving Nootka Indian culture. This scene was painted by the expedition's artist, John Webber.

a pup and kill the parents when they came to investigate its cries. Other sea mammals were harpooned offshore or driven inland from the rocks and dispatched with clubs or arrows.

Like all Northwest tribes, the Nootkas relied heavily on the salmon, the fall run of dog salmon providing the bulk of their food supply. Hung from the rafters of Nootka houses in winter, the salmon were smoked, almost inadvertently, by the fire that warmed the room. To the Nootkas this smoky, fishy atmosphere represented the good life—the security of the family hearth and the bounty of an ample food supply. To white nostrils, however, the stench was overpowering, as Captain Cook's men attested on their visit in 1778.

Of all the Nootkas' seafaring exploits, the most impressive were their whaling expeditions in great oceangoing canoes. Meriwether Lewis (speaking of the smaller canoes of the Chinooks, three hundred miles to the south) expressed his admiration: "I have seen the natives near the coast riding waves with safety and, apparently, without concern, where I should have thought it impossible for any craft to live a minute."

One can imagine the excitement of the sea hunt. Since the fatal harpoon is to be thrust, not thrown, the canoe must be maneuvered close alongside the behemoth. The struggle begins as the harpooner drives his twenty-foot weapon behind the left flipper. Its shell blade shatters, and elkhorn barbs lodge in the whale. Enraged, the animal dives. Crewmen brace themselves, letting out fathoms of line with sealskin floats attached. The line is not fastened to the canoe; the floats slow the whale and enable the paddlers to keep pace with its flight.

Onshore the women begin a chant inviting the "noble lady" to visit their beautiful village. The whalers strike the "noble lady" again and again, whenever she surfaces for air, and the floats tire her when she dives. If everyone has done his part in the rituals, she will expire right in front of the village, not several days out to sea.

Special lances complete the kill by severing the tendons of the flukes and piercing the heart. The mouth is sewn shut to prevent the great creature's waterlogging, and she is towed home to be feted like a visiting chief. This is no Moby Dick, but a generous provider of many days' food and a heroine in an ancestral village drama.

The Nootkas were rich in another way. They had access to what every coastal Indian desired—dentalia, the shell-money used for trade between tribes. These shells grew at an accessible depth in only a few places along the west coast of Vancouver Island. The precise location of a dentalia bed and the technique for making delicate pincers to pluck the shells from the bottom were closely guarded family secrets.

Adjusting to the whims of weather and water creatures, the Nootkas had three homes: one facing out to sea for the summer fishing season, another in a sheltered cove for the violent winter cross seas, and a third upriver

A Makah whaler: Sealskin buoys on the harpoon line kept the whale afloat. (Edward S. Curtis photo.)

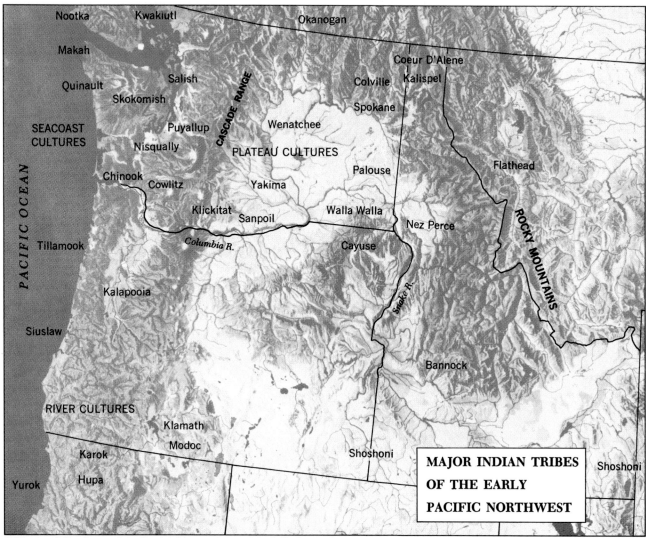

Nootka
Kwakiutl
Okanogan
Makah
Coeur D'Alene
Quinault
Salish
Colville
Kalispel
Skokomish
Spokane
CASCADE RANGE
SEACOAST
CULTURES
Puyallup
Wenatchee
Flathead
Nisqually
PLATEAU CULTURES
Chinook
Palouse
PACIFIC OCEAN
Cowlitz
Yakima
Klickitat
Walla Walla
ROCKY MOUNTAINS
Sanpoil
Nez Perce
Columbia R.
Cayuse
Snake R.
Tillamook
Kalapooia
Siuslaw
Bannock
RIVER CULTURES
Klamath
Modoc
Karok
Shoshoni
MAJOR INDIAN TRIBES
Shoshoni
Yurok
Hupa
OF THE EARLY
PACIFIC NORTHWEST

© Jeppesen & Co., Denver, Colo. Reprinted by permission of the H. M. Gousha Co., proprietors, San Jose, Calif.

at the salmon run. Unlike most hunting-gathering societies, they built at each site a permanent house frame, 20 to 40 feet wide and 50 to 100 feet long. Overlapping red-cedar planks were attached to the frame— loosely, for the families took their wall and roof boards with them when they moved. Each plank, wrought from a log with stone tools, was an heirloom.

Cedar is one of the few woods that can be worked with such crude implements. It is so soft and straight-grained that a stone maul striking a hardwood wedge is enough to split it into thick boards. Sometimes boards were split by driving wedges into the living tree and letting wind-sway split off the desired pieces.

The Indians used a controlled fire to fell the standing tree, split it with wedges, then finished the wood with an adz or chisel. Adz blades were usually nephrite, elk-horn, or shell, depending on local resources; when available, rare materials like jadeite from the Fraser River and iron from white explorers (and from some mysterious earlier source—perhaps Japanese fishing boats carried east on the Kuroshio) were prized for their cutting strength.

A single house served an entire group of relatives, all sharing the one large room. A person's rank determined his area of the house; here he piled his belongings and slept, on a cedar plank laid with a cedar-bark mat.

Indeed, the fibrous inner bark of cedar was used everywhere: twisted into strips, it held the house walls together, secured shaft and blade of tools, and provided material for women's capes and skirts.

A UNIQUE FEATURE of coastal Indian life from Juan de Fuca Strait northward was the *potlatch*. Literally the term means "gift-giving," but the potlatch was much more. It provided the basic framework for conducting social relations and affirming status. At the potlatch a person acquired the names that identified him at different stages of his life, and here, with the guests at witnesses, he could exercise his inherited rights to certain rituals and privileges.

Planning for a typical potlatch might begin on the death or retirement of a prominent member of a clan.

The individual who is to inherit the deceased's title arranges a feast for several hundred guests, with gifts to be distributed to all according to their ranks. A totem pole is carved in the host's honor, with a series of animal crests that tell his lineage. The preparations may take as long as a year, and the expense is tremendous. However, the host's kin help to share this burden, for the potlatch will redound to the glory of every member of the clan.

When the gala day arrives, guests land their ceremonial canoes in order of rank. (There are legends of hosts who would club a slave to death and use his body as a roller to beach the canoes—the slave being just one more evidence of expendable wealth.) Sumptuous feasting begins almost at once, and the fires roar with costly dousings of oil.

After a few days' suspense the totem pole is hoisted

The coastal Indians' cedar canoes were sleek, beautiful, and sturdy enough for whaling in the open Pacific. Here Frederic Remington shows one on a more festive mission—"Going to the Potlatch."

Ocean-going canoes, well-constructed houses, gracefully carved totem poles — Northwest Indian culture was literally built of cedar. (Kwakiutl village photographed in the 1880s.)

into place, and a speaker explains the significance of its figures, recounting the clan's supernatural heritage, powers, and deeds. More feasting and dancing follow until the potlatch reaches its climax—the distribution of the gifts.

By the number and quality of his gifts the host both displays his own affluence and flatters his guests (who will remember and reciprocate when they give a pot-latch). Through the years blankets have been one of the traditional gifts, whether from native looms, the Hudson's Bay Company store, or the Sears Simpson catalog. The most precious gifts were sheets of beaten copper, 2 to 2½ feet long, each considered to be worth many canoes and slaves. Individual coppers were given names, such as "Making-the-house-empty-of-blankets" and "All-other-coppers-are-ashamed-to-look-at-it."

Among the Kwakiutls, neighbors of the Nootkas, a copper doubled in value every time it changed hands.

The potlatch was in effect an investment. Recipients of gifts were honor-bound to repay the presents, with interest, at the risk of losing their totems, their songs, even their freedom, by becoming slaves. In a surplus economy the potlatch served as a means of stimulating production. Among the Kwakiutls, who practiced it most intensively and were among the few tribes to engage in destructive potlatches, it became a substitute for warfare: "We used to fight with bows and arrows,

with spears and guns. We robbed each other's blood. But now we fight with this here (pointing at the copper he was holding in his hand), and if we have no coppers, we fight with canoes or blankets."

Another important social institution of the tribes around Puget Sound was the dancing society. Based on a shamanistic religious view, the initiation rites of these societies provided some of the most important cere-monials of tribal life. Among the Nootkas, whose novices were children, the more macabre aspects of the rituals were played down, and the events had more of a festival air. Among the Kwakiutls, however, the adult novices often went berserk when "possessed by spirits," with destructiveness and even cannibalism frequently though unreliably reported. (So much deception accom-panied these staged rituals—masks, trap doors, voices traveling mysteriously through kelp stems concealed under the floor—that it is hard to know how frequently cannibalism actually occurred.)

WHEREAS SHEER COASTAL MOUNTAINS kept the Noot-kas close to the sea, farther south, near what was to become the Oregon-California border, the mountains were more rounded and the river valleys habitable. Thus, the Yuroks who lived there, and their neighbors the Karoks and the Hupas, became river people rather

At the White Deerskin Dance, unlike the potlatch, the Hupas displayed wealth without destroying it.

to that of the ancient Greeks, who also lived among a maze of mountain ranges. It provided a stage for world-renewal rituals like the White Deerskin Dance, in which the participants would visit traditional trees or stones, reciting prescribed accounts of the ceremony's origin among prehumans and ritually reenacting the deeds of the ancient race.

The thrifty Yuroks had no potlatches. They affirmed their status in the community, not by extravagant gift-giving, but by display of their possessions, gathered over the years by abstinence, hard work, and care in courting the favor of the spirit world. The prime occasion for this display was the White Deerskin Dance. As the tempo of the dance gradually increased, the dancers would appear, bearing the Yurok treasures: scarlet woodpecker scalps, obsidian blades, and finally, at the climax, the albino deerskins themselves.

Consistent with their acquisitive value system, the Yuroks were careful about money. They distinguished five grades of dentalia, based on size and freedom from flaws, and so standardized the grading that it approached a modern currency system. Every adult male had a mark tattooed on his arm by which he could measure strings of dentalia.

In a sense, every Yurok was a lawyer, because every offense was considered to be against an individual and had to be atoned for with a negotiated payment. (There were no crimes against society, no existing authorities to impose punishment.) Intent was irrelevant; manslaughter and murder required the same payment—the "bride price" of the deceased's mother (that is, the amount paid to the bride's family by the groom's family at the time of marriage)—a fair appraisal, in Yurok society, of a person's value.

This sense of personal liability extended to other aspects of life. A man had to provide free ferry service even for an enemy; but if his house burned down while he was away, the passenger was liable. If a trespasser broke his leg at another man's fishing grounds, he could immediately lay claim to the territory because of his injury. Often, Yurok slaves were not prisoners of war but debtors—fellow Yuroks without sufficient means to pay for some insult.

Except for kinship, the distinction between rich and poor provided the only measure of social organization the Yuroks possessed. The rich made possible those two

than ocean people. Their redwood canoes were made for river travel, so sea-mammal hunting was out of the question. But there was plenty to be gathered along the shore and at the river mouths. Besides the ubiquitous salmon, they caught eels, sturgeon, and steelhead. The acorn was also a staple for these people, as for most other California Indians; in fact, the Yuroks held a First Acorn Ceremony as well as a First Salmon Ceremony each year. After the fall harvest the women pounded the tanbark-oak acorns into flour, leached it in a sand basin to extract the bitter tannin, and served it as a thin mush.

The Yuroks' world extended only a few miles each side of the Klamath River, surrounded on all sides, they believed, by ocean. Their language reflected their narrow horizon, for they had no expressions for the points of the compass, only terms for "upstream" and "downstream." The land abounded with sacred sites—similar

Yurok canoes hewn of redwood were crude compared to the Nootkas' cedar masterpieces; but for a tribe that fished the coastal rivers rather than the open sea, they were adequate.

basic institutions, the White Deerskin Dance (for which they lent the treasures) and the sweathouse (which a rich man would build for the use of all his kin). The poor were of another world—the Yurok words for "man" and "woman" did not even apply to them.

The sweathouse was both a social center and a place of ritual purification. Men would spend the night there rather than with their wives, since it was believed that sexual activity would drive dentalia out of the house. (Practically all children were born in spring, since men and women slept together only outdoors, in summer.) The sweathouse was arranged with seven positions around the fire, which were occupied according to rank. Each man had a redwood stool and headrest. It was believed that feeding the fire with wood from the tops of certain tall firs would produce luck in the quest for wealth. Whatever their potency, these branches did

produce a smoky fire, and the men had to lie close to the ground to avoid suffocating. To stay awake in the heat, they used strong tobacco or took an icy plunge in the river, then rubbed their bodies with herbs.

One highly desirable role in Yurok society was reserved for women—that of shaman, with its attendant high fees for cures. During her trial period the aspiring shaman was visited in a dream or trance by a guardian spirit in the form of a dead shaman, a chicken hawk, or perhaps a whale, who put a "pain" into her. Since "pains" came in pairs, she would ascend a mountain, dance, and wait for the second "pain." When it came, she went into a trance and was carried to the sweathouse of her male relatives (the only time a woman might enter). There the "pains" were "cooked," or made tractable, during several days of dancing and trancing. Now mistress of her first set of pains (the best shamans

Functionally designed, the Chinooks' cedar houses had sleeping bunks along the walls and a raised platform for sitting. The cooking fire, center, also served to smoke salmon hung on the racks above.

acquired several sets in the course of their careers), she was ready to attempt cures. Standing by a patient, she would make one "pain" rise in her throat and, passing her mouth over the patient's body, send the "pain" into it. If all went well, it would link up with his "pain" and both would return to the shaman, who would then vomit up the bad one and send it away.

Unlike some other tribes, the Yuroks never killed the doctor if the patient died.

THE CHINOOKS occupied the strategic valley of the Columbia, a mixed blessing that gave them economic wealth and power in aboriginal times but placed them directly in the path of the white man.

The Columbia offered the best trade route between coastal and inland tribes, and the Chinooks, not sur-

prisingly, became prosperous middlemen in this commerce. They traded continuously at the mouth of the river and held a yearly trade fair at The Dalles that was the largest in the entire Northwest. Goods from as far as Alaska and the Great Plains found their way to The Dalles. The warlike Modocs of California brought slaves taken in combat; Coast Salish from Puget Sound brought tule-mat rain capes, as well as dentalia and canoes from their neighbors farther north; the Nez Perces brought hides and other items from the buffalo hunters of the plains east of the Rockies; the Chinooks themselves brought their own great surplus of salmon.

The language of trade became known among whites as the "Chinook jargon." Primarily a blend of Chinook and Nootkan, it originally developed from the Indian Babel at The Dalles; later it was infused with some English and French. To many white settlers, the Chi-

A venerable Chinook woman stands on the southern Washington shore, where her scattered, decimated people were once proud and prosperous traders. (Edward S. Curtis photo, ca. 1910.)

nooks were *the* Indians, and their name was used in a number of rather misleading contexts — Chinook salmon, Chinook wind, Chinook canoe.

Exposed to so many influences from outside their own society, the Chinooks tended to be importers rather than innovators. They wore Nootkan rain hats with whale crests, and rabbit-skin robes from the Great Basin. They carved their bowls from the horns of mountain sheep secured from Indians of the high mountains to the east. In truth, not much is known about the customs and daily life of these people. When they were shunted off to reservations, their social patterns were so profoundly disrupted that they lost their racial and cultural identity. But even before that, as early as the 1850s, so many had succumbed to alcohol and the white man's diseases that an observer could say their "race is nearly run." Five thousand strong when Lewis and Clark encountered them fifty years earlier, the Chinooks had been reduced to a hundred "miserable, whiskey-drinking vagabonds."

The other cultural groups of the Northwest fared somewhat better than the Chinooks. The Yuroks, hidden in the mountains of northern California, were off the thoroughfare of westward movement. Today, they have at least a tribal memory of the time when their narrow homeland seemed sacred, although modern distractions have put them adrift between two cultures. The Nootkas and their neighbors also continue to live on some of the same land and in somewhat the same fashion as they have for centuries. On their reserves they practice rituals derived from their cultural heyday, but, to be sure, the details have changed; adz blades are no longer stone but metal; potlatch gifts now include sewing machines and pool tables; and, in obedience to the white man's law, slaves are no longer held, much less killed to demonstrate wealth. The temptations of progress are strong, and these people, who in the eighteenth century beat off the white explorers and hunters, are now succumbing to the enemy's world and relinquishing the culture of their ancestors.

CHAPTER 10

PLATEAU PEOPLES

*Peaceful tribes of the inland deserts, where the choice
was between gathering food in harmony or going hungry*

THE GREAT INTERIOR PLATEAU of the Northwest—
the high desert, rolling hills, and rising mountain area between the Cascades and the Rockies
—was the home of Indian tribes who, whatever their
differences, shared the task of surviving in a land less
bountiful than that to the west. Gatherers and hunters,
they roamed a region marginally hospitable, and their
cultures reflected the austere imperatives of the plateau.

The Sanpoils, who lived in the Big Bend of the
Columbia River, may be taken to represent the plateau
culture—though it must be remembered that variations
in the response to environment were nearly as important
to the early red man as to the latter-day anthropologist.
In a land that to the first whites seemed desolate, the
Sanpoils found food for survival and the roots of a
special culture. Whereas coastal tribes moved short
distances between summer and winter villages, the
Indians of the interior plateau followed food over a
circuit so wide that they had not villages but campsites.

The flowers led them. When the earth's surface in late
March or early April began to yield to the growing
thrust of the camas beneath, the women left the winter
camps and started the long dig for sustenance. The
men, too, stirred themselves, though in spring, when
game was scarce, their efforts were rewarded with little
more than snails and slow rabbits.

In May or June the salmon, yielding to the blind
urges of sex and impending death, struggled upstream
to the spawning grounds. The Sanpoils knew they were
coming and moved to the banks of the Columbia and
its tributaries, where they could most easily intercept
them. The men were in charge of the salmon harvest.
They waited in rapids and at falls, spears at the ready.
In time they found a way to impound protein: they
built fencelike weirs to guide the fish into traps.

Among the coastal peoples individuals were accorded
by inheritance the right to particular fishing grounds,
though in most tribes they were expected to share with
the tribe the bounty of their favored spot. But on the
plateau fishing was a community task. Among the
Sanpoils and other tribes, it was customary to choose a
salmon chief to direct the harvest. The salmon chief was
usually someone who had the salmon as guardian spirit,
someone, therefore, whose family was steeped in the lore
of the salmon run, though room was left for accident or
genius. The salmon chief interpreted the rules, which in
general barred women from approaching the sites of
great catches, lest scents of menstruation drive away
the quarry. A salmon chief, like a president, took credit
for periods of prosperity. When runs failed, he, again
like a president, blamed a foreign power. He became
shaman and practiced magic. Sometimes the salmon run
came late; sometimes it did not.

Waiting for the salmon run was a period of tension.
Survival depended on it. The first salmon was greeted,
not just with gratitude, but with reverence. The Sanpoils, like other tribes, felt that a reincarnated ancestor
had surmounted the hazards of a dangerous passage to
bring his people sustenance. He was welcomed with
ceremony, his flesh shared among all, his bones interred
with appropriate ritual.

As the days grew short and the yield of the waters

*With the acquisition of the horse, many plateau Indians became wide-ranging hunters and
warriors, often adopting the trappings of Plains tribes—as here in "Indian Encampment,
Shoshone Village" by Albert Bierstadt.*

A Nez Perce warrior by Paul Kane—the bone through his nose may be courtesy of the artist's imagination.

slackened, the Indians left their sites by the river. The women gathered the soft berries of autumn. The men stalked deer and elk, antelope and mountain goat. Like hunters everywhere, they had their superstitions; rituals developed. They abstained from sex; they retired to the sweathouse; they extrapolated results and drew deductions—most, probably puritanical and poorly founded.

The dark, tough winter on the plateau was a time to think about life; a time to propitiate the spirits who might determine the yield of the digging stick, the heft of the fishnet, the path of the arrow; a time to reflect, to take stock of shortage, and to celebrate success. Among the Sanpoils, winter was the facing of necessity, a religious experience.

The quest for a guardian spirit was the most important event in the lives of most Indians—central, coastal, or plateau. The young man—or sometimes, but rarely, a young girl—would retreat to some spot beyond human contact. There, after exposure to hunger, cold, and isolation, he would experience a dream or halluci-

nation in which appeared the animal or creature that would represent his special relationship to the world. At a guardian spirit performance during the winter, he would hint to his people of this relationship, letting them know enough to understand the name he chose as his adult name, but keeping private unto himself its special significance and power.

Cooperation was essential to the lives of the plateau people. They recognized few ranks in their society and had little concept of status or wealth. Every adult man and woman had a voice in the village councils. A village chief was elected primarily to settle disputes. Candidates were often less than eager for the office: a chief had few privileges and many responsibilities; he had to give presents from his own possessions to pacify those who were quarreling. Tribesmen seriously dissatisfied with village life simply left to form an alliance with another group of families. The village actually was just a group of families.

The Sanpoils constrained no one and compelled no one. Their treatment of outsiders reflected this willingness to live and let live. Slaveholding was anathema to them, as was war; sometimes they even refused to avenge attacks. They were pacifists, but pacifists without moral fervor. Such was the balanced and humane culture of these early people of the plateau.

T HE HORSE, introduced to America by the Spanish and stolen by the Indians of the Southwest, reached the Shoshonis, southernmost of the plateau peoples, around 1700. The animals thrived in the immense grazing land north of the Great Basin. In a land where scarcity had been shared, the horse became the mark of distinction. "Many horses" meant status.

The horse changed the pattern of tribal warfare. Once men had contested fields where camas grew or valleys where deer abounded, now they raided for women and portable wealth. The horse made warfare more flexible, more sudden, more rewarding. Even a peaceable tribe like the Nez Perces changed under the impact of its threat and its opportunity.

The Nez Perces had developed a fairly peaceful pattern of life. A relatively sedentary people, they lived along the Clearwater, Snake, and Salmon rivers, gathering roots throughout the digging period, harvesting the salmon runs, trapping and sometimes felling with arrows the elk, deer, and mountain sheep of the high country. They had found their niche in the ecology of the plateau.

The horse was not of as much immediate benefit to the Nez Perces as to some of their neighbors. Nevertheless they adapted themselves to its possibilities—and the horse to theirs. Lewis and Clark proclaimed them the only Indians to practice selective breeding of livestock. By castrating inferior stallions and trading off inferior brood stock to rival tribes, the Nez Perces developed herds of strong, durable animals that eclipsed their neighbors' and were said by white visitors to rival the prize stock of the white breeders on the Atlantic Coast. In the course of their trading, they acquired some strangely marked horses from the Southwest which, when interbred on the rolling hills of the Palouse country, provided the strain now celebrated as the Appaloosa.

The horse made the root-digging Nez Perces mobile, thus permitting them contact with other cultures. They borrowed and adapted many things and attitudes developed by the Plains Indians across the mountains, including dances, burial practices, and styles in clothing, such as the handsome, cumbersome eagle feather warbonnet. They learned to hunt buffalo, and they had to learn new ways to fight.

In the mid-1700s, the white man's guns came into the hands of the Nez Perces' rivals, the Blackfeet, upsetting the balance of power along the continental divide. When their eastern rivals obtained weapons that could kill beyond the range of bow and arrow, the Nez Perces were forced to adapt. They became more organized, more oriented to defense. Among their leaders, priority no longer went to the medicine man or hunter but to the war chief. When the white men first came among the Nez Perces, what the Indians asked for was weaponry.

At the opposite edge of the interior region, the Indians near the bustling native trade center of The Dalles were becoming as status-conscious as the wealthy natives of the coast. The horse accelerated this cultural change. It was a valuable item in trade and could be exchanged, for example, for a slave. Bands like the Wishrams found themselves holding slaves, first because they were acting as middlemen in the trade between the coast and the interior, and later because they were

Walla Walla chief Peopeo Moxmox, whose tribal lands were diminished by Isaac Stevens' doubletalk.

proud of the status of slave owner. Even the distant Nez Perces were affected. On their magnificent horses they journeyed to The Dalles to obtain treasures like sea shells and, in later times, trinkets of white traders.

THE SHOSHONI spanned the spectrum of Indian existence and experience across the intermontane region. Before the coming of the white man, Shoshoni peoples were found across the Great Basin, northward onto the plateau, and eastward into the Rockies. They were hunters and gatherers, grubbing in the soil for roots, collecting seeds and nuts, and hunting the small game and insects of their arid home for bare survival. Tribes to the south, where the climate was drier, the grass shorter, the rivers meager, fared the hardest; while those to the north, on the plateau, found a better living from lusher vegetation, larger game, and the seasonal salmon migrations.

The Shoshonis of the plateau lived much like the

This scene near Fort Colville, painted by Paul Kane, shows Indians along the Columbia drying the annual salmon catch—the year-round staple of their diet—on the poles of their lodges.

Sanpoils, changing with the cycle of the year, adapting themselves to the natural world, living in communal harmony and relative peace with their neighbors. But sometime in the last decades of the seventeenth century a wedge was driven between the Western (or basin) Shoshonis, and the Northern (or plateau and mountain) Shoshonis; as with the Nez Perces, it was the horse that caused the change.

The Shoshonis of the mountains and plateau took to the horse with amazing ease. The range of their foraging was extended across the Rockies and onto the plains. But the basin Shoshonis, though like their northern relatives in language and original culture, continued to roam the deserts on foot, digging in the earth, gathering seeds, munching grasshoppers, and stoning an occasional rabbit. For some, like the Snake River Shoshonis, the change was gradual, incomplete, or intermittent, to the point where an individual's designation as Northern

ethic of the plains.

But the Shoshonis were quickly pushed back to the mountains by the Blackfeet, Crees and Assiniboins armed with rifles supplied by British and French fur traders. By the time Lewis and Clark (in the company of the Shoshoni girl Sacajawea) crossed over Lolo Pass to their rendezvous with the Shoshonis and their all-important horses, the Lemhis had been confined to the safety of the mountains for a number of years by their fierce and well-armed neighbors to the north and east. Because they lacked modern arms for many years, the Northern Shoshonis lost some of the advantages of mobility that the horse conferred. Nonetheless they ranged faster and farther in their annual cycle of fishing, hunting, and occasional root-digging.

Some of the Northern Shoshonis never made the transition to the horse, most notably the Sheepeaters. Found in the highest country of what is now eastern Idaho and Yellowstone Park, the Sheepeaters persisted as furtive remnants of the neolithic era, living in brush shelters, eating mountain sheep, and hiding in the most inaccessible high country to escape hostile Blackfeet. Despite their cautious avoidance of neighbors, the Sheepeaters were wiped out in the end—by smallpox.

T HE PREHISTORY of the plateau peoples was simple. In their acquisition of food and in their relations inside and outside the tribe, they followed the dictates of nature. They were peaceful and cooperative from the necessity to survive in a land that required almost constant attention and effort to food-gathering. But for many of the tribes the life they had led for thousands of years began to change about 1700—a change caused by men most Indians would not see for nearly another hundred years. By trade from Indian to Indian, horses and metal tools and firearms—the hallmarks of white culture—reached the plateau Indian, changing his way of life and his cosmology as well.

At a time when, for the white man, the Northwest was a land shrouded in coastal mists and mythical geography, the natives of the plateau were embarking on a new life—one that would climax and decline in less than two hundred years. To the white man the Northwest was the stuff that dreams were made of; to the Indian, that dream was the beginning of a nightmare.

or Western Shoshoni might change daily—depending upon whether or not some raiding Ute had stolen his horse. Afoot he was Shoshoko (Western) ; mounted he was Shoshoni (Northern) .

The Shoshonis of Idaho's mountain country, especially the Lemhis and the Bannocks, adapted to the horse with a vengeance. They ranged widely across the Rockies and onto the plains in search of buffalo and, like the Nez Perces, adopted the trappings and warrior

PART THREE

CHALLENGING THE UNKNOWN

A remote edge of the North American continent, the Northwest lay shrouded in the mists of legend and speculative cartography for centuries. But eighteenth-century man's compelling urge to discover — plus the obvious riches in furs waiting for any who would take them — finally eroded the mystery and isolation. Successive waves of maritime explorers, sea traders, overland expeditions, and fur trappers washed over the land, probing its secrets. In time, even the soul of the heathen became a lure that drew agents of discovery and, eventually, settlement.

*Lewis and Clark on the Columbia
by C. M. Russell.*

CHAPTER 11

SHIPS FLYING MANY COLORS

Seeking commerce, empire, and an illusory Northwest Passage
in the name of Spain, England, Russia, and America

THE GEOGRAPHY OF THE NORTHWEST succumbed slowly to the fickle curiosities of Europe. The region lay in a dark and distant corner of the last great sea to challenge the mercantile and territorial ambitions of the western maritime powers, nations that would spend 250 years occasionally poking and probing at its fringe before they came to know it well enough to contest for possession with any reasonable understanding of what they were fighting over. Even then, the vast interior remained an enigma, for the long first chapter of discovery was the story of the coast—the domain of men with ships and of nations that found their livelihood, power, and prestige in the commerce of the seas.

They came first for discovery and empire, later as the outriders of Enlightenment science that made eroding the unknown an end in itself. But the real progress was made on the keels of commerce, for the explorers found in the course of their voyages an engaging sea mammal with a luxurious pelt that could be converted into a small fortune in the Orient.

The sea otters that ranged the rocky shores and kelp beds of California, northern Washington, British Columbia, and Alaska (Oregon's coast being a less favorable habitat) possessed a thick, fine, brown-black fur that fairly shimmered with long, silver guard hairs. Warm and beautiful, the pelts—sometimes measuring two-by-five feet—were highly prized by the Chinese, who would trade favorably with their spices, tea, and cloth to get them. As a consequence, these playful, gregarious critters were ruthlessly and vigorously pursued by traders, who did not hunt themselves but offered en-

ticing trade goods to the Indians who did. In the course of their search, the trading ship captains thoroughly and minutely examined the shoreline of the Pacific Northwest. The long-languishing, intermittent exploration of the coast was quickly brought to a crescendo of activity by the fur trade, an activity which was abandoned just as abruptly when the hunters succeeded in very nearly exterminating the sea otter.

IT WAS MYTH that first brought white men to the broken Northwest coast: the self-generating hope of golden cities awaiting conquest, or the persistent belief in a Northwest Passage through the new continent just waiting to be found. The Spanish nurtured both fictions to varying degrees. When experience proved that neither the gilded city of Quivira nor the Strait of Anian lay in the northern reaches of their Mexican domain, the dreams were simply shifted—undiminished —farther north. In 1542, Bartoleme Ferrelo, as a pilot for Cabrillo, chased the retreating phantoms as far north as the southern coast of Oregon before turning back. Energy and resources were scarce on the frontier, and the Spanish dream had to convalesce for nearly half a century. Besides, there was time; after all, the Pacific was Spain's private lake.

In 1579, Sir Francis Drake, flying the English flag, jarred that complacency. This rascally upstart appeared with the *Golden Hind* on the western coast of South America, raiding towns and shipping at will, and disappearing to the north. He left the Spaniards anxiously

Empire and industry in the making: Captain Cook's "Resolution" and "Adventure" in 1778 at Nootka Sound,   125
where his crew acquired the otter furs which focused British trade interest on the Northwest.

speculating over his intentions, but he was as much in the dark as they. He sailed up the coast, apparently to a point near the mouth of the Rogue River, where he turned back south again, discouraged in his search for the Northwest Passage by "thicke and stinking fogges." Drake found little to remark on concerning the Northwest coast, save the cold and foul weather, and eventually made landfall for repairs just north of San Francisco Bay.

Because nothing definitely negative was found, imaginary cosmography continued to proliferate, probably reaching its zenith in 1596 with the publication of a delightful fabrication by a Greek explorer in the service of Spain, named Juan de Fuca. This latter-day Ulysses claimed that in 1592 he sighted a broad inlet between 47° and 48° north latitude (fortuitously, quite near the latitude of the strait which now bears his name), and, sailing up it for twenty-odd days, found a land rich in gold, silver, and pearls. This claim was periodically revived by everyone who *wanted* to believe in a Passage.

In 1602, Spain commissioned Martín Aguilar to search for Quivira and the Strait of Anian along the coast. Although he mentions a "rapid and abundant river" that some have speculated was the Columbia, it is unlikely that he got any farther north than Coos Bay. The paucity of his discoveries was hardly noticed, however, for the Spanish became sidetracked by a growing trans-Pacific trade with the Philippines and Japan. For over a century and a half after Aguilar, Spain ignored this backyard section of her empire, only showing an interest when it appeared that the Russians were casting covetous glances—and a few settlements—upon the lands in that region.

R USSIA'S APPEARANCE on the Northwest coast came by a slow and circuitous route. In 1725, Peter the Great's aspirations for Westernization and a place in world commerce led him to commission explorations seeking an Arctic Sea route from Archangel in the West to the Pacific. Vitus Bering was sent north from Kamchatka in the Pacific but was turned back by the ice after finding passage through the strait named for him. In 1741, this time urged by Catherine I, Bering returned with two ships to probe for the continent to the east. Wandering across the Pacific, the ships became sepa-

rated, but both made landfalls on the far north coast: Bering at Prince William Sound in Alaska; the other, commanded by Alexei Chirikov, possibly near Lituya Bay. Chirikov, after having two landing parties swallowed up by some unexplained peril, retreated to Kamchatka. Bering did not fare as well. Abruptly pulling out of Prince William after less than a day, he sailed blindly in fog and storms until he was shipwrecked on a tiny island off the end of the Aleutian chain. A desperate winter followed, which saw Bering and half his crew perish, before a crude craft could be built to carry the survivors back to Kamchatka.

During that bleak winter the survivors warmed themselves in the skins of sea otters they killed along the shore, and when the remnants were seen on Kamchatka, they touched off a wild stampede of hunters and traders. The *promyshleniki* were the Siberian counterparts of the American mountain men—tough, capable, freespirited misanthropes who worked the frontiers, gathering furs for Russia and for trade with the Chinese. Recognizing the potential bonanza and utilizing anything that even looked like it would float, they set out by the hundreds to backtrack Bering's ill-fated crew to the hunting grounds. A frightening number of these novice sailors in precarious crafts were lost in the treacherous seas, but others, lured by the potential wealth, were not to be deterred. The profits were incredible: one ship returned with a cargo valued at 112,000 rubles (almost a million dollars in today's currency); another reputedly, with the equivalent of almost 200,000 rubles in pelts. They worked their way through the Aleutians, stripping island after island of every animal, and their scourge was not limited to the sea otter.

Originally, the *promyshleniki* hunted the otter themselves, but they soon found that native Aleuts would do it for them in exchange for trinkets. Failing that, the Russians took Aleut women hostage, forcing the men to hunt to guarantee the return of their wives and daughters. Excess led to outrage, and soon the *promyshleniki* were wantonly killing and pillaging along the entire north coast. The Russian government finally intervened to curb the brutality, and Catherine, her interest in the region piqued, ordered three explorations southward down the coastline between 1765 and 1768.

Although none of the Russian expeditions reached as far south as Spanish colonial territories, this foreign

Captain James Cook began mapping the Northwest coast during his third, and fatal, voyage to the Pacific.

Before the last quarter of the eighteenth century, England had flexed her maritime muscles and garnered an empire that stretched over three quadrants of the globe; the time had come to reach into the Pacific. On two voyages between 1768 and 1775, Captain James Cook, the nation's preeminent seaman, had sailed the southern Pacific, mapping the coasts of New Zealand and Australia and making scientific observations. On his third voyage, lasting from 1776 to 1780, he was charged with exploration of the northern waters, to find the elusive western end of the Nórthwest Passage. The hope of the passage died hard in English hearts—the crown had been induced to put up a prize of £20,000 for its discovery; moreover, regardless of results, exploration was an integral element of the Age of Enlightenment's "need to know."

Cook's geographic discoveries in the Northwest were something short of momentous: sailing north from near Yaquina Bay, he missed both the Columbia River and the Strait of Juan de Fuca. But he did come to harbor in Nootka Sound, where eager native Indians bartered with his crew for bits of metal, exchanging hundreds of furs that the sailors used for bedding and cloaks. After refitting his ship, Cook continued north to the Bering Strait, then south to the Sandwich (Hawaiian) Islands, where he was killed in a skirmish with the locals.

The ships tried to reach Europe by sailing north of Siberia. Failing, they turned south, stopping in China en route home, where the sailors discovered that their makeshift bedding—sea otter pelts—were worth as much as $120. The revelation nearly caused a mutiny, since the crew wanted to return immediately to Nootka for more furs, while the officers, as navy men, felt a higher obligation to complete the scientific voyage free from degrading charges of profiteering. Although Cook's voyage failed to turn up a Northwest Passage, British merchants consoled themselves with the zoological discovery—and scurried off to the Pacific like so many white-collar *promyshleniki*.

The English traders found their ambitions momentarily blunted by their own nation's habit of restrictive trade: monopolies granted to the South Sea Company and the East India Company (giving sole right of trade in the Pacific and China, respectively) excluded any vigorous independents. But men like Charles Barkley, who in 1787 discovered the "long lost strait of Juan de

presence did not escape the notice of the Spanish, and in 1774 the first of a succession of voyages was launched to explore and consolidate the lands Spain regarded as her own. Juan Perez sailed up the coast to about 54° before scurvy decimated his crew and he turned back. Subsequently, Bruno Heceta and Juan Francisco de la Bodega y Quadra took two ships north, only to have their efforts blunted by the same disease. Returning, Heceta paused in a bay which he presumed to be the outlet for a great river; but his weakened crews precluded any possible exploration, and Heceta proceeded south, denied the discovery of the Columbia River. Perez, Heceta, and Bodega gave a rough outline to the coast, mapping and naming some points, bays, and mountains, providing the first semblance of a systematic cartography of the Northwest. But while they had set out to blunt the advances of the Russians, the Spanish would soon find that the real threat to their dominion came from an unexpected source: the British.

Yankee trader Robert Gray named a river for his ship and established an American claim to the Northwest.

Fuca," evaded the ponderous bureaucracy by assuming foreign registration. Within three years more than fifteen British ships using this polite fiction were bartering along the Northwest coast. A few affiliated with Richard Etches to purchase a kind of mini-monopoly from the larger companies, but most independent newcomers could not afford the price of admission immediately.

One such was John Meares, who arrived unlicensed in 1786. Tossed out of Northwest waters by the earliest Etches' men, Meares returned in 1788 flying Portuguese colors. He built a small storehouse (which he later called a fort) at Nootka Sound, launched a coastal trading schooner, and with a year's profits bought his way into the Etches circle. But Meares was destined for a more important role on the coast than that of mere trader—he, his "fort," and his ships would become the focus of a controversy that very nearly ignited a war.

The Spanish had grown nervous of the British presence in the north, and in 1788 José Martinez was dis-

patched to reinforce Spain's claim. When Meares' ships returned to Nootka in 1789, Martinez undiplomatically seized ships and crews and carted everything portable off to Mexico under a charge of unauthorized settlement and trading. Spain, chagrined at Martinez' hasty action, returned ships and crews, but Meares howled to Parliament for redress and an indemnity of $500,000. The motives and mechanics of what followed were intricate and multi-faceted; suffice it to say that the belligerents had barely squared off, when an aged and declining Spain found herself alone against an awesome adversary. The Spanish conceded the right of free trade and access "in places not already occupied" and promised to pay Meares $210,000 for his trouble. Fifty years later, the precedent set by Britain would be turned against her by the Americans in this same Oregon country— and it would cost the imperial lion a choice piece of real estate.

To iron out the details of the Nootka controversy, each government sent envoys to the scene: the Spanish, Bodega y Quadra; the English, Captain George Vancouver. Arriving on the coast in 1792, Vancouver took his time reaching the negotiations. He sailed up the Oregon shore mapping and taking voluminous notes and passed the mouth of the Columbia, which he discounted as unworthy of investigation. Shortly, he met an American trading captain named Gray who speculated optimistically on the river ignored, but Vancouver continued north to the Strait of Juan de Fuca. Entering the sound that would be named for a lieutenant in his command, Peter Puget, Vancouver conducted two months of intensive exploration in the entire inland waterway. His curiosity satisfied and the logs bulging with data and newly named landmarks, Vancouver took the *Discovery* north between Vancouver Island and the mainland, dropping off his smaller companion vessel *Chatham* and its commander William Broughton to continue exploration of the Inland Passage and adjacent lands.

After completing his chores in Nootka, Vancouver returned for Broughton and coasted south to the river he had disregarded earlier; in Nootka, Bodega had told him that the optimistic Captain Gray had indeed found a great river. Because his 340-ton *Discovery* was too large to hazard the bar at the river's mouth, Vancouver sent Broughton and the 135-ton *Chatham* to investi-

The fruit of Meares's efforts: A British painting of the era re-creates the "insult" at Nootka Sound.

Captain George Vancouver charted the Northwest coast en route to his peacemaking duties at Nootka.

John Meares was a trader-without-portfolio at Nootka whose presence almost ignited a war.

Gray and Vancouver met at sea, where the Englishman rejected the idea of a great river to the south.

gate. Behind the bar, Lieutenant Broughton found not only a fine harbor but a small British trading schooner. Adopting his captain's thoroughness, Broughton spent three weeks in a longboat exploring nearly a hundred miles upriver, finding there "the most beautiful country that can be imagined"—and laid a tardy, though thorough, claim to the region for England.

Vancouver's efforts at Nootka had not been conclusive —he and Bodega amiably agreed to leave some contested points in limbo. His investigations of the coast marked the last great maritime exploration of the region by the British. But it was all largely a moot point: Nootka became a dead issue because the otter had been nearly exterminated, and no one really wanted the region. British traders were rapidly disappearing on the coast, victims of the lethargic monopolies, and of a redirection of capital and energy to the conduct of growing European wars. Into the vacuum would sail a vigorous new group of traders: Yankee merchants seeking a place in world commerce for their new nation.

T HE SCRIPT for the American pageant on the Northwest coast was outlined by a young vagabond named John Ledyard, orphan of a Yankee sea captain. He had sailed as a marine corporal on Cook's third voyage and seen the fabulous wealth to be made in the fur trade with China. In 1783, he published a description of the journey, emphasizing the commercial discoveries, and cast about New England for financial backing. But Americans knew nothing of the China trade and shied away. Ledyard followed his dream, and occasional whimsy, to England, the Continent, halfway across Siberia, and ultimately Africa, where he died in 1788. But while he never found support, his writings and enthusiasm were to be capitalized upon by others.

In 1784 the merchant Robert Morris, who had rejected Ledyard's overtures, sent his *Empress of China* to Canton in a blind probe for fiscal possibilities that might exist. The venture was successful, and others immediately followed, but Americans had nothing to exchange for Chinese goods except hard cash—a scarce commodity in the infant nation. Then, in 1787, a group of Boston merchants, remembering Ledyard's story, launched two ships, the *Columbia Rediviva* and the smaller *Lady Washington,* to try the merits of the trading pattern he described. Commanding the *Columbia* was John Kendrick, while a younger Robert Gray took the *Washington.*

Kendrick, a seasoned merchant seaman, had seemed a good choice for command, but in transit to the Northwest he dawdled until Gray left him behind in disgust. Reunited on the coast in 1788, both wintered in a harbor on Vancouver Island, resuming trade again in the spring. They had arrived amidst the height of British activity on the coast (they were present at Nootka when Martinez impounded Meares' ships—but managed to retain a semblance of neutrality) and found the Indians had grown into more sophisticated bargainers than those Ledyard had encountered.

The natives had always placed a high priority on sea otter skins—two would buy a slave in the prewhite society—but they were readily seduced by the metal products of an industrial world. Originally content with bits of metal and cloth, they soon began demanding finished garments and knives. By the time the Americans arrived with a hull full of gewgaws, the Indians were angling for guns and powder. Kendrick and Gray found trading slow—subsequent Americans would find it even more difficult—and an impatient Gray fell to squabbling with his plodding, lethargic captain. They traded ships; Gray was ordered to finish the season and then make for China and home, while Kendrick stayed

This romanticized mural in Oregon's capitol rotunda depicts Gray's discovery of the Columbia. As a trader he was more interested in furs than exploration and underestimated the import of his find.

behind, embarking on a career of sloth and theft from his sponsors, drifting back and forth across the Pacific as fancy moved him.

Gray's arrival in Boston, while not an overwhelming financial success, was widely heralded. Gray was immediately dispatched again, and more Americans followed in his wake as quickly as they could be outfitted.

It was on this second voyage that Gray made the discovery which would bring him fame. He wintered in 1791 at Clayoquot on Vancouver Island and began closely probing the coast of Washington and Oregon seeking Indians less jaded by contact. He found the mouth of a river that he named for his ship, the *Columbia*. He assessed the stream to be a large one, but discouraged by bad weather, he turned north where he met Vancouver. His interest once again stimulated, he returned and on May 11, 1792, made his way over the treacherous bar. Because he saw himself as a trader, not a man of destiny, Gray's examination was only cursory; finding trade slow and unpromising, he only coasted the harbor and apparently failed to stake a claim of possession for his country. His laxity would

later provide the rationale for a proprietary claim by the British on the strength of Broughton's activities later in the year.

Americans who followed Gray (over eighty-five American ships would pursue the trade in the next fifteen years) struggled with hard-bargaining Indians and a rapidly declining otter population. Covetous glances were cast at the fertile California shores, but Spanish restrictions made trade there risky. In 1810, hoping to check the declining fortunes of the business, Nathan Winship proposed to establish a trading depot in neutral territory, and to send Aleuts into Spanish waters. He settled on the Columbia River for his post and had even begun construction before hostile Indians drove him away. The venture fizzled, but it marked the first attempt at permanent settlement by Americans in the Pacific Northwest.

The American trade was saved from an agonizingly slow decline by the outbreak of hostilities with Britain in 1812. After the war the trade never regenerated, and the contest for empire subsequently shifted from the coast to the valleys and rivers of the interior.

131

CHAPTER 12

THE GREAT RIVER OF THE WEST

Explorers and traders along the Columbia:
Mackenzie, Thompson, Astor, and Lewis and Clark

CAPTAIN COOK, while off the Northwest Coast, confided to his journal that he did not believe the Northwest Passage existed; but the quest for a shortcut across the continent did not cease. The famous seagoing explorers Drake, Frobisher, and Cook had their counterparts on land in the men who sought a legendary River of the West.

One searcher was an indomitable Scot named Alexander Mackenzie. Migrating with his family to New York and—during the Revolutionary War—to Quebec, he fell under the spell of the fur trade and the lure of the vast unknown extending west and northwest from Montreal.

By the age of twenty-three, Mackenzie was a full partner in the North West Company, a new and daring association of Scottish entrepreneurs and French-Canadian *voyageurs,* or wilderness men, left over from French dominance of the fur trade on the St. Lawrence and Great Lakes before 1763. They operated from Montreal westward along the narrow passageway between the Hudson's Bay Company's monopoly and the new republic of the United States. Their competitor, in controlling Hudson Bay, had an enormous geographical advantage: HBC ships could sail deep into the interior of the continent, to 92°W 57°N—farther west than the Great Lakes and far enough north to find chilly, hence thickly clad, beaver. "Nor'Westers," on the other hand, had to maintain their supply lines to Montreal over "an infinite number of portages"; thus, as they moved west, the idea of a Pacific depot looked more and more attractive.

Mackenzie set out to find a route from the middle of the continent to the Pacific. He began with a map wishfully based on the tame and orderly geography of eastern Canada. From one height of land in beautiful symmetry, it was believed, ran four rivers in four directions. The River of the East was the St. Lawrence (and the Great Lakes) ; the River of the South was the Mississippi; the River of the North was the Nelson, which emptied into Hudson Bay; and the River of the West, which led to the Pacific, was still to be found.

Mackenzie spent the winter of 1788–89 at Fort Chipewyan, where he was exposed to American trader Peter Pond's contagious enthusiasm for discovery and Indian rumors about routes to the Pacific. When summer came, Mackenzie followed the river that leaves Slave Lake in a westerly direction. Though plagued by reluctant Indian guides, he managed to reach a strange, foggy place with peculiar currents. As the mist cleared, he and his men saw some whales sporting and realized that their canoes had been tossed by ocean tides. But their latitude was 69°N, and the sun had been up at midnight—they had reached the Arctic Ocean. It was 14 July 1789: the Bastille was being stormed, and Mackenzie was in the wrong ocean. Understandably, he named this river the Disappointment, though in all of North America it was second in length only to the Mississippi-Missouri system. (Today it bears the name Mackenzie.)

In 1793, Mackenzie and his men tried again, proceeding from Fort Chipewyan up the torrent known as the Peace River. They portaged along the sides of cliffs much of the way to the Continental Divide, tried the

An early lithograph of the mouth of the Columbia. Cape Disappointment,
the point from which Lewis and Clark first viewed the Pacific, juts out at left.

Visionary, often frustrated, Alexander Mackenzie made the first continental crossing north of New Spain.

which included a long-range program for the fur trade. He warned that the Americans would soon seize the advantage if the British continued to cut each other's throats. Merge the HBC and the North West Company, Mackenzie asked Parliament, or at least grant the North West Company use of Hudson Bay for shipping; break the East India Company's monopoly on the China trade, so that Nor'Westers could trade in China and properly compete with the Americans; and finally, secure the Columbia River for Britain by fixing the Canadian boundary at 45°N.

P RESIDENT THOMAS JEFFERSON was among those who read Mackenzie's *Voyages*. He had been interested in westward exploration since 1785, when, as ambassador to France, he encouraged John Ledyard in his plan to hitchhike to the Northwest Coast on a Russian fur ship, then walk back to the Atlantic. From the time he became president, he had advocated an expedition from the Missouri to a Pacific-flowing river—undeterred by the fact that the United States had no claim to the land west of the Mississippi. A decade later, when the Lewis and Clark Expedition was authorized, Louisiana Territory was still foreign soil. In fact, Lewis and Clark had actually started west before word of the Louisiana Purchase reached Washington. They carried passports from France and Britain, and the Spanish minister had been asked if their expedition would give offense. He replied that it would, for he saw through Jefferson's assurance that the expedition would be purely for "the advancement of geography."

Jefferson did indeed have other purposes in mind. In his secret address to Congress on January 18, 1803, the President noted that "the country [on the Missouri] is inhabited by numerous tribes, who furnish great supplies of furs & peltry to the trade of another nation carried on in a high latitude, through an infinite number of portages and lakes, shut up by ice through a long season. The commerce on that line could bear no competition with that of the Missouri, traversing a moderate climate, offering according to the best accounts a continued navigation from it's source, and, possibly with a single portage, from the Western ocean." This was Jefferson's answer to Mackenzie: the United States must find a better route than the North West Company's.

Tacoutche-Tesse—the southward-flowing Fraser, which the Indians said reached the sea and which Mackenzie took to be the Columbia. Declaring it unnavigable, Mackenzie took the Indians' advice and struck out overland to the sea.

At first, as Mackenzie stood triumphantly on the shores of the Pacific, trying to fix the end point of his transcontinental journey, his reception by the Indians was warm; but within a few days he began to reap what other white men had sown. He was just north of Vancouver Island in a land of intensely proud and creative peoples, some of whom had been underestimated by previous visitors. A group of Indians approached him and his party: "One of them in particular made me understand, with an air of insolence, that a large canoe had lately been in this bay, with people in her like me, and, that one of them, whom he called *Macubah* [Vancouver] had fired on him and his friends."

Nevertheless, Mackenzie returned to tell his tale,

Quiet and studious, Meriwether Lewis was the titular head of the first American overland exploration.

Practical and extroverted by nature, and schooled in frontier skills, William Clark shared the command.

With the acquisition of Louisiana in the spring of 1803, the Lewis and Clark Expedition acquired belated legitimacy. The American explorers began to talk frankly of the extent of their country's rights. For example, how far north into the North West Company's rich fur districts did tributaries of the Missouri extend? This was an important question, because America might claim that Louisiana included all land drained by the Mississippi-Missouri system. The antagonism of British and American plans for the fur trade was becoming clear.

The map of 1797 on page 136 represents the geographical knowledge generally available in Jefferson's day. Though it claims to incorporate "all the new discoveries," it ignores Mackenzie, Vancouver, and Gray. The legendary River of the West follows its fictitious course, and the Rockies are mostly invisible. Aware of these shortcomings, Lewis and Clark bought the only copy of Vancouver's survey of the Pacific Coast available

in America. They also carried with them Mackenzie's reliable *Voyages*.

By the time they left civilization, Lewis and Clark had made themselves perhaps the most informed geographers of their time. Even so, they continued to nourish the hope of an easy connection ("a single portage") between two easily navigable rivers. They were in for many surprises.

Their care in geographical research was matched by their other preparations and by their work in the field. For example, Meriwether Lewis, in the months before his departure, improved the remarkable education he had received as Jefferson's private secretary by studying with leading Philadelphia scientists. Botanists, geologists, ethnographers, physicians, and other specialists provided lists of questions for the expedition to investigate; nature, Lewis would find, provided even more. For example, Lewis and Clark discovered or described for the first time 122 new species or subspecies of ani-

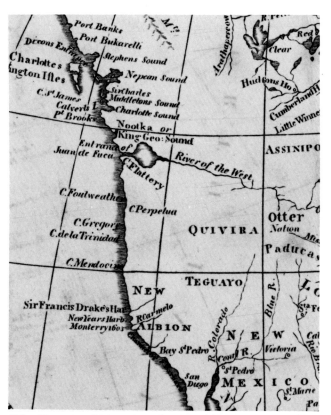

The West in 1797: No Rocky Mountains, no Columbia River, but a mythical "River of the West."

mals and 178 plants, not counting the cache of plants at the Great Falls of the Missouri that flood waters destroyed.

Red-headed, openhearted William Clark was the perfect counterpart to the introverted, scientific Lewis. They were both expert woodsmen and intelligent leaders, and shared command for three years apparently without a quarrel. The idealistic Lewis, who was always planning, theorizing, and philosophizing, was perhaps the more gifted of the two. However, he was doomed to an early death in 1809, only three years after the expedition's return, either at the hands of an unknown murderer or at his own. The more practical Clark was to live for many years in St. Louis, his advice and mediating skill constantly sought by his Indian friends as tensions with white settlers increased.

Clark was naturally at ease with the Indians. He was esteemed as a friend and as a negotiator; he won one tribe after another to the American cause by showing the Indians respect and occasionally firmness. Apparently, he was also esteemed by their women, for he left at least one red-headed son among the Nez Perces.

Clark was also a remarkable geographer. His maps and advice guided Americans of the next four decades into the Northwest. Unlike other maps of the period, which show the interior of America almost blank, Clark's map published in 1814 is filled with details, just as Lewis and Clark's journals are. The explorers found no superhighway across America for the fur trade, but they did make the options clear for the Astorians and their successors. They also gave the United States a powerful claim to the Columbia River and the Pacific Northwest. Most important, in William H. Goetzmann's words, Lewis and Clark "succeeded in making the West itself an object of desire."

The Corps of Discovery (a name the expedition richly deserved) was frequently hard-pressed. Witness the party's crossing of the Bitterroots, the rugged gateway to the Northwest:

AUGUST 20TH 1805

I now asked Cameahwait [Shoshone chief] by what rout the Pierced nose indians, who he informed me inhabited this river below the mountains, came over to the Missouri; this he informed me was to the north, but added that the road was a very bad one. . . . And that they had suffered excessively with hunger on the rout being obliged to subsist for many days on berries alone as there was no game in that part of the mountains which were broken rockey and so thickly covered with timber that they could scarcely pass. however knowing that Indians had passed, and did pass, at this season . . . my rout was instantly settled in my own mind. . . .   [Lewis]

SEPTR. 15TH 1805

Several horses Sliped and roled down Steep hills which hurt them verry much   the one which Carried my desk & Small trunk Turned over & roled down a mountain for 40 yards & lodged against a tree, broke the Desk the horse escaped and appeared but little hurt   after two hours delay we proceeded on up the mountain Steep & ruged as usial, more timber near the top,   when we arrived at the top As we Conceved, we could find no water and Concluded to Camp and

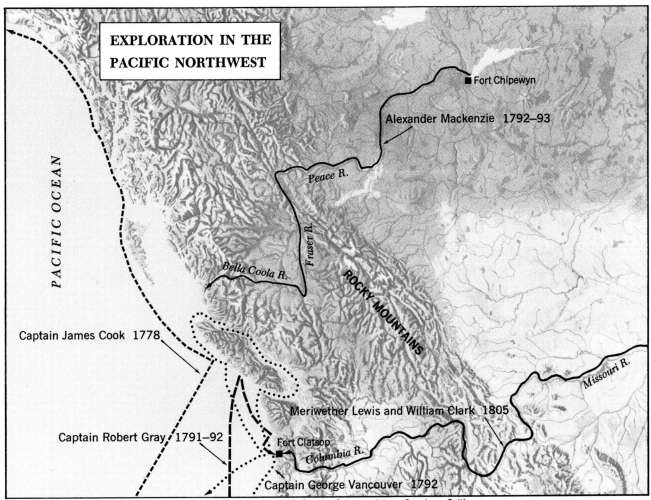

EXPLORATION IN THE PACIFIC NORTHWEST

© Jeppesen & Co., Denver, Colo. Reprinted by permission of the H. M. Gousha Co., proprietors, San Jose, Calif.

make use of the Snow we found on the top to cook the remns. of our Colt & make our Supe, evening very cold and cloudy. Two of our horses gave out, pore and too much hurt to proceed on and left in the rear. nothing killed to day except 2 Phests.

From this mountain I could observe high ruged mountains in every direction as far as I could see

[Clark]

SEPTR. 16TH 1805

began to Snow about 3 hours before Day and con-tinued all day the Snow in the morning 4 inches deep on the old Snow, and by night we found it from 6 to 8 inches deep, I walked in front to keep the road and found great difficulty. . . . I have been wet and as cold in every part as I ever was in my life,

indeed I was at one time fearfull my feet would freeze in the thin Mockirsons which I wore. . . . I took one man and proceeded on as fast as I could about 6 miles. . . halted and built fires for the party agains. their arrival which was at Dusk, verry cold and much fatigued, Killed a Second Colt which we all Suped hartily on and thought it fine meat. [Clark]

SEPTR. 17TH 1805

We hear wolves howl some distance ahead . . . .

[Sgt. Ordway]

Down to eating an unappetizing army ration called "portable soup" and dividing a single crow among them, the men emerged from the Bitterroots into a Nez Perce village stacked high with dried salmon and camas roots. But the change in diet was catastrophic: "Several 8 or 9 men sick, Capt. Lewis sick and complain of a *Lax* & heaviness at the stomack. . . . Capt. Lewis scercely able to ride on a jentle horse which was furnished by the Chief, Several men so unwell that they were Compelled to lie on the Side of the road for Some time others obliged to be put on horses."

The party approached The Dalles after the height of the fishing and trading season. Nevertheless, Clark wrote with awe of the river "crouded with salmon" to a depth of twenty feet and of the shore crowded with "great numbers of Stacks of pounded Salmon," which "kept Sound and sweet Several years." The division near The Dalles between plateau and coastal Indians did not escape Lewis and Clark, who were recording vocabularies in every village: "Not withstanding these people live only 6 miles apart, [they understand] but fiew words of each others language."

At The Dalles itself Lewis and Clark displayed the extraordinary care that had become routine for the expedition:

OCTOBER 24TH 1805

The whole of the Current of this great river [the Columbia] must at all Stages pass thro' this narrow chanel of 45 yards wide.

  as the portage of our canoes over this high rock would be impossible with our Strength, and the only danger in passing thro those narrows was the whorls and swills arriseing from the Compression of the water, and which I thought (as also our principal watermen Peter Crusat) by good Stearing we could pass down Safe, accordingly I deturmined to pass through this place notwithstanding the horrid appearance of this agitated gut swelling, boiling & whorling in every direction, which from the top of the rock did not appear as bad as when I was in it; however we passed Safe to the astonishment of all the Inds. . . . [another] place being verry bad I sent by land all the men who could not Swim and such articles as was most valuable to us such as papers Guns & amunition . . . .   [Clark]

As they neared the mouth of the Columbia in early November, Clark wrote from alongside the north bank:

We have not leavel land Sufficient for an encampment and for our baggage to lie cleare of the tide, the High hills jutting in so close and steep that we cannot retreat back, and the water of the river too Salt to be used, added to this the waves are increasing to Such a hight that we cannot move from this place. . . . We are not certain as yet if the white people who trade with [the Indians with sailor's jackets] or from whome they precure their goods are Stationary at the mouth, or visit this quarter at stated times. . . . The seas roled and tossed the Canoes in such a manner this evening that Several of our party were sea sick.

Lewis and Clark portaging around the falls at The Dalles en route to the Pacific, from a mural in the capitol rotunda at Salem.

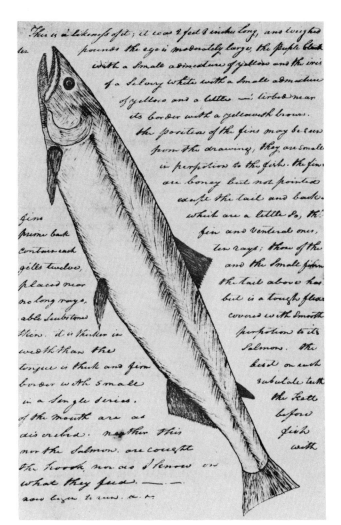

A page from Clark's journal of March 1806, embellished with a fine drawing of a steelhead.

The rain &c. which has continued without a longer itermition than 2 hours at a time for ten days past has distroyd. the robes and rotted nearly one half of the fiew clothes the party has. . . .

At last, the party escaped and established a fifty-foot-square winter headquarters, Fort Clatsop, on the south side of the Columbia. One trading ship crossed the Columbia sandbar during their stay, but the Indians failed to inform Lewis and Clark. The rainy monotony at Fort Clatsop remained unbroken; January 29 was a typical day: "Nothing worthy of notice occurred today. our fare is the flesh of lean elk boiled with pure water, and a little salt. the whale blubber which we have used

very sparingly is now exhausted. on this food I [Lewis] do not feel strong, but enjoy the most perfect health." With time on their hands, the men made salt, candles, and 338 pairs of moccasins from their accumulated elk-hides. Lewis filled page after page with precious botanical and zoological observations. Clark completed his map and deduced a shortcut between the Missouri and the Columbia. The decision to split up to explore alternative crossings of the Bitterroots was made.

Come spring, the expedition departed without regret. They headed east to the Indians who had welcomed them to the Northwest with the region's great blessing, the salmon. The Nez Perces returned the explorers' horses that they had held in trust for them that winter, and Lewis and Clark spent the month of June with this people waiting for the mountain snows to melt. During this time, the whites marveled at the Nez Perces' practice of selective breeding of horses by gelding; found the Indians "expirt marksmen and good riders"; and deemed them "the most friendly, honest, and ingenuous" of all the tribes they had met. The esteem was mutual. The Nez Perces assured Lewis and Clark "of their warmest attachment and that they would alwas give us every assistance in their power; that they were poor but their hearts were good."

As Mackenzie had spurred Lewis and Clark into action, so the Americans' dramatic thrust to the Pacific now awoke the British North West Company. The results of this awakening appear in the fine print of a map by Nor'Wester David Thompson. As many as nine trading houses labeled "NW Co" may be distinguished east of 120°. The one built on the Sheewap River was called Fort Kamloops and was the link between the Columbia department, where the Nor'-Westers were confronting the Astorians, and the more northerly districts.

Lewis and Clark's news that the Columbia turned northward from its junction with the Snake excited the Nor'Westers. They were already trapping in the area where the great River of the West was thought to originate. They sought the river repeatedly.

The very first attempt is represented in the upper left of Thompson's map by a dotted line labeled "Mc-Kenzie's Road to the Sea." It was here that Mackenzie

Simon Fraser, a North West Company employee who revised and affirmed many of Mackenzie's discoveries.

John Jacob Astor, whose enterprising challenge to British ascendency in the Northwest failed.

declared the southward-flowing river unnavigable. However, one of the new generation of Nor'Westers, Simon Fraser, faulted Mackenzie for giving up too easily and tried the Tacoutche-Tesse himself. He pursued it to the sea, and the river acquired his name. But brash young Fraser had to make two admissions: the first appears as a single word on Thompson's chart—"unnavigable"; the second was that the Tacoutche-Tesse was not the Columbia! Gray had discovered that river at 46°N, and Fraser's river emptied into the ocean at 49°.

Meanwhile, another Nor'Wester, David Thompson, was also seeking the elusive Columbia. In 1807 he built the Kootenai House trading post just north of Lake Windermere on the Columbia. The river rises about twenty-five miles to the southeast, at Canal Flats, a bleak stretch of glacial till that also gives rise to the southward-flowing Kootenai. The Columbia continues its Arctic-bound course for another hundred miles beyond Windermere before turning south. It took Thompson four years to establish trade with the local Indians, work out the complicated geography of the ranges and rivers,

and gather men and equipment for a trip down the Columbia to the Pacific.

Near the river's mouth Thompson found that the Americans had arrived and were constructing a trading post. They represented the Pacific Fur Company, ambitious enterprise of a German-immigrant storekeeper named John Jacob Astor. Hoping to neutralize the Russian threat to the Columbia, he agreed to ship their Alaskan fur harvest to China. Astor had offered to help evade the monopoly privileges of the East India Company in British trade with China by selling North West furs as American. When they refused, he simply hired away some of their men with higher salaries.

Astor outfitted an overland party and a ship, and directed them to meet at the Columbia. Unfortunately, the captain of the *Tonquin* was mad and led his captive passengers into successive disasters. He sent two boatloads of men to their death trying a find a channel past the Columbia sandbar and later antagonized the Indians on Vancouver Island into butchering every man on board save one. That one concluded the sad history of the *Tonquin* by setting a match to the powder room, taking several Indians with him to their deaths.

The people Thompson encountered at the mouth of the Columbia were the three dozen men, one-third of them Sandwich Islanders, who had providentially left the *Tonquin* at the Columbia. Rumors of the ship's disaster were beginning to reach the Astorians. And where was the overland party?

Hells Canyon of the Snake River had scattered the party of fifty led by Wilson Price Hunt and Donald McKenzie (not to be confused with his relative Alexander Mackenzie) across the barren lava landscape in a struggle for survival. At times a mile above the drinking water of the Snake, they drank their own urine and, for food, chewed strips of beaver skin. At last, in January 1812, McKenzie and ten others stumbled into Astoria and within a month most of the rest had appeared. Soon the Astorians were competing with the Nor'Westers across the Northwest, from Fort Kamloops to Spokane House. Meanwhile, their respective countries became embroiled in something more serious than economic competition: the War of 1812 had begun.

Word of the war made the already fuzzy situation in the Northwest chaotic. Both the Nor'Westers and the Astorians were isolated at the end of communication and supply lines half a continent long. Neither could be quite sure what the implications of war—economic, political, or pragmatic—would be for the Northwest. News from the centers of corporate and national decision, when it came at all, was sparse and garbled.

The first report of the war included information that the North West Company was about to dispatch the *Isaac Todd* to seize Astoria and destroy it. Anticipating this, a party of Nor'Westers came down from Spokane House and camped outside Astoria's stockade. The Astorians, most of whom were British subjects, saw no need to die for the United States or even to drive a hard bargain with their former colleagues. Their supply ship was long overdue; whether it had failed to run the British blockade or whether Astor had simply abandoned them, as they feared, they were desperate and on the verge of flight overland to St. Louis. (Astor actually had outfitted four ships in separate but ill-fated attempts to get supplies through under the flag of some nonbelligerent nation.)

Astor's "Tonquin" was overrun by Indians. The last survivor blew up the ship and the attackers.

After their first bold maneuver, the Nor'Westers, too, became uneasy. *Their* supplies were also late, and there was still no sign of the *Isaac Todd*—what if it had fallen victim to the American navy? For many of the same reasons that the Astorians put up little resistance to siege, the Nor'Westers did little to press their advantage. Both groups were temperamentally traders, not soldiers; and a military struggle for the post would result in such destruction that neither side could return to profitable trading for a long time.

Responding to practical realities, the two groups negotiated a sale of Astoria to the North West Company, and on October 16, 1813, ownership was transferred. Six weeks later, in a grand anticlimax, the British sloop of war *Raccoon*, which had been convoying the *Isaac Todd*, arrived at the Columbia. Disappointed at finding Astoria already in British hands, her commander went through a comic-opera ceremony of taking possession for the crown. On the basis of this gesture, the Americans were able, after the war, to invoke terms of the Treaty of Ghent and force the British to raise the American flag over the post in recognition that the United States retained its claims in the Oregon country.

CHAPTER 13

THE BEAVER BRIGADES

*Furious competition for furs as the resourceful Nor'Westers
challenge the power of the giant Hudson's Bay Company*

WHEN AMERICAN ASTORIA became British Fort George in 1813, the British North West Company found itself in undisputed control of the Columbia and all the land west of the Rockies between Spanish California and Russian Alaska. Although the company had thrived on severe competition with the Hudson's Bay Company (HBC) and later the Pacific Fur Company, it now collapsed. It seemed to inherit the natural disasters and penchant for poor decisions that had plagued Astor's men.

From 1813 to 1816, while the Nor'Westers clung to their forts, complaining of the rain and hostile Indians, their company lost money. They pretended to be consolidating their gains along the Columbia while actually refusing to explore new beaver territory. By 1816 there was talk of abandoning Fort George.

At this juncture, Donald McKenzie, a former Astorian, accepted a North West Company contract to develop fur-trapping in the interior—in the harsh Snake River country that had broken Astor's overland expedition, McKenzie included, when that party tried to cross it. The pessimists at Fort George gave him only the dregs of the fur trade as companions—a few dozen Iroquois and half-breeds. McKenzie, a stumpy three-hundred-pounder, took this motley crew to the Cascades of the Columbia, where his first labor was the delicate one of making friends with his Indian enemies. He faced the problem head on by wintering with them.

In the spring McKenzie encountered a similar challenge as he approached the Snake. Previous trappers in the region had been belligerent to friendly Indians like the Nez Perces because the nations refused to hunt beaver, saying (truthfully) that they needed all their time for gathering food. On his earlier trip, McKenzie himself had countered supposed Indian stubborness with brutality. This time, by wooing the natives, praising their children, and distributing presents, he won forgiveness.

By the end of 1817, McKenzie's plan for trapping had evolved, and headquarters back on Lake Superior told the Fort George contingent to cooperate. The following spring one hundred men left Fort George to construct a post at the junction of the Snake and the Columbia. They had to float timber from a hundred miles away to this treeless point, but eventually they completed a post: Fort Nez Perce.

No snug haven, the fort was only a base for McKenzie's operations. While other Nor'Westers waited for Indians to bring furs to them, McKenzie led brigades of trappers into the wilderness. If the Indians would not trap, the whites would. At a time when other Nor'Westers were importing birchbark around the Horn instead of adopting the cedar canoes of the natives, McKenzie turned to horses. Trying to find a canoe route along the Snake remained a company temptation, however; and in 1819, McKenzie ascended the Snake through Hell's Canyon. He survived—and appreciated horses even more.

While McKenzie was trapping the interior Northwest, his company was engaged in a bloody struggle with the HBC in the Red River district, mid-continental supply center for the trappers.

Lord Selkirk, allied with the HBC, had founded a

*The free trapper, knight-errant of American civilization in the far West,
met the British presence head-on. (Engraving from a Frederic Remington drawing.)*

143

settlement in Red River—a settlement, however, that straddled the North West Company's supply line and endangered the peddlers' supply of pemmican, which fueled their canoe brigades. The resulting struggle contributed to the North West Company's problems along the Pacific Coast. For a time, supplies had to come to the Northwest around the Horn or not at all. Worse, the best men were sent to Red River to resist the HBC.

After five years of bloodshed, parliament in 1821 ordered a shotgun wedding of the rival giants. They were required to share power under a single name, the older one—Hudson's Bay Company. McKenzie, former Astorian turned Nor'Wester, thus completed his circuit of the beaver companies by retiring under the aegis of the HBC. His enterprising expeditions into the Snake wilderness had revitalized the fur trade and altered the pattern of development of the Northwest. Henceforth, the interior would be the base for trapping and exploring regions even more remote—the focus of the British-American struggle for furs and for the land itself.

Donald McKenzie, 300 pounds of perpetual motion, led fur brigades deep into the Northwest.

WITH THE MERGER of the North West Company and the HBC, part of the dream of that earlier Mackenzie, Alexander, had come true: the British could now show a united front to the Americans. Their unity came none too soon. Brigades of American trappers were already ranging far up the Missouri; the British, no longer tied to their posts, were trapping as far east as the Bear River, the Green River, and the Tetons. A confrontation was imminent. Only the Blackfeet held the Americans at bay, and in 1824, after a British punitive expedition dampened the ferocity of the Blackfeet, American trappers crossed the Rockies.

The Americans were a great worry to George Simpson, first governor of the expanded HBC. Despite McKenzie's rich hauls and the imposition of strict economies, Simpson could not seem to pull his Columbia department out of the red. The HBC might justify a small loss in this region because their presence north of the Columbia strengthened Britain's claim to the area and forestalled American designs on the richer fur lands farther north. But his losses were not small, and he was moved to desperate measures. He decided that by literally stripping the Snake country of furs, he might create a barren buffer zone against the advance of American

trappers from St. Louis. "While we have access thereto, it is our interest to reap all the advantages we can for ourselves, and leave it in as bad a state as possible for our successors."

In the 1820s diplomats argued two ways to fix the boundary between British and American holdings: extend it along the 49th parallel all the way to the Pacific, or extend it along that parallel only to the Columbia, then follow the river to the Pacific (see chapter 14). Simpson made preparations for either eventuality, leaving imposing John McLoughlin to carry them out. He was to abandon Fort George on the south side of the Columbia, lest that river become the boundary, and erect Fort Vancouver on the north side across from the mouth of the Willamette. As a hedge against a 49° boundary, he was to build a base, Fort Langley, about thirty miles upstream from the mouth of the Fraser River, north of the 49th parallel. All other forts in danger of falling to the Americans were to be phased out or severely curtailed—a measure that also promised

Hardy Nor'Westers and HBC voyageurs were accustomed to traveling by canoe, but they often found Northwest rivers dangerously unsuitable. (Charles Deas painting.)

economy. For example, Spokane House, where Simpson had found the traders "eating gold" (European provisions), was shut down and replaced by Fort Colville, which met all of Simpson's specifications: it stood on the north bank of the Columbia, fish were there for the taking, and there was room for a potato garden.

Simpson also moved the base of operations for the Snake region from Fort Nez Perce to Flathead Post, well located though disturbingly close to American territory. One encounter with the Americans proved a costly embarrassment for both the HBC and trader Alexander Ross, who commanded the post. Some Snake Indians in Idaho, irate at Ross's trading tactics, had fallen upon a party of his Iroquois trappers and robbed them. When a group of Americans under Jedediah Smith happened along, the distraught Iroquois pleaded with the Americans to give them supplies and safe conduct back to Ross's camp, offering in return some cached furs the Snakes had not found. Rising to the opportunity, Smith accompanied them not only to the camp but, along with

Ross, on to Flathead Post—learning much along the way about HBC operations.

Ross, in disgrace with the company as a result of this episode, was promptly relieved of his responsibilities and shipped off to be a schoolteacher at Red River. His successor at Flathead Post was Peter Skene Ogden, able and ruthless.

But even Ogden was unable to overcome the central weakness in the British system, its class structure. The highest class of trapper was known as a "freeman"— a misnomer because in reality he was a company serf, forever in debt to the HBC because of low premiums for beaver and high prices for necessities at the company store. No amount of pelts would improve a freeman's lot, and after a while he stopped caring about beaver skin and started worrying about his own.

The Indians, too, were soon bound to the HBC by their debts and dependency on company stores even for food. When these posts closed for reasons the Indians did not understand, they readily believed American sug-

Fort Okanogan, erected on the Columbia in 1811 by Astorians under David Stuart, marked the deepest penetration of the interior by Astor's Pacific Fur Company.

gestions that the "King George men" were deserting them. The small bands of Americans, on the other hand, were flexible; these "big hearts of the East" could afford to please the Indians with generous prices when the British were nearby.

The nature of the American and the British operations gave each certain advantages with the natives. The highly organized British had the advantage of security: business was conducted either at the fort window or with the backing of a large brigade in the field. Since chief factors and chief traders were held accountable for events in their districts, they strove to administer justice in a way that the Americans, lacking a clear chain of command, could not. The British punished white as well as Indian, and the Indians respected this proverbial British fairness.

Many Americans, however, treated the Indians as social equals, camping with them and adopting their dress to some extent. Although this may have been a genuine democratic inclination, the American system of trapping left little choice. A small brigade had to make friends or die. Over five hundred Americans did die in little more than a decade.

The American rendezvous delighted the Indians, too; it had much the character of their own trade gatherings. The institution of the rendezvous is usually attributed

Built by Donald McKenzie in 1818, Fort Nez Perce became the North West Company's
trade and supply center in the Snake River country.

to William H. Ashley, who gave Jedediah Smith and many other future giants of the fur trade their start. Every year, beginning in 1825, Ashley came from St. Louis to a site in the Rockies. The meeting date was always sometime in the summer, when travel was easy and beaver coats were too thin to be worth trapping for. At the rendezvous, Ashley reaped enormous profits, just as the HBC traders did at their forts. Despite Ashley's outrageous prices, however, the gathering appealed to the mountain men. It relieved a long winter's loneliness and provided for their two strongest passions: domestic articles for their squaws and liquor for themselves. Mountain men had the option of returning to civilization after the rendezvous, but most managed to carouse themselves into debt and another winter in the mountains before the affair was over.

Thus the American trappers were only slightly more independent than their HBC counterparts, but they could, with great luck and effort, make their fortunes. George Simpson remarked on their independence:

Erstwhile Astorian Alexander Ross, who ultimately failed to measure up to North West Company standards.

Sir George Simpson, the businesslike Scot who administered the reorganized Hudson's Bay Company.

"Leaders of parties are men who have been common Trappers, and therefore posses no influence: and the Trappers themselves are, generally speaking, outcasts from Society. . . . this 'motley crew' acknowledge no master, will conform to no rules or regulations. . . . We might repeatedly have broken up their parties, but the spirit of insubordination which characterises those fellows, is particularly infectious in the plains."

As BRITISH AND AMERICAN BRIGADES leapfrogged along the beaver streams of the Northwest, the quest for furs often led them to unravel parts of the complex geography of the wilderness. In 1826 and 1827, American Jedediah Smith, one of the grand personalities of the fur trade, made a remarkable loop from the Great Salt Lake. His journey took in present-day Zion National Park, the Mojave Desert, the Spanish settlement of San Gabriel (now Los Angeles), and the San Joaquin Valley. On his return he made the first recorded eastward cross-

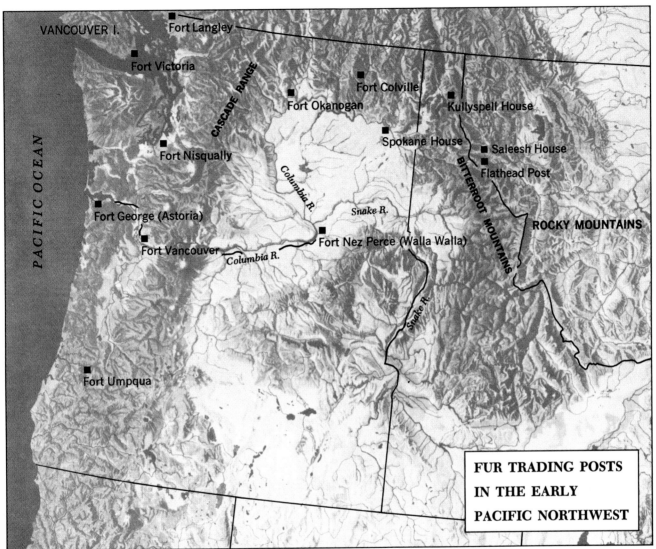

VANCOUVER I.
Fort Langley
Fort Victoria
CASCADE RANGE
Fort Colville
Fort Okanogan
Kullyspell House
Spokane House
Saleesh House
Flathead Post
Fort Nisqually
Columbia R.
Snake R.
BITTERROOT MOUNTAINS
ROCKY MOUNTAINS
PACIFIC OCEAN
Fort George (Astoria)
Fort Vancouver
Columbia R.
Fort Nez Perce (Walla Walla)
Snake R.
Fort Umpqua

FUR TRADING POSTS IN THE EARLY PACIFIC NORTHWEST

© Jeppesen & Co., Denver, Colo. Reprinted by permission of the H. M. Gousha Co., proprietors, San Jose, Calif.

ing of the Sierra Nevada and a first trek across the Great Basin. Small wonder that the mountain men were far ahead of the map makers of their day; for example, they knew the Great Salt Lake's contours intimately at a time when map makers drew it as a perfect rectangle.

The HBC's Peter Skene Ogden was also wandering around the mysterious inland sea about this time, wondering what other secrets might be revealed. There were reports of a river called the Buenaventura flowing westward from the Great Salt Lake, and Ogden speculated that it might be the upstream waters of the Umpqua, which emptied into the Pacific. In 1828 he discovered that the Buenaventura was a myth but that a major

river, the Humboldt, traversed the forbidding Great Basin. His discovery gained nothing for the British but ironically helped American settlers reach California two decades later. Ogden, like other HBC traders, also explored routes from the Columbia south through mountain mazes into Spanish California. But his greatest accomplishment was the first north-south crossing of the Far West. In 1829 he left Fort Vancouver, crossed the Humboldt River and the Sierra, and eventually reached the Gulf of California.

By this time the growth of Fort Vancouver, Ogden's base, reflected a change in the HBC's plans. Simpson, like Simon Fraser and Alexander Mackenzie before him,

As chief factor for the HBC, Dr. John McLoughlin dominated Northwest affairs for a quarter-century.

Stern and competent, Peter Skene Ogden was the wheelhorse of HBC operations in the field.

had discovered firsthand that the Fraser River was unnavigable ("I consider the passage down to be certain Death in nine attempts out of Ten"). This meant that Fort Langley, safely above the 49th parallel, could not be used to supply other HBC forts and that Fort Vancouver would have to do.

John McLoughlin made it do very nicely indeed, as the ubiquitous Jedediah Smith, the fort's surprise guest one winter, reported: "The crop of 1828 was seven hundred bushels of wheat; the grain full and plump, and making good flour; fourteen acres of corn, the same number of acres in peas, eight acres of oats, four or five acres of barley, a fine garden, some small apple trees and grape vines. The ensuing spring eighty bushels of seed wheat were sown: about two hundred head of cattle, fifty horses and breeding mares, three hundred head of hogs, fourteen goats, the usual domestic fowls. They have mechanics of various kinds, to wit, blacksmiths, gunsmiths, carpenters, coopers, tinner and baker; a good saw mill on the bank of the river five miles above.

. . ." The HBC threw these resources into a vicious trade war with the Americans. By 1829 the sea otter, mainstay of the costal fur trade, was virtually extinct, and American merchant ships were offering rum, guns, and good prices for upriver Indians who would bring their beaver skins to the coast. The British countered by dropping prices for trade goods lower and lower, using the Fort Vancouver inventory as their trump card. During the 1830s the HBC constructed a series of trading posts along the coast as a further hedge against the threat of the American merchantmen.

Smith's uninvited presence at the British stronghold foreshadowed a new kind of threat to British dominance of the Northwest: American settlement. Governor Simpson, on his second whirlwind tour of the Northwest, questioned this mountain man who knew the geography of the American West better than anyone else: What about "the flattering reports which reached St. Louis of the Wilhamot Country, as a field for Agricultural speculation"? Would "people in the States" attempt to cross

Fort Vancouver, one hundred miles above the mouth of the Columbia, surrounded by McLoughlin's treasured farms and pastures, was HBC headquarters in the Northwest.

overland to the Northwest? Smith responded cooly that he had "discovered difficulties which never occurred to their minds"—the "Sandy desert," for example.

To the American government, however, Smith gave a somewhat different account of his travels: "This is the first time that wagons ever went to the Rocky mountains; and the ease and safety with which it was done prove the facility of communicating over land with the Pacific ocean. The route from the *Southern Pass,* where the wagons stopped, to the Great Falls of the Columbia, being easier and better than on this side of the mountains."

That report, confirmed by those of the missionaries of the 1830s, would soon lure thousands of Americans onto the Oregon Trail. It was a threat that the British beaver magnates would come to understand only gradually.

THE GREAT NORTHWEST

The Story of a Land and its People

By the Editors of American West

From its earliest exploration, a sense of remoteness has pervaded the Pacific Northwest. Shielded by distance from easy discovery by Europeans, sheltered from early travel by mountains, desert, and ocean, the region has long offered a vision of challenge, a sense of freshness and isolation, that continues even today.

In this book, the authors take the reader on a unique journey, combining intellectual discovery of the area's natural history and human history with a visual experience of scenic splendors unsurpassed by any other place in the world. Profusely illustrated with more than 90 full-color pictures and over 150 black-and-white photographs, diagrams, and maps, *The Great Northwest* traces the awesome forces of nature from earliest geological times, documents its human triumphs and disasters, and shows this dramatic region as it is today.

Here the reader can visit such renowned places as the Lost Forest, the mysterious Mima Mounds, the John Day Fossil Beds, the mighty Columbia and Snake rivers. Here are historic Hells Canyon, sites of Northwest Indian cultures, Puget Sound, and a rain forest unlike any other on earth. Included are spectacular views of the mountains, rivers, desert, and coastline, as well as the great cities and industries in the Northwest today.

As the noted Northwest historian, Murray Morgan, says in the foreword, the special merit of this book is that it shows how geology and geography have shaped the area's history and influenced its economics and the attitudes of its people.

Enhanced by beautiful color reproductions, by historic paintings and engravings, by authentic portrayals of wildlife in natural habitats, by first-hand accounts from historic documents, here unfolds a comprehensive view, yesterday and today, of this magnificent land and its people.

CHAPTER 14

...ERS IN THE WILDERNESS

...ies who adapted to the British and the Indian; ...ho paved the way for American settlers

...ineteenth century ...iced far from civi-...isk one's skin for ...'s Bay Company, ...the two concerns ...traders—survival

...were like Donald ...ay facts about his ...ving off the land ...of the giants of ...l men, their eco-...th touches of ...on, for decades ...s Bay Company ...lt of a pair of ...wilderness that ...ction of God's ...and the Amer-...ristians.

...s ordinarily a ...y was likely to ...life-style and ...pper develop-

...ts were begin-...l of the trap-...itain and the ...r way. In this ...und it politic to declare its support for missionary efforts to civilize the Indians.

The fur trade, up to this point, had profited by keeping the wilderness and the Indian savage, preserving both the beaver and the beaver hunter. George Simpson, no praying man, now speculated that converting the Indians might be profitable, because an Indian who settled down became dependent on the HBC store. (The Church of England's Missionary Society would have been appalled.)

Simpson instructed Alexander Ross, who was about to leave Flathead Post to become a schoolteacher at Red River, to select two Indian boys for Christianizing there. They were Kootenai Pelly and Spokan Garry, surnamed for two officials of the HBC. It was 1829 when the two returned to their tribes. Little is known of Pelly, who died within two years, but Garry created a sensation. Upon his return he succeeded his father, the most respected Spokan headman, and acted as an extraordinary shaman who could call upon the miraculous "talking book" (the Bible) and the white man's other powers. Envy rippled through the neighboring tribes. The next year five more sons of chiefs left their homelands for the tutelage of the Anglicans.

Meanwhile, warriors from tribes that had not been favored by the HBC invitation mulled over what to do. Four Indians from the Nez Perce and Flathead tribes resolved to appeal for religious teachers (whether Catholic or Protestant is much debated) to the Americans in St. Louis, in particular to William Clark whose friendship they remembered from 1805 and 1806. In 1831, having obtained the protection of an American Fur Company caravan while passing through Blackfoot

Greeted by a dour but courteous John McLoughlin, Narcissa Whitman and Eliza Spaulding—first women to arrive overland—portended an American migration of overwhelming proportions.

country, the four arrived in the white man's metropolis. The news of their pilgrimage electrified American missionary societies. A religious revival was brewing, and this cry from the wilderness brought it to a ferment.

The Methodists acted first, in 1833 authorizing Jason Lee, his nephew Daniel, and three laymen to establish a mission among the so-called Flatheads. In Boston the Lees fortunately encountered Andrew Wyeth, an entrepreneur of sorts in the Northwest, and found him willing to transport their heavy equipment in his ship, lend them his two Indians for fund-raising (a Nez Perce with a deformed skull pulled the heartstrings and purse strings of the coldest), and guide them to the Northwest the following summer. The journey of 1834 disabused Lee of the romance of his mission. Not only did Flatheads have normal skulls, he reflected, as he shuddered through that devil's revel, the trappers' rendezvous, but their degradation (and that of his fellow whites) was blacker than he had dreamed.

At Fort Vancouver, Chief Factor McLoughlin further dissuaded Lee from working among the nomadic Flatheads. Lee then cast his eye over the landscape for a mission site and saw "a central position from which missionary labors may be extended in almost every direction among the natives and those emigrants who may hereafter settle in that vast and fertile territory." He was referring to the Willamette Valley. No matter that Indians were scarce and sickly from an influenza epidemic; the land was ripe for settlement.

The first missionary to the Northwest was face-to-face with the dilemmas that both plagued American Protestant missionaries and gave them their strength: the Methodists and later the Presbyterians found first that their own survival was a full-time secular pursuit, and second that converting the Indians was synonymous with civilizing them—providing them with material comforts. Both missionary boards ordered their Northwest missions closed at one time or another because of the difficulty of distinguishing a mission from a store or a family farm.

The arrival of thirteen additions to Lee's party in 1836 and the "Great Reinforcement" of 1840—fifty men, women, and children—meant the fulfillment of Jason Lee's purposes. A station was established at The Dalles, the Indian trade center and the key point on all the Columbia transportation routes. New missionaries

Jason Lee, first of the Oregon missionaries, found more hard work than inspiration.

went from Willamette to the mouth of the Columbia and to Fort Nisqually on Puget Sound. The latter were practically the only Americans to settle north of the Columbia before the resolution of the boundary dispute with Britain. Methodist headquarters remained in the Willamette Valley ready to catalyze settlers into forming a provisional government loyal to the United States.

Meanwhile, the Hudson's Bay Company acted on its own to try to provide a ministry for the natives. In 1835 George Simpson, governor of the HBC northern department, appointed Herbert Beaver to go to Fort Vancouver, with his wife Jane, as "chaplain and missionary for the education and the religious instruction for the Indians."

Other than his name, Beaver had few qualifications for the frontier. He was a country gentleman and an Anglican—a bitter anti-Catholic at a post where most men of any religious affiliation were Catholic. He asserted he had "raised my wife to my station" by marriage and felt she was demeaned by the company of

The missions, such as Jason Lee's at The Dalles (painted by W. H. Tappan in 1839), attracted numbers of interested Indians but seldom converted many souls.

Indians. On discovering that most of the company men living with Indian and mixed-blood wives were not married to them, he wrote letters to London complaining about the moral situation.

One of the offenders was the Chief Factor, Dr. John McLoughlin. Never having had an opportunity to marry Mrs. McLoughlin, he understandably resented Beaver's talk about concubines. The feud climaxed when Beaver swung at McLoughlin with his walking stick. McLoughlin, a head taller and a hundred pounds heavier, took away the stick and chased Beaver back to his quarters, where he stayed until the next ship arrived to take him home to England.

In 1835 the Presbyterians followed. Scholarly Samuel Parker, old for the wilderness at fifty-six, and a doctor by the name of Marcus Whitman traveled to the trappers' rendezvous to investigate the prospects for a mission in the Northwest. En route they were treated to tales of trappers selling decks of cards as Bibles and to the ridicule that moralizing greenhorns invited. Whitman adapted well, winning the respect of the mountain men by doctoring the caravan during a cholera epidemic and by removing an arrowhead from Jim Bridger's back.

Parker, a man with no wilderness skills but escorted by Indians who considered him a precious burden, continued to Fort Vancouver over the Lolo Trail, which thirty years before had brought the Lewis and Clark Expedition to the brink of starvation. Parker, like Captain Bonneville, the amateur fur trapper and professional observer, claimed that the Nez Perce and Flatheads were ripe for conversion. Some observed the Sabbath, used Christian gestures, and, most remarkably, disavowed war. Bonneville was furious at this change of heart when he needed their martial skills, but Parker of course approved: "They do not now believe that all who fall in battle go to a happy country. They now believe there is no other way to be happy here or hereafter, but by knowing and doing what God requires." These Christian aspects and the Indians' initial receptivity to their teachings misled missionaries of all sects.

But Parker understood better than many that the natives and the missionaries had different expectations of the advantages of Christianity: "They also think [the religion] has power to elevate them on the scale of society in this world, and place them on a level with intelligent as well as Christian white men."

From the rendezvous Whitman returned east to assemble a missionary force. The importance of personalities in the Presbyterian effort begins here. Whitman was engaged to marry Narcissa Prentiss on the condition of their going to Oregon, and their going depended on finding another missionary couple. Whitman agreed to allow Henry Spalding, a rejected suitor

of Narcissa's, and his wife Eliza to accompany them. Jealousy, resentment, and purging of guilt became the order of the day among the Presbyterians.

The 1836 journey of the Whitmans and the Spaldings was very much a pioneer trek. Marcus dragged a farm wagon to Fort Laramie and then a pair of wheels as far as Fort Boise. Wagons and women *could* cross the Rockies. Narcissa wrote enthusiastically: "If anyone wishes to come by land (& by the by it is the best for health & the cheapest) let them send all their outfit to Oahu by ship & take only the suit they wish to wear & a few changes of undergarments, packing their provisions only & they will make an easy pleasant trip & less expen-

MISSIONS IN THE EARLY PACIFIC NORTHWEST

sive than we made. . . . *We see now* that it was not necessary to bring anything *because we find it all here."* Words like these stimulated a succession of wagon wheels that left nearly indelible ruts across the continent.

The Presbyterian missionaries founded missions in areas of great Indian need, but not without regard for the previous pattern of trading posts or for the future pattern of settlement. Against McLoughlin's advice, the Whitmans settled among the Cayuse at Waiilatpu, "the place of rye grass." It lay twenty-five miles east of Fort Nez Perce (also called Walla Walla), McKenzie's old base for his Snake Country forays. Here on March 14, 1837, Narcissa gave birth to the first white child in the Northwest, a girl named Alice Clarissa. Here the Whitmans began to take over some of McLoughlin's humanitarian responsibilities for succoring desperate settlers, for Waiilatpu lay in the path of the Oregon Trail from the Snake to the Columbia, just before settlers transferred themselves and their goods to boats.

In Lapwai, or "Butterfly Valley," near the junction of the Clearwater and the Snake, the Spaldings also found fertile ground for growing crops and saving souls. Elkanah Walker, a later arrival, would formulate this Presbyterian dictum: "We must use the plough as well as the Bible, if we would do anything to benefit the Indian. They must be settled before they can be enlightened."

One other person accompanied that unlikely pair of pioneer couples, the Whitmans and the Spaldings. He was William Gray, an acerbic, self-important man, who was later to write a strongly biased history of Oregon. Gray very much wanted a mission of his own. In 1837, without Whitman's blessing, he went north from Waiilatpu to find a site. Gray decided to locate among Spokan Garry's people and headed east to recruit more missionaries and funds.

At the rendezvous of 1838, Gray returning west met Jason Lee going east. Around them, the fur trade was in its death throes. Beaver were almost trapped out, and the demand as well as the supply had vanished. The beaver hat was being driven out of fashion by cheaper felts and silk.

Meanwhile, the missionaries talked of the dawn of a new era. Lee was headed for Illinois to gather men and material for the "Great Reinforcement." He would bring $40,000 from the Methodist board and stay six months lecturing to raise part of it with two genuinely flat-

Father De Smet, Jesuit leader of the loyal opposition in the Almighty's Oregon vineyards.

headed Chinooks by his side.* One of the Indian boys would tell of lush farms and fat salmon, and prompt the formation of the Peoria Party. Lee himself would prepare public opinion for the Great Migration of 1843 that Whitman would guide.

A frenzy of expansion was overtaking the Presbyterians, too. Lee showed Gray a letter from Whitman and Spalding requesting an incredible 220 assistants and tons of necessities. The request foreshadowed the rush of civilization into the Northwest, but in 1838 such assistance was out of the question. Gray wondered if the eight helpers and a few horseloads of supplies he had in tow would suffice.

The arrival of Gray's party, despite its small numbers, permitted the establishment of Tshimakain near Fort Colville and Kamiah on the Lolo Trail. It also brought

---

*The Chinooks flattened the skulls of newborn children by fastening a board across the forehead while the head was still soft. This was a mark of aristocracy, denied to the slaves.

*Indian parishioners provided their own housing;
this scene shows Elkanah Walker's Spokane mission.*

the conflict of personalities to a crisis. Unlike the Methodists, who more or less followed Jason Lee's orders, the Presbyterians attempted to govern themselves. But even on the trail the Elkanah Walkers, the Cushing Eellses, the Asa Smiths, Cornelius Rogers, and the Grays (for Gray had married) had made, in the words of the waspish Mary Walker, "a strange company of missionaries. Scarcely one who is not intolerable on some account."

Then there was the difference between Spalding and Whitman. It was intellectual as well as personal. Spalding at out-of-the-way Lapwai hoped to convert the Indians to agriculture and Christianity before the whites arrived, to give them roots to withstand the waves of civilization that were surging past Whitman's station. Whitman felt the Indians' salvation lay in submerging them as soon as possible in white culture. History would prove Whitman wrong: the Indians did not survive this sudden baptism.

THE CATHOLIC MISSIONARIES were much slower to try to change the Northwest. They were, after all, dependent on the old patterns. Fathers Blanchet and Demers came in 1838 in response to the invitation of the French-Canadian *voyageurs* who had retired to farms in the Willamette. They traveled in HBC canoes and, thanks to McLoughlin, could rely on HBC stores and largely avoid the secular necessity of farming.

The French priests brought no wives or families and were not interested in settlement, though they appreciated the connection between conversion and civilization. They hoped to establish "far from the settlements of the whites, missions like those in California." Since they were not interested in the land itself but exclusively in the souls of the whites and Indians, they were admirably suited for their task.

From the Willamette, Blanchet circulated through the vast countryside, and from the Cowlitz Valley, another HBC settlement, Demers did the same. Reinforcements came singly, if at all, though the fathers wrote eloquently to their superior, the Bishop of Quebec. Unlike the Protestants, the Catholics were careful in selecting missionaries. Laymen—another name for inexperienced volunteers—were not sent. Personality clashes and quarrels with missionary boards were absent, largely because of the hierarchical nature of the priesthood, which was anathema to the democrats of the Willamette. The cooperation between the French priests and the HBC, the other foreign, antidemocratic institution in Oregon, bristled American pioneers even more.

The two Old World monoliths had their troubles, too. When Blanchet and Demers sought more priests, they found George Simpson unwilling to give the essential protection of the "Honourable Company." Though the company's workers were Catholic, most of its higher-ups were Anglican and, as products of British history, fearful of popery. Blanchet pointed to a different menace—the Americans—in his correspondence with Simpson. More priests, especially English-speaking ones, Blanchet argued, would counteract the influence of the American clergy. Nevertheless, Simpson continued to refuse to let the priests accompany the trapping brigades—until priests began to come via the St. Louis diocese with *American* help.

The Jesuit De Smet was one of the first to travel from St. Louis to the Northwest with the American fur-trading caravans. He came in response to the appeals of several delegations of Indians for religious teachers. De Smet reconnoitered present-day Idaho in 1840 and founded St. Mary's on the Bitterroot River in 1841. The following year De Smet met Blanchet and Demers at

Fort Vancouver, and the Catholics were on the way to coordinating the branches of their world-wide organization, though their reinforcements would never equal those of the Protestants.

In dealing with native traditions like polygamy and shamanism, the Catholics showed a willingness to accept sin in all its blackness, while the Protestants were inclined to be shocked into moralizing and imposing their ways. Both Whitman and Spalding whipped their Indians for thievery not understanding that to the Indians the punishment seemed cruel and unusual. As desirous as the Indians were to have missionaries live with them, they got along far easier with visiting Catholics than with resident Protestants.

Eventually the Cayuses would wonder what Whitman was doing for them. The mission crops were feeding white settlers, who trampled on Indian land and pride, and scores of Indians were dying from the new diseases the whites brought. Finally, in November 1847, incensed at Whitman's success in healing white children

suffering smallpox and failing to heal Indian children, who had no resistance to the disease, the Cayuses made Marcus, Narcissa, and about a dozen mission workers pay the price of the shaman who fails to cure—death.

The Whitman Massacre brought the missionary era to a close. Spalding and other Presbyterians fled for their lives. The Catholic effort waned as American settlers wrongly blamed the priests with complicity in the massacre and as the "Honourable Company" withdrew north of the 49th parallel.

The Protestants for the most part failed as missionaries but, as agents of Manifest Destiny, wrought great changes. Having less singleness of purpose than the British fur traders or the European priests, the American missionaries recognized that the future of the Northwest lay with the settler. With regret they abandoned their Indian charges and prepared the way for the first wagons, broke ground for the first communities, and helped organize the first American government in the vast disputed land known as Oregon.

A lurid lithograph of the day depicts the Whitman Massacre, which ended the missionary era. Despite the artist's sense of drama, Narcissa was not in the room at the time.

PART FOUR

CLAIMING THE LAND

Rich in promise and free for the taking, the Oregon country drew immigrant homeseekers by the thousands, who came to shape the land in their own image. As harbingers of civilization, women, children, and farmers drove the taproot of family life deep into the soil and staked for America an irrevocable claim to the Northwest. They were followed by miners, fishermen, loggers, and rail barons who helped to build a broad-based and freestanding economy. Theirs was a migration of dreams, made real in a toil of optimism.

Emigrants on the Oregon Trail.

161

CHAPTER 15

THE OREGON QUESTION

A flood of immigrants, the beginnings of local government,
and settlement of an important and long-disputed boundary

THE EPIDEMIC OF OREGON FEVER that set thousands of Americans on the trail of Lewis and Clark may be traced to a paranoid Bostonian visionary named Hall Jackson Kelley, who by 1823 had a virulent case of the fever himself and was communicating it with glowing circulars designed to enlist a huge party of emigrants. For nearly ten years he assaulted eastern ears —including those of Congress—with his entreaties.

Whether it was his shrillness, or his self-righteousness, or his superb talent for alienating all with whom he came in contact—Kelley's grandiose scheme fizzled. He finally did start for Oregon, but his followers robbed him and deserted him at New Orleans; Mexican authorities taxed away most of his remaining funds at Vera Cruz; and when he at last caught a boat north from San Blas, he could pay for passage only to San Diego. His faith undimmed, he preached the glory of Oregon to other American wanderers, among them Ewing Young, a mountain man who only the year before had been in the land of Kelley's dreams.

While the prophet of Oregon was proselytizing in California, one of his earlier converts was testing the business climate on the Columbia. Nathaniel Wyeth had an eye for the unlikely: he had made money shipping New England ice to Africa in overaged whaling vessels. Now, having made his way to Fort Vancouver and charmed Dr. John McLoughlin, the chief factor, he variously tried to go into the business of supplying independent trappers, running a fort in competition with the Hudson's Bay Company, and pickling salmon. All failed. Eventually he settled down to farming, but

not until he had made his most lasting contribution to Northwest history: providing transport and protection for the first party of missionaries, Jason Lee and his Methodists.

Just as Hall Kelley had incited Wyeth to go west from Boston, he finally convinced Ewing Young that his future lay not in sunbaked San Diego but in the rainy valley of the Willamette. After first refusing to accompany Kelley, Young changed his mind, joined him at Monterey, and, to the great relief of most Americans there (who considered Kelley "King of Beggars" and "the Great Bore"), consented to lead him and a hundred horses north to the promised land. En route they met some horse thieves, and by the time they reached Fort Vancouver, word had preceded them that *they* were the thieves. John McLoughlin gave them an understandably chill reception, so antagonizing Young that when Kelley left for good in the spring, the trapper stayed on to challenge the power of the HBC.

"The settlers are so entirely dependent on us," an HBC official had said, "that every man must go down to Vancouver to sharpen his share, his coulter, and his mattock." Ewing Young contested this economic stranglehold—and the Methodists' cooperation with it—by taking up farming and launching a miniature whiskey rebellion. Buying a big kettle left over from Wyeth's salmon pickling venture, Young started to build a still to convert the settlers' surplus wheat into alcohol. The enterprise alarmed not only the Methodist Mission's temperance society but also the less abstemious pioneers who worried about Indians with hangovers. The situa-

The epochal meeting at Champoeg, where the Willamette settlers met to discuss a bounty on wolves
and ended up creating an independent government for the Oregon country.

tion was resolved by William Slacum, a secret agent sent by President Jackson to report on the Oregon Country. Slacum loaned Young money, persuaded Mc-Loughlin to allow him to buy at the post commissary, and eventually led the mountain man into an enterprise of great importance to the American community: a cattle drive from California.

Young started from Monterey with about 1,000 head of barely domesticated, wide-horned, slim-flanked Spanish heifers and *toritos,* and reached the Willamette with 630. These were the first cattle Americans owned in Oregon. An old-timer recalled, "They were better than no cattle at all."

Bᵧ 1838 these first stirrings of independence had crystallized into a petition, which Jason Lee carried east, asking Congress to "take formal and speedy possession" of the land in order to change their ad hoc, lawless settlement into a community that would attract the right type of settler. "We flatter ourselves that we are the germe of a great state," the settlers wrote; but Oregon, held jointly by the United States and Britain, was a decade away even from territorial status.

In 1841, Ewing Young died the wealthiest American on the Willamette as a result of his cattle venture. He left no will and no apparent heir, and the desirability of his estate emphasized the need in Oregon for law and a court system. At a meeting called by Lee, a probate judge and several constables were elected, and the Catholic priest Blanchet was chosen to chair a committee to organize a full-fledged government. His support was essential because he had great influence with his French-Canadian parishioners, the retired HBC employees who constituted fully half of the settlers on the Willamette. Blanchet, however, failed to call a meeting. Like others, Blanchet felt that government by gentlemen's agreement—by McLoughlin and Lee, that is—was sufficient for 125 families. Lieutenant Charles Wilkes, in charge of the United States Exploring Expedition, then visiting the area, counseled the Americans against forming a provisional government lest they be outvoted by the British.

Back east, however, Oregon fever was raging, largely because of a bill pending in Congress which offered 640 acres of free land in Oregon to each settler. In

Nathaniel Wyeth found business unrewarding in the Northwest but remained to prosper as a farmer.

Missouri, Illinois, and Ohio, especially, there were enthusiastic town meetings to discuss migrating en masse to Oregon. Settlers already on the Willamette braced themselves for the expected hordes.

At a settlers' meeting in Champoeg (pronounced Cham-*POH*-eg or Cham-*POO*-eg), called in March of 1843 to discuss the financing of a wolf bounty, Presbyterian missionary William Gray brought up dangers "worse than wild beasts." Gray was referring to the Indians, the British, and the settlers that were massing in Missouri. How would the established settlers defend their land claims and their public positions against the newcomers, who might outnumber them?

On May 2, 1843, a study committee recommended a government and (even more controversial) a militia. Some thought a militia would be an invitation to trouble, given the vastly superior numbers of the British and the Indians, but the meeting proceeded to a confused voice vote on the combined issues. The nays seemed to have it, when (according to legend) trapper

Joe Meek boomed out, "Who's for a divide? All for the report of the committee and organization follow me." A counting of heads showed the ayes in a slight majority.

The day after the Fourth of July, a government took shape modeled on the Iowa Code, the current standard for territories. Land titles were confirmed to the extent of six square miles for the Methodist mission and 640 acres for each individual. An apparatus of government including rifle companies was set up, although taxes to pay its expenses were left voluntary. Provisional Oregon was bravely divided into counties theoretically extending through British claims to the Russian holdings above 54°40'.

In the fall the arrival of nine hundred settlers roughly tripled the population. Naturally the majority redrew the laws to their own liking. They pared Methodist holdings to one square mile and initiated property and sales taxes that discriminated against the established wealth of the community, namely the HBC and the first settlers.

The fall of 1844 brought twelve hundred more settlers, who replaced the executive committee with a

Mountain man Joe Meek carried Oregon's appeal for a territorial government to Washington, D.C.

Oregon City, 1845: Seat of the provisional government, boasting five hundred inhabitants and four water-powered mills, it was the only settlement worthy of the name "city."

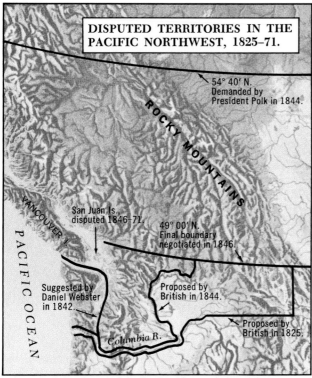

DISPUTED TERRITORIES IN THE PACIFIC NORTHWEST, 1825–71.

54° 40' N.
Demanded by
President Polk in 1844.

ROCKY MOUNTAINS

VANCOUVER I.

PACIFIC OCEAN

San Juan Is.,
disputed 1846–71.

49° 00' N.
Final boundary
negotiated in 1846.

Suggested by
Daniel Webster
in 1842.

Proposed by
British in 1844.

Columbia R.

Proposed by
British in 1825.

© Jeppesen & Co., Denver, Colo. Reprinted by permission of the
H. M. Gousha Co., proprietors, San Jose, Calif.

governor and convened the first legislature in Oregon City. By the summer of 1845 the British, thanks to Jesse Applegate and other moderates, were participating in the government for the purpose of maintaining peace and protecting their claims until the boundary could be settled.

Settled it was, the following year, and in 1848, Joe Meek in full trapper's regalia arrived in Washington to lobby for an Oregon Territory. The sensational news of the Whitman Massacre persuaded Congress to act. President Polk signed the bill on August 14, 1848, only two years after he had concluded the treaty with Britain that defined Oregon's status. In March, Governor Joseph Lane and United States Marshal Joe Meek reached Oregon, and the provisional government ceased to be necessary.

WHILE AMERICAN PIONEERS were forming a government on the Willamette, American negotiators were attempting to win the Northwest from the British. Since 1818, all the land from Spanish California to Rus-

sian Alaska had been under joint occupation by Britain and the United States—how would they divide it?

Oddly enough, American settlers had little influence on the final decision. They felt the land south of the Columbia was certain to go American in any division. From the first, diplomatic negotiations centered on the area south of the 49th parallel and west of the Columbia River—what is now western Washington. In this area, as late as 1845, there were only a score of Americans scratching at farms in contrast to the establishments of the Hudson's Bay Company.

The Oregon Question—would Britain or the United States control the Northwest?—was ultimately answered amid the shuffling of papers in the conference room and the niceties of diplomatic protocol. For example, Secretary of State John Quincy Adams regained Astoria, the former Astor establishment on the Columbia, by successfully arguing that its purchase and occupation by the British during the War of 1812 had been an act of war. Under terms of the Treaty of Ghent, property that changed hands as a result of the War of 1812 was to be restored.

A Punch cartoon of 1846 lampoons the Oregon situation.

In 1818 formal negotiations on the Northwest began. The United States suggested that the boundary be extended along the 49th parallel, beyond the Rockies, to the Pacific. It was a reasonable offer, for it split the Northwest approximately in half and gave each power valuable harbors. The British objected that two great rivers, the Columbia and a fictitious stream they called the Caledonia, would be cut by such a boundary. The negotiators deadlocked and agreed on joint occupation of the Northwest for ten years. The British were left free to exploit beaver, and the Americans to dream of an independent Pacific republic.

During the initial negotiation, the American delegation had little information about the lay of the Northwest land. One background report by a former Astorian assured them that the Puget Sound area was worthless, deficient even in timber—of all things; the American delegate Albert Gallatin at one point indicated a willingness to give the British all land not drained by the Columbia. But the British, too, coveted the river, the North West Company fur traders insisting that it offered the only freight route to the interior. The English turned down a settlement which would have left them in control of the saltwater ports.

In 1824 the Monroe Doctrine made it clear that the United States would not tolerate further European colonization in the Americas. President Monroe intended his manifesto merely to encourage independent republics on the farther reaches of the continent, not to clear the way for annexation, which he feared would tempt the United States into colonial vices. Two of his cabinet members, however, John Quincy Adams and John C. Calhoun, were enthusiastic about acquiring distant lands. Adams envisioned the glory of a United States expanding to cover all of North America, and Calhoun saw hope of more lands for slave owners.

When the time came for renewing the joint-occupation convention, Adams, now president, was not in a conciliatory humor. He prided himself on his success in limiting the claims of the Spanish and the Russians (see map), especially the latter, who in 1806 had talked of a colony at the mouth of the Columbia and in 1821 had tried to exclude non-Russians from the territory north of 51°. Adams was hoping for further diplomatic triumphs with the British and barely permitted Gallatin to offer 49° again.

A British bastion during the "Pig War," this blockhouse on San Juan Island now flies American colors.

The newly aggressive Americans met their match in George Canning, the British foreign secretary. To fuel his determination not to yield further to Britain's former colony, he sifted through HBC governor George Simpson's assessments of the area in dispute. With facts in hand, Canning maintained the British demand for a boundary at the Columbia and added only an offer of the Olympic Peninsula north of Grays Harbor and Hood Canal as an enclave for American vessels. The two sides were farther apart than ever. Joint occupation was continued indefinitely with the proviso that either country could cancel after a year's notice.

During these London negotiations in the 1820s, the Puget Sound ports were not overly prized; but by the Washington negotiations of the 1840s, railroads had captured the country's imagination and offered the sheltered deep-water ports of the sound a potential means of communicating with the interior. At the same time, Lieutenant Wilke's reports reviling the Columbia bar where he lost the *Peacock*, and lauding the harbors of the sound were reaching Washington. American resistance to the persistent British offers of arbitration stiffened; New England shipping interests in particular felt that these ports must not be lost in a compromise settlement between 49° and the Columbia.

Daniel Webster and Lord Ashburton met in 1842 and resolved a host of outstanding difficulties between their countries. But by the time they reached the Oregon Question, which perhaps seemed the least important of the issues at the time, Webster and Ashburton, both ailing old men, were wilting in the summer heat of Washington. Worse, Ashburton's instructions on Oregon were anachronistic, having been written by a disciple of Canning; they led Ashburton, who was quite willing to compromise, to revive an offer even Canning never had the gall to make.

By the time British diplomats came to their senses and offered a variety of concessions, including free ports north of the Columbia, Calhoun had replaced Webster as secretary of state. In his devotion to Southern expansion, Calhoun urged annexation of Texas but "masterly inactivity"* with regard to Oregon. James K. Polk sympathized with Calhoun, but he had been elected to the presidency in 1844 on a pledge to acquire Texas and "all Oregon." To keep the Northern expansionists happy, he echoed their cries of "Fifty-four Forty or Fight!" and made belligerent gestures toward Britain, though, in truth, both Polk and the British negotiators wanted peace and a boundary at 49°. The final stage of negotiation focused on Congress's wording of the notice to terminate joint occupation. It could be an invitation to war or to peace. At last the Senate sent a conciliatory message, and a treaty agreeing to 49° was forthcoming.

B UT THE WILD NORTHWEST resisted the mathematical simplicity of the 49th parallel—as the surveyors learned when they tried to follow the line through lakes and down cliffsides. The treaty makers learned a similar lesson: the treaty they had tried to obtain since the War of 1812 did not magically resolve all the conflicting interests of Britain and the United States in the Northwest.

For one thing, the treaty of June 15, 1846, did not erase the British presence south of 49°; it allowed the HBC to continue to use the Columbia and provided compensation for HBC forts and supplies left behind. For over fifteen years, the United States avoided paying

Joseph Lane, first governor of Oregon Territory.

the HBC until the specter of British aid to the Confederacy made the settling of old debts seem wise.

From where the 49th parallel reached saltwater, the boundary was to follow the main channel through the San Juan Islands to the Strait of Juan de Fuca and to the Pacific. But for twenty-five years the British and Americans could not agree whether Haro Strait or Rosario Strait was the main channel, and the San Juan Islands remained in dispute. When an American settler killed a British pig on one of the islands, the United States and Britain came ridiculously close to war. The arbitration of the German Emperor William I in 1871 finally brought an end to the crisis and ushered in an era in which the 49th parallel would become known as one of the most tranquil borders in the world.

Oregon had once been a nebulous region, a blur in the corner of a poorly drawn map; now it was being defined with such precision that nations could quarrel over the zig and the zag of its boundaries. The Oregon of the settler had once been one man's obsession; now it was the reality of hundreds of hardworking families. Oregon had once been held together by the understanding of two gentlemen; now it was sanctioned by international law. One claimant to Oregon, however, had been ignored. He was the original owner of the land, the red man.

---

*It might be mentioned that Calhoun's policy of "masterly inactivity" was not quite as passive as it sounds. He contended that since Americans were sending families to Oregon while the HBC sent mostly single men, the United States would win the struggle in our bedrooms, outbreeding the British and filling the land up to Russian America.

For Indians of the upper Columbia, the year's food supply depended on the fall run of salmon, which they trapped in weirs or speared. This fishing scene at Kettle Falls was painted by Paul Kane.

Among the Chinooks and related tribes, the bodies of the dead were "buried" in elevated canoes; paddles, utensils, and other belongings were included for use in the afterlife.

Artist John Mix Stanley, like his contemporary Paul Kane, painted a highly romanticized view of Indian life in the Northwest; this is a village on the Columbia, looking toward Mount Hood.

A sloping forehead was a mark of aristocracy among Indians of the lower Columbia Basin. The infant's head was shaped by strapping it firmly to a carrying board, as in this painting of a Cowlitz mother and child.

A vivid blend of art, culture, and religion, the totem poles carved by coastal Indians north of the Strait of Juan de Fuca commemorated the owner's ancestry or important remembered events.

The finest weavers in the Northwest, the Salish developed the whole loom and yarns of such varied materials as down, cedar bark, and dog hair.

A reconstruction of a typical communal house of Vancouver Island Indians: the rectangular design above the doorway represents a "copper," their major symbol of wealth.

Captain Robert Gray's "Columbia Rediviva" rides at anchor near the mouth of the Columbia River, May 15-18, 1792.

The treacherous bar of the Columbia discouraged some and scuttled others; here the Astorian ship "Tonquin" hazards a crossing in 1811.
(Paintings by Northwest artist Hewitt Jackson.)

Perched above the churning seas, North Head Lighthouse marks the point where the Columbia River meets the sea.

Artist Charles Russell commemorates Lewis and Clark's meeting with the Salish-Flatheads at Ross's Hole near the head of the Bitterroot River in 1805.

*"Fort George, formerly Astoria"—a fur trade center
on the lower Columbia, painted by H. J. Warre.*

*Fort Vancouver, headquarters for the HBC located at the confluence
of the Columbia and Willamette, was painted about 1845 by an unknown artist.*

The Catholic mission of St. Paul's in Oregon's Willamette Valley was rendered in watercolor by frontier artist Paul Kane in 1847.

The frontiersmen who opened the interior of the Northwest are celebrated, albeit unflatteringly, in Alfred Jacob Miller's "The Lost Trapper."

The long, often grueling overland migration that secured Oregon to the American nation seldom proved as idyllic as Benjamin Reinhart envisioned it in "Emigrant Train Bedding Down for the Night."

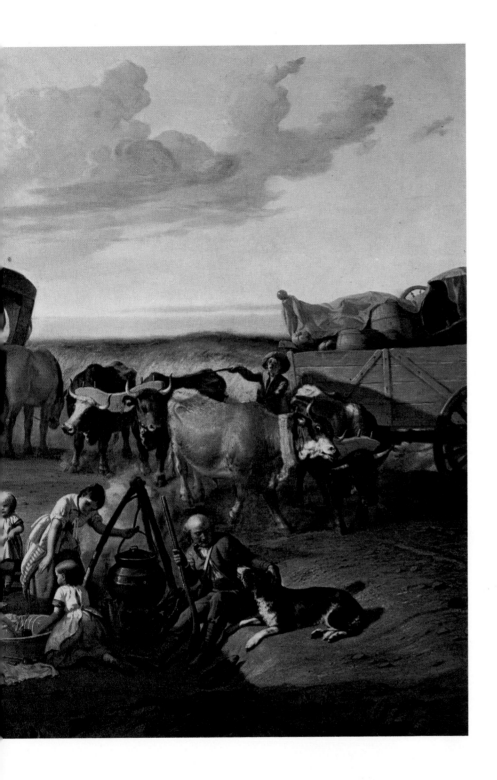

Carving their own memorial, wagon ruts are still visible on parts of the Oregon Trail.

*"Discovery of Gold at Last Chance Gulch," by Charles Russell, recalls
the placer diggings that grew into the enduring city of Helena, Montana.*

Rusting ore cars and decaying mills provide mute
testament to vanished hopes of Zincton, British Columbia
(above), and Cornucopia, Oregon (left).

*Its members left when the ores ran out, and now the Fraternity
Hall of Elkhorn stands drying in the Montana wind and sun.*

TREATIES AND MISUNDERSTANDINGS

The unbreachable gulf between Americans who held the land as masters and Indians who loved it as sons

AMERICANS CAME WEST TO RULE. Their faith in Manifest Destiny boiled down to belief in Progress and the white Protestant. Conscious of virtue, they expected reward. It would come from possession of new land that a scout reported "lies like a beautiful young heiress, waiting to be appropriated and enjoyed."

There was an impediment to progress, however, a threat to enjoyment. The red man lived with the land and loved it as son, not master. Shown a plow and told its use, a shocked Yakima asked, "Does a man tear the breast of his mother?" A Duwamish, sadly placing his mark on the treaty that turned over tribal lands to the whites, told the new proprietors, "The very dust under your feet responds more lovingly to our footsteps than to yours. It is the ashes of our ancestors."

But the advance agents of civilization were untouched and impatient. They could hear the approach of juggernaut progress in the creak of the covered wagon, in the only slightly more distant wail of locomotives and in the scream of steam-driven saws. The Indian was in the way; he must turn white or disappear.

The missionaries made a short-order effort at transformation, seeking to lift the Indian from darkness, save his soul, and convert him from a pagan who roamed the prairies and oceans seeking food to share with his fellows into a Christian farmer who cultivated a plot of his own for the primary benefit of his family. To the Indians this did not promise a better life; many considered farming an abomination, a rape of the Earth Mother who, unforced, provided all the Indian needed.

The mission at Waiilatpu in the Cayuse country became the cleavage point, where the westward movement of white concepts collided with an established way of life. Held in check briefly, it soon overrode the old order, leaving as a fault line on the consciousness of both races the Whitman Massacre. (See page 159.)

The murders of Marcus and Narcissa Whitman and a dozen other whites and mixed-bloods at the Place of the Rye Grass shattered the dream of accommodation. After the killings, red-white relations became a test of numbers, power, and technology. The Indian's destiny was, to be displaced.

At the time of the massacre, the United States possessed the Oregon Country south of the 49th parallel but had not extended the authority of American law beyond the Rockies. Oregon was run by a provisional government, an administration whose powers depended on the consent of the citizens. It responded to the crisis by dispatching the colorful mountain man Joe Meek (whose half-Indian daughter had been among the victims at Waiilatpu) to Washington to ask for troops; it also called for five hundred volunteers to go punish the Cayuses and appointed a three-man peace commission to negotiate. The soldiers and diplomats were left to argue the priorities of their missions while they tried to catch up with the Cayuses.

Volunteer Colonel Cornelius Gilliam led the chase. He found it like trying to catch fish barehanded. The Cayuse braves hit, ran, and avoided major engagements; their noncombatants, when encountered, posed as friendly Indians and acted as spies. More bloodthirsty

Chief Joseph of the Nez Perces surrenders for his people following their epic flight north toward Canada. (Painting by O. C. Seltzer.)

Conflict of interests strained Indian-white relations; here, John C. Fremont's 1846 fight with the Klamaths.

the whites determined to starve them out. A fort was built at the site of the destroyed mission; from it, soldiers policed the bottomlands and low hills which had supported the Cayuse herds. In the spring of 1848, provisional Governor George Abernathy "in consideration of the barbarous and insufferable conduct of the Cayuse Indians," declared their tribal lands forfeit and "justly subject to be occupied and held by American citizens."

So it went. The Cayuses hid in the lean hills, ever hungrier, ever fewer; the whites settled in the fat valley. After two years the remaining Cayuses agreed to surrender five tribesmen involved in the murders. They were formally tried, found guilty, baptized, and hanged. Said one of the condemned, "Did not your missionaries teach us that Christ died to save his people? So do we to save our people."

But the remnants of the tribe of great horsemen were not saved. The whites were in the valley to stay.

than competent, painfully aware of limited supplies and the short attention span of volunteers, Gilliam wanted to destroy tribes as met, whether or not they had been involved in the massacre.

The peace commissioners struggled to keep the volunteers from driving the neutral Nez Perces and Walla Wallas into the ranks of the hostiles. Gilliam, who blamed his failures on delays caused by the commissioners, removed himself from the controversy when he pulled a lariat from a supply wagon, accidentally discharging a rifle, which killed him. But his successor could not catch the Cayuses either.

The hostages taken at the time of the massacre were ransomed by Peter Skene Ogden of the Hudson's Bay Company. His success reflected Indian preference for the British, who had been less concerned with making over the Indians than with making money off the furs they brought in. It reflected, too, Ogden's bargaining shrewdness. For fifty blankets, fifty shirts, ten guns, ten fathoms of twisted tobacco, ten handkerchiefs and a hundred rounds of ball and powder he extracted from the Cayuses their one important bargaining counter: forty-six prisoners.

The punitive expedition settled into an occupation of the Walla Walla Valley. Unable to catch the Cayuses,

JOE MEEK'S TRIP to Washington did not bring federal troops west to round up the Cayuses—the army was otherwise occupied with the Mexican War—but his pleas and personality did speed establishment of a territorial government, effective March 3, 1849. With Oregon a territory, Congress in 1850 passed a Donation Land Law allowing a male who had settled west of the Rockies during the period of joint occupation to claim 320 acres, with another 320 for his wife, were he wed by December 1851—a provision that made bachelorhood doubly unrewarding. Settlers who arrived up to 1855 could qualify for 160 acres.

Legally the land that Congress was giving away still belonged to the Indians. So Congress passed a second bill, the Indian Treaty Act, which set up machinery for properly quieting the Indian title.

The task of persuading the tribes to give up their land and move onto reservations fell first to Superintendent of Indian Affairs Anson Dart, a political appointee of considerable character. He was assigned to bunch up the western tribes and send them to share a reservation east of the mountains in country the whites could see no use for, far enough away so they would be no threat to the new landlords of their old homelands. But Dart recognized the Indians' need to be on land where they were spiritually and technologically at home, not grouped with enemies on a hostile terrain. The treaties he drew assigned the tribes a portion of the land that had produced their culture. The settlers, fearful of the Indian presence, protested; the Senate failed to ratify the treaties. Dart resigned. The Indians were left to puzzle the difference between the Hudson's Bay Company, whose officials had power to sign binding agreements on the spot, and the United States government, whose agents could not commit the Great White Father by their promises.

The discovery of gold in California touched off a rush through tribal lands in southwestern Oregon toward the valley of the Sacramento. There were incidents and provocations aplenty, with Rogues, Klamaths and Modocs defending their lands and women against trespass, and whites shooting Indians as casually as crows.

In 1853 several southwestern tribes rose in frustration and attacked scattered white settlements. Territorial Governor Joe Lane, a hero of the Mexican War, led a volunteer force against them and was shot through the shoulder. Later the governor and Joel Palmer, Dart's replacement as Indian agent, in an act of bravery and generosity, went unarmed to the Indian stronghold atop Table Rock Mountain and negotiated a treaty which left the Indians with part of their homelands in the west as a temporary reservation. This treaty was ratified the following year and went into effect in 1855. It preserved a fragile peace for two years.

WHILE THE GOVERNOR OF OREGON was negotiating at Table Rock, the newly appointed governor of Washington Territory, which had just been carved out of the northern portion of the Oregon Country, was heading west. Isaac Ingalls Stevens came not only as governor but as head of a railroad survey authorized by the War Department, and as superintendent of Indian Affairs for the Interior Department. Later, at his own request, the State Department named Stevens treaty commissioner and assigned him to get the Washington tribes on reservations.

Stevens' multiple assignments were a mark of the man; able, ambitious, individualistic, supremely self-confident, he was unwilling to delegate authority even when his time and energy were stretched taut. The cen-

tralization of authority in the vast territory stretching from the continental divide to the Pacific avoided a conflict of administrative personalities but created, as far as his Indian assignment was concerned, a conflict of interest.

As superintendent of Indian Affairs, Stevens represented the red man; as governor, the white settler; as treaty commissioner the State Department; and as railroad surveyor, the War Department—and he was not unmindful of the growth a transcontinental line would bring the area he governed. Thus, Stevens had multiple reasons for wanting the Indians to sign away their lands. He had to quiet their title so that white settlers could claim farms. He hoped to group the Indians away from possible areas of settlement to reduce friction. He also wanted to remove them from the probable route of a rail line across eastern Washington, lest they interfere with the trains, legally or physically. He needed to do this swiftly so progress could get amoving.

Stevens did feel some responsibility for the Indians.

Governor, surveyor, and Indian superintendent, Isaac Stevens created more problems than he solved.

Gustave Sohon captured the pageantry as 2,500 Nez Perces arrived in full regalia for the 1855 Walla Walla Council, there to be relieved of ancestral lands by Stevens' chicanery.

He admired most Nez Perces and certain individuals of other tribes; a fighting man himself, he respected their bravery and their skills as horsemen. Yet, he never doubted that theirs was a less worthy civilization which must yield to that of the white man. He did what he thought best for all concerned, but he was an instrument of white power and white policy. When he had to choose between white and Indian needs, the Indians inevitably lost.

Treaty making in Washington Territory began during the Christmas holidays of 1854. Stevens, as treaty commissioner, summoned the tribes and bands of southern Puget Sound to a council under an old fir on a low hill beside Medicine Creek, between today's Tacoma and Olympia. In three days of discussion—which Stevens had translated not into the Indian languages but into the imprecise Chinook trade jargon—he convinced the tribes that they should give up the land comprising the present Thurston and Pierce counties, plus parts of Mason and King counties. In return the Indians were promised two reservations of 1,280 acres (two square miles) each, payments of $32,000 in trade goods over a twenty-year period, and a free school, a blacksmith shop, and a carpenter shop.

Colonel Benjamin Franklin Shaw, who served as translator at Medicine Creek and some later negotiations, considered the treaties "humbugs," and explained that "the Indians did not understand them, although we endeavored to do it." James Wickersham, later one of Alaska's great federal judges, studied the Medicine Creek treaty in a paper for the Washington State Historical Society. He branded it "a contract obtained through over-persuasion and deceit; through promises not in the record; by imposition upon minds unaccustomed to written contracts; a contract obtained from the weak by the strong; from the ward by the guardian; from the child by the parent, and wholly without consideration—unfair, unjust, ungenerous and illegal."

But the Indians signed it—that was the important fact to Stevens. He swept on to other tribes, explaining, promising, cajoling, until most of the saltwater tribes accepted reservations. Some Indians like Seattle, lamented in classic phrases:

"It matters little where we pass the remnant of our days. They will not be many. A few more moons; a few more winters—and not one of the descendants of the mighty hosts that once moved over this broad land or lived in happy homes, protected by the Great Spirit, will remain to mourn over the graves of a people once more powerful and hopeful than yours. . . ."

Sometimes the Indians balked. "When you first began to speak, we did not understand you," Narkarty of the Chinooks told Stevens at a conference on the Chehalis. "Now our hearts are enlightened and what you say is clear as the sun. . . . We are willing to sell our land, but we do not want to go away from our homes. Our fathers, and mothers, and ancestors are buried here, and by them we wish to bury our dead and be buried ourselves. We wish, therefore, each to have a place on our own land where we can live and you may have the rest; but we can't go to the north among the other tribes. We are not friends, and if we went together we should fight, and soon we would all be killed." Eventually, they signed. And the Chinooks are no more.

Stevens faced more formidable problems east of the Cascades. The horse Indians of the intermontane country were more numerous, more mobile, less vulnerable; their villages and hunting grounds could not be brought under the guns of warships. They knew how Stevens had dealt with the saltwater tribes; knew too, from eastern Indians who were members of the Hudson's Bay Company brigades, about the treaties in the Atlantic states and the later removal of the betrayed tribes to distant lands beyond the Mississippi. They looked on the declared forfeiture of Cayuse lands as a broken promise. They resented that the innocent had been punished with the guilty for the Whitman massacre; resented the swelling flow of settlers along the Oregon Trail. They feared the white man's ways, his diseases, his magic. They knew Stevens would come to them with small presents and great demands.

The leaders of the interior tribes conferred on strategy and tactics. Some, like Peopeo Moxmox of the Walla Wallas and Kamiakin of the Yakimas were inclined to fight; others, especially the Christian converts, Lawyer of the Nez Perces and Spokan Garry of the Spokanes, favored negotiation. As a stop-gap they settled on the idea of demanding as reservations all the land they customarily roamed. But the tribes remained divided by old hostilities and conflicting interests. In their meetings with the Americans they suffered the handicaps of any alliance dealing with a single power.

Stevens summoned the tribes of the southwest interior to a parlay late in May of 1855. He agreed to the suggestion by Kamiakin of the Yakimas that the gathering be in the Walla Walla Valley. The site selected was at Mill Creek, six miles upstream from Waiilatpu.

Stevens and Joel Palmer, the Oregon Indian superintendent (tribal boundaries did not coincide with state and territorial lines), arrived on May 21, accompanied by forty-seven dragoons. A brave man, Stevens looked on the soldiers not as bodyguard but as a police force. He noted in his diary that if any Indians stirred up resistance to the proposals, "the malcontents must be seized; the well-affected would then govern in the deliberations."

Arrests proved unnecessary. The differences between tribes and stresses within tribes assured Stevens a diplomatic triumph, however ephemeral. The tribal rivalries showed even in the manner in which Stevens' summons were answered. Kamiakin refused the presents Stevens forwarded to him, explaining that he never took from the Americans "the value of a grain of wheat" without paying. The Walla Wallas sent word they were bringing their own food supplies and did not need those promised by Stevens. The Nez Perces swept onto the treaty

Looking Glass, Nez Perce war leader who scoffed at Stevens' entreaties to sell his homeland.

C. C. Nahl's painting commemorates the 1866 duping of the Shoshonis by Idaho Territorial Governor Caleb Lyon, a land cession deal so shady the government later renegotiated the terms.

grounds with a grand display of horse power. "A thousand warriors," wrote Stevens' son Hazard, "mounted on fine horses and riding at a gallop, two abreast, naked to the breech-clout, their faces covered with white, red, and yellow paint in fanciful designs, and decked with plumes and feathers and trinkets fluttering in the sunshine." But not all the Nez Perces were on hand. The aged, intransigent Looking Glass gave Stevens the snub direct: he took many of his best men on a buffalo hunt in Blackfoot country. Some of the smaller tribes materialized quietly, sullenly. By May 29 some five thousand Nez Perces, Yakimas, Cayuses, Walla Wallas, Umatillas and smaller bands were camped at the treaty grounds.

The council opened under threatening skies and was soon interrupted by a thunderstorm. The rain-washed air remained electric with tension and mistrust. Lawyer, the christianized Nez Perce, resplendent in a gray top hat, struggled to bridge the gap, but with each speech by Stevens or Palmer, Indian resistance hardened.

Stevens spoke of the Great White Father's desire to find places where the Indians would not be preyed upon by bad white men. Palmer warned that beyond the Rockies the whites were "numerous as grasshoppers on the plains" and would soon sweep over the land. "If we enter into a treaty now, we can select a good country for you; but if we wait till the country is filled up with whites, where will we find such a place?"

Time after time the Indians urged the Americans to "speak straight" and complained they did not "see in a true light the object of your speeches." Again and again they demanded time to think and to consult among themselves. The council fires burned through the night. Rumors spread of a plot to kill the treaty commissioners. But Stevens kept pressing for acceptance.

At the end of a week's talk, Peopeo Moxmox brought matters to a head. "You have spoken for our lands generally," he told Stevens. "You have not spoken of any particular ones."

Guardedly Stevens replied that he was thinking in terms of two reservations. He described them: one between the Yakima and Columbia rivers in which would be assembled all the tribes along the Columbia from The Dalles to the Okanogan and Colville valleys; the second in Nez Perce country from the Blue Mountains of Oregon to the Bitterroots of Idaho, from the Palouse to the Grand Ronde and Salmon.

Perhaps the Indians did not realize that under the proposal the whites would get the most obviously valuable agricultural land and would control the Spokane, Palouse and Yakima areas through which Stevens' proposed railroad would be routed. If they did, such considerations were lost amid the complaints from the tribes that would be bunched together.

But Stevens had picked the reservation areas shrewdly, leaving the most powerful tribes—the Nez Perces and the Yakimas—on their own lands. He sweetened the proposal with offers of grist mills, sawmills, schools; with promises of houses for the chiefs and annuities. He agreed to some shifts in the proposed boundaries. He pledged that the Indians would remain on their present lands undisturbed until "our chief the President and his council sees this paper and says it is good, and we build the houses, the mills, and the blacksmith shop."

Resistance began to crumble. Peopeo Moxmox said he would move to the reservation when his house was built, and Kamiakin was at the point of accepting for the Yakimas when, in the phrase of Lieutenant Lawrence Kip of the dragoons, "a new explosive element dropped into this little political caldron." An Indian runner arrived with word that the redoubtable Looking Glass, seventy-year-old war chief of the Nez Perces, was approaching.

Looking Glass arrived accompanied by three elderly chiefs and twenty young warriors fresh from the buffalo hunt. They wore buffalo robes and war paint. A Blackfoot scalp dangled from one lance. Coolly brushing aside Stevens' gesture of welcome, Looking Glass addressed the Nez Perces:

"My people, what have you done? While I was gone, you have sold my country. I have come home, and there is not left me a place on which to pitch my lodge. Go home to your lodges. I will talk to you."

He talked in vain. Stevens simply by-passed Looking Glass and dealt with Lawyer, designating him as the spokesman for the Nez Perces. The tactic worked. The long council had drained the Indians' energy. They could not be rallied. On July 11, they signed—Lawyer first as "head chief," followed by the others, even Looking Glass.

"Thus ended in the most satisfactory manner the great council," said Stevens in his summary of the proceeding. Well might he be satisfied. Under the treaties sent east for ratification, the Indians were to yield title to 45,000 square miles. Beyond that, Stevens' plans called for him to swing through the rest of the territory, first bargaining for the ancestral lands of the friendly

Flatheads; then, after a detour to the plains to talk the Blackfeet into behaving better toward the Nez Perces, to pick up the lands of the Kalispels and the Coeur d'Alenes; with a final great parley to be held with the Kettles, Okanogans, and Spokanes. He was in Blackfoot country in October when word reached him that his treaties had led to war.

Before leaving Walla Walla, Stevens had dispatched a triumphant message to the Oregon *Weekly Times* with a request that other papers please copy it. The statement, over Stevens and Palmer's signatures, told the land-hungry whites that "by an express provision of the treaty, the country embraced in these cessions and not included in the reservation is open to settlement."

The haste of the whites to get to the interior was made greater by reports of gold on the Colville. As men looking for land and gold came into their territory, the Indians felt betrayed. Americans were violating the treaty before the Great White Father had even read it. When prospectors raped some Indian women, the Yakimas killed them. When A. J. Bolon, just appointed agent for the Yakimas, went to investigate, they killed him and his horse.

Charles Mason, a twenty-three-year-old lawyer with soft beard and granny glasses, was acting governor while Stevens made treaties. He begged the army to protect travelers in the Yakima country. Major Granville Haller left The Dalles with eighty-four men and a howitzer, while Lieutenant William Slaughter started east from Puget Sound with fifty men.

To the Yakimas this was an invasion. They ambushed Haller, killed five soldiers, wounded seventeen, captured the supplies and pack animals, and forced the survivors to spike the howitzer, then flee for their lives. Lieutenant Slaughter retreated back across the Cascades without casualties. The stories of the Yakimas chasing soldiers from their land spurred on other tribes.

The express rider who brought Stevens news of the disasters that trailed in his wake advised the governor that the best way to get back to the territorial capital at Olympia would be by way of New York and Panama. Stevens rejected the grand tour and went directly west through hostile country. After struggling through a snow-clogged pass, he faced down several tribes by sheer boldness. Even Spokan Garry, long-time friend of the whites, proved hostile. "When you look at red men, you think you have more heart, more sense than those poor Indians. I think the difference between us and you Americans is in the Clothing; the blood and body are the same. Do you think because your mother was white and theirs black that you are higher or better?" Nonetheless Stevens was able to keep the Spokanes from joining the Yakimas in the war.

Back in Olympia he addressed the legislature, defending his treaties, blaming the war on a few malcontents. ". . . Nothing but death is a mete punishment for their perfidy—their lives only should pay the forfeit. . . . The tribes now at war must submit unconditionally to the justice, mercy, and leniency of our government. The guilty ones should suffer, and the remainder be placed upon reservations, under the eye of the military."

Major Gabriel Rains at Fort Vancouver shared Stevens' feelings. Setting out after Kamiakin he promised, "We will . . . war forever, until not a Yakima breathes in the land he calls his own. The river only will we let retain this name, to show to all people that here the Yakimas once lived."

This was not all talk. Volunteers under Lieutenant James K. Kelley took Peopeo Moxmox of the Walla Wallas prisoner while he was negotiating under a flag of truce. When a skirmish started they killed him, scalped him, and took his fingers and ears as mementoes.

Such talk and action sat poorly with the commander of the Department of the Pacific, the gallant, seventy-one-year-old John Ellis Wool. A veteran of both the War of 1812 and the Mexican War, and one of the officers who had shepherded the Cherokee nation along the Trail of Tears, Wool admired Indians. He suspected settlers of stirring up trouble simply to get on the government payroll as Indian fighters. The army's duty, said Wool, was not just to protect settlers from Indians, but also Indians from settlers. And he ordered the interior closed to white settlement.

The feud that developed between General Wool and Governor Stevens for a time overshadowed action in the field. Stevens urged a winter campaign to smash the tribes before seed time. Wool preferred a waiting game. He saw no need to chase Indians to make the land safe for whites who had no business on the Indians' land. Stevens complained to the War Department that the commander of the Department of the Pacific was impeding the war effort; Wool warned the

War Department that times were tough and the settlers looked on Indians as a cash crop. Stevens, trying to carry on his campaign with volunteers, simply drove more Indians into taking up arms.

There were other sideshows. Stevens ordered some former Hudson's Bay Company men at Nisqually, who had married Indians and felt safe on their farms, to join the other settlers holed up in blockhouses. The farmers refused to leave their land. Stevens had them arrested, but attorneys got writs of habeas corpus demanding their release. Stevens declared martial law and suspended the courts. When a federal judge tried to hold court in Steilacoom, Stevens had him arrested. When the judge was released, he promptly declared Stevens in contempt and fined him. Stevens, as territorial governor, suspended the fine on Stevens, the defendant. President Pierce finally decided martial law was not warranted. Friends paid Stevens' fine.

The war slowly faded away. There was little fighting in the west after the Indians were repulsed in an unsuccessful attack on Seattle. Leschi of the Nisquallies stopped fighting and was turned over to Stevens by a traitor. The governor had the war chief tried as a civilian for murder. Leschi was vigorously defended by regular army officers who had fought against him, but a civilian jury found him guilty. On the day Leschi was to be executed, army officers arranged to have the sheriff arrested for bootlegging, thus blocking the hanging. The trick worked, but a new date was set, and this time Leschi went to the scaffold. He was so calm the hangman was moved to say, "I thought I was hanging an innocent man."

Not until 1858 did the fighting stop east of the mountains. In the last flare-up the Spokanes routed a small force under Colonel E. J. Steptoe. Regular army troops under Colonel George H. Wright then chased the Yakima and Spokane warriors into the hills, slaughtered the grazing horses, kept the women from the camas fields and berry patches, and starved the tribes into submission. When the warriors surrendered, Wright hanged their leader without trial.

The struggle was over. The tribes had been broken and humbled. General Wool was transferred east, and his successor, the half-mad W. S. Harney, reversed his policies and declared the interior open to settlement.

All that remained was the rewriting and reinterpre-

Modoc Indians resisting the removal policy were finally subdued after a long siege in the lava beds of Northern California.

tation of treaties to suit the whites as gold was found on Indian reservations, or new techniques made farming possible on land considered worthless, or use was found for timberlands, or the development of canning made the salmon runs commercially exploitable.

The Nez Perces were rewarded for their neutrality by having their reservation cut in half, then halved again. When Old Joseph of the Wallowa Nez Perces refused to sign a new treaty, the whites had the ever-obliging Lawyer sign for him, planting the seeds of a new tragedy. President Grant wrote an executive order granting Joseph's group exclusive use of the valley, then another executive order rescinding the first. Old Joseph stayed on with his people, and his dying words to his son, Hinmay-too-yah-lat-kekht, whom the whites called Young Joseph, were "Do not ever sell the bones of your ancestors."

In southwest Oregon, the Modocs tried for a time to live with the Klamaths on a reservation chosen by the whites. In 1868 they balked and went to their former homes. There they found too many whites, too much liquor, too much outrage. In 1873 Captain Jack led his remaining people across the California border to the lava beds near Lassen Peak. In that natural fortress of interlocking caves and passageways, sixty warriors held

off a thousand soldiers for five months. It was gallant and hopeless and tragic. When at last the survivors surrendered, some were executed, the rest exiled to Oklahoma.

Now it was the turn of the Nez Perces, the Americans' favorite Indians, the tribe which had welcomed Lewis and Clark. Good farm land was becoming scarce. The whites coveted the rich Wallowa where the non-treaty Nez Perces grazed large herds. An Oregon weekly suggested a solution: "If some Christian gentleman will furnish a few blankets from a smallpox hospital well inoculated, we will be distributing agents and see that no Indian is without a blanket. This kind of peace is better than treaties."

But the treaty signed by Lawyer for people he did not represent proved good enough. Under its provisions General Oliver Otis Howard, a man of good intentions and considerable capacity for muddle, ordered the non-treaty Nez Perces to leave their ancestral lands and move onto the Lapwai reservation on the Clearwater with the other Nez Perces. He gave them thirty days.

Reluctantly, bitterly, hopelessly the Indians agreed. "I knew we were too weak to fight the United States," said Young Joseph. "We had many grievances but I knew that war would bring more." The Salmon and the Snake

rivers ran high with the spring melt but the Nez Perces got across with most of their livestock. As the displaced Indians neared their new home, a handful of young braves, led by a youth whose father's murder had not been punished under white man's law, reversed the decision of the tribal elders. They went on a raid and killed four whites. The settlers called for protection. General Howard sent out cavalry to bring in the Nez Perces. The die was cast for war.

The leaders of the Wallowa Nez Perces jointly determined to flee to Canada and join Sitting Bull, who had escaped there after smashing Custer. Though the whites credited Young Joseph with leading the long retreat, the decisions were made by the chiefs in council. Together they improvised one of the most remarkable marches in history.

The first battle was fought in White Bird Canyon on the Salmon with the Indians routing two companies of cavalry and a force of volunteers. The Nez Perces forded the swollen Salmon and moved toward the Clearwater. General Howard with 500 men, two light cannons and a Gatling gun caught up with them. Outnumbered two to one, the Indians fought the professionals to a standstill and fled toward Lolo Pass while the whites regrouped.

General William Sherman said that Lolo Pass was universally admitted to be "one of the worst trails for man and beast on this continent." Joseph crossed it with some 700 Indians, including more than 400 women and children, 1,500 horses, and some cattle. When a detachment, notified by telegraph of the Indians' approach, blocked their path, they outmaneuvered the soldiers and escaped through a canyon where "rocks on each side came so near together that two horses abreast could hardly pass."

The Nez Perces emerged in Montana to the dismay of settlers there—dismay that turned to astonishment when the Indians politely paid in gold for the supplies they demanded.

Canada lay near to the north, but the open country in that direction was dotted with settlements, and Joseph feared there would be military posts. The Nez Perces turned southwest through the Bitterroots. They crossed the continental divide. At Big Hole in Montana a force of regulars and volunteers under General John Gibbon, author of the *Artillerists' Manual* and a veteran

Chief Joseph, Nez Perce hero, statesman, and victim.

of Gettysburg and the wilderness, surprised them in camp. On a field cluttered with Indian women and children—fifty-three of whom were killed—the Nez Perces fought off the first charge, counterattacked, captured a howitzer, and took off for the Yellowstone with part of Gibbon's pack train.

The whites had the advantages of the telegraph, fresh troops, abundant supplies, even Indian scouts recruited from among the Crows and Bannocks. Yet the Nez Perces outdistanced Howard's pursuit. After a flight of two thousand miles in four months they made camp at Eagle Creek in the Bear Paw Mountains. Canada was only forty miles away. But a fresh and unsuspected force under Colonel Nelson Miles was even closer.

On the morning of October 1, with snow drifting from a dull sky and sticking to the slopes, cavalry burst into the camp. Again the Nez Perces rallied. The troops were driven off in hand-to-hand fighting, but they had captured the Nez Perces horses. The tribe was on foot and surrounded, without supplies, without hope. The long flight was over. After six days, Joseph acknowledged the Nez Perces' defeat. General Howard's aide described the surrender and recorded one of the most moving of Indian speeches.

"Joseph's hair hung in two braids on either side of his face. He wore a blanket . . . and moccasin leggings. His rifle was across the pommel in front of him. When he dismounted he walked to General Howard and offered him the rifle. Howard waved him to Miles. He then walked to Miles and handed him the rifle. Then Chief Joseph stepped back and began his formal speech:

" 'Tell General Howard I know his heart. What he told me before I have in my heart. I am tired of fighting. Our chiefs are killed. Looking Glass is dead. The old men are all killed. It is the young men who say yes or no. He who led the young men is dead. It is cold and we have no blankets. The little children are freezing to death. My people, some of them, have run away to the hills and have no blankets, no food; no one knows where they are, perhaps they are freezing to death. I want time to look for my children and see how many of them I can find. Maybe I shall find them among the dead. Hear me, my chiefs, I am tired; my heart is sick and sad. From where the sun now stands, I will fight no more, forever.' "

He was as good as his word. The white men were not. Joseph had understood that the Nez Perces would be returned to the Northwest. Instead they were sent first to Kansas, later to Oklahoma. A third of their remaining number died in the strange, hot land so unlike the Wallowa. Many of those who had fought the Nez Perces became their advocates and called for amnesty. Joseph became a popular hero in the East, but the whites on his land did not want the Nez Perces back. When, after twelve years of exile, the remnants of the tribe were returned to the Northwest, it was not to the lush Wallowa but to the sagebrush reaches of the Columbia's big bend. And there Joseph is buried.

The history of Indian-white relations in the Northwest is not a story of grand military engagements. It is a chronicle of conflicting assumptions, of words unheard or misunderstood. Joseph observed:

"The Indian's Portion": a **Puck** *cartoonist's acid commentary on usurpation of Indian lands.*

"It makes my heart sick when I remember all the good words and all the broken promises. . . . Too many misrepresentations have been made, too many misunderstandings have come up between the white men about the Indians. If the white man wants to live in peace with the Indian he can live in peace. There need be no trouble. Treat all men alike. Give them all the same law. Give them all an even chance to live and grow. All men were made by the same Great Spirit Chief. They are all brothers. The earth is the mother of all people, and all people should have equal rights upon it.

"You might as well expect the rivers to run backward as that any man who was born free should be contented penned up and denied liberty to go where he pleases.

"Whenever the white men treat the Indian as they treat each other then we shall have no more wars. We shall all be alike—brothers of one father and mother, with one sky above us and one country around us and one government for all. Then the Great Spirit Chief who rules above will smile upon this land and send rain to wash out the bloody spots made by brothers' hands upon the face of the earth."

CHAPTER 17

THE SEARCH FOR BURIED TREASURE

Mining and the road-building it triggered,
which opened up the interior and made coast cities boom

ROM THE FIFTIES TO THE EIGHTIES, the miners were the true pioneers in the Northwest. For them, the whisper of "gold!" could transform a forbidding wasteland into the end of the rainbow. The pot of gold that the hopeful found was meager compared to the riches of California or Nevada. But it was enough to keep hordes of miners on the move, and their ramblings after treasure would have far-reaching consequences.

Nothing could stand in their way. The miners wrecked the Indian cultures in their path and built towns near the diggings without regard for the quality of the soil, availability of timber, or access to shipping. The stern test of time turned many of their glittering settlements—Golden Age, Ruby, Quartzburg, Bonanza City, and Comeback—into ghost towns. Others have survived marginally on the dollars of summer residents and history-minded tourists. A few, by virtue of their strategic location—Boise and Helena, for example—blossomed into the population centers of their regions.

Lust for treasure led the prospectors into the Bitterroots and the Rockies, where they forced the inhospitable peaks and ravines to play host. Only a few got rich, but many found consolation in the new communities where they shared their dreams and sufferings.

Equally numerous and important were the suppliers, the necessary corollary to any mining venture; the miners, like Midas, found that man cannot live on gold alone. They offered their gold to anyone who could bring them food and equipment in the wilderness. Suppliers prospered as well or better than miners, and the old pioneer towns along the Columbia became com-mercial boomtowns. Supplying was such good business, in fact, that the Northwest profited as much from supplying other regions' mineral rushes as from uncovering its own precious metal.

The Northwest's first attack of gold fever came with all the suddenness of the California rush. In the fall of 1848 the Oregon legislature failed to muster a quorum, because the legislators were busy combing the California gold fields ahead of the easterners. David Lavender has estimated that in 1849, $2 million of badly needed gold found its way into the economy of the Northwest. Even before the wanderers returned, the economy began picking up. Ship captains with purses of gold were calling at the Columbia and demanding timber, wheat, and produce for California. Oregon was well-prepared. The Willamette Valley had an established population of farmers, merchants, and even professional men, as well as continuing reinforcements of family men, who refused to be diverted by California gold from the Oregon Trail. Suppliers around Puget Sound, too, cashed in on the bonanza.

A boom, of course, followed the new demand for the Northwest's products, and with the boom came speculation. New towns were promoted and planned; most proved ephemeral, but one, derisively called Stump Town by the Oregon City establishment, grew to eclipse its denigrators. In 1851, Stump Town entrepreneurs began a corduroy road (a road made of logs strapped together) to the rich wheat fields of the Tualatin Plains. This road and a port for ocean vessels were an unbeatable combination; Stump Town—or Portland—boomed.

Idaho gold brought hopeful argonauts by the thousands, like these men on the Coeur d'Alene in 1884, who pooled their efforts to construct and work a large sluicing system.

Instant city, mining camp style: Murraysville, Idaho, blossomed with stump-lined streets.

Meanwhile, the forty-niners' demand for produce sent shallow-draft boats farther and farther south along the Willamette's fertile shores. The new towns of Salem (which in 1851 replaced Oregon City as the capital), Albany, Corvallis, and Eugene sprang up, and the stagecoach initiated at Oregon City in 1846 hastened south to serve them. By 1860 the stagecoach line extended all the way from Portland to Sacramento.

Soon after miners from the Northwest returned home with their pockets full of gold, the Californians—men whose home was where the gold was—began to drift into the Northwest in search of better diggings. Southwestern Oregon produced several flurries of excitement, enough to maintain Jacksonville as a local gold-seeking and Indian-fighting capital in the fifties and sixties. Elsewhere, gold and Indian conflict also went together. In 1855 miners rushed through Indian lands to Fort Colville (north of present-day Spokane) and found far more trouble than treasure (see chapter 15).

In 1858 miners again crossed Washington and Oregon, this time on their way to the Fraser River in British Columbia. Local merchants lightened a few pockets, but the old nemesis of the American entrepreneur, the Hudson's Bay Company, succeeded in cornering the market. James Douglas, HBC chief factor and governor of Vancouver Island, ordered all miners to buy licenses at five dollars a month. Since these were available only in the British town of Victoria, Victoria soon became the chief port of entry for the rush, even though, as the enraged Americans pointed out, their town, Whatcom (the forerunner of Bellingham, Washington), was closer to the gold country. Miners were paid to build their own trail from Whatcom to the Fraser, but to little avail; Douglas was financing a British road on a grander scale. The purpose of the frenzied road building was to lower freight charges from the coast to the mines, which were running $1,400 a ton. Further strikes in 1860 and 1861 —richer than the Fraser diggings and farther inland— gave Douglas the impetus he needed to complete his road. He called in the Royal Engineers, and they extended the Fraser Trail into the Cariboo Road, a road worthy of the name. Freight charges dropped immediately to $300 a ton, and the British were assured a virtual monopoly in supplying the Cariboo. American efforts to profit from the Canadian rushes bore some fruit, however. Joel Palmer, former Indian superintendent for Oregon, pioneered a new pattern of trade in livestock by his trail drives through Washington's interior into Canada.

Comparatively rich mineral finds were made along Oregon's Powder and John Day rivers, but these were overshadowed by strikes farther east; and deservedly so. Oregon and Washington would yield less than $20 million in the thirty years after the California gold rush. On the other hand, the virgin diggings in present-day Idaho would produce about the same haul in treasure in only five years.

Idaho's mineral rush history began when several whites sneaked onto the Nez Perce reservation late in 1860 and panned some gold. When the word spread ("gold!"), no treaty or Indian agent could dissuade the miners from massing in Walla Walla and newly founded Lewiston (founded not only on Nez Perce land but on land from which whites were specifically excluded by treaty). There they awaited the first thaw and the start of the rush. A few Christianized Nez Perces met the miners in white man's fashion, as capitalists ready to supply the miners' wants. These few grew wealthy, but they eventually signed away more than three-fourths of their tribe's remaining land.

Oro Fino and "Fabulous" Florence were the sparkling creations of the miners' first flush of enthusiasm. But there were many names to follow. As the historian H. H. Bancroft explained, "The miners of Idaho were like quicksilver. A mass of them dropped in any locality, broke up into individual globules, and ran off after any atom of gold in their vicinity. They stayed nowhere longer than the gold attracted them." By 1862 miners were scurrying southward from Oro Fino and Florence in pursuit of an old legend, the legend of Blue Bucket Diggings. The story was that in 1845 pioneers along the Oregon Trail had filled a blue bucket with a yellow metal whose value was then unappreciated. The legend happened to coincide with the truth. The Boise basin, a small circle of open land hemmed in by forests and mountains, was soon filled to overflowing, with the new metropolises of Boise City and Bannock City (later Idaho City) sitting on opposite rims. By the end of the second mining season, Bannock City was the most populous city in the Northwest, larger even than Portland. In its first winter the city was transformed into a labyrinth of ditches in preparation for the spring sluicing operations. Nearly eighty miles of ditches were dug, and Main Street was not spared. But spring after spring justified the peculiar landscape, since $3 to $5 million a year in gold settled to the bottoms of the sluices.

THE SERENE WILDERNESS became a mining camp, then a town, with a roar. In the first weeks, it was every man for himself. Then the community bustled and shook as miners and merchants cooperated in around-the-clock industry, occasionally relieved by around-the-clock debauchery. The din, especially on Sundays, the miners' day of relaxation, was unearthly.

Sawmills ran twenty-four hours to supply the miners with sluices and the merchants with stores. Soon the camp became a town, complete with a main street and perhaps a brick building expressing hope for the future. Celebrating the present, however, was more common: every third establishment was a saloon, where miners found male and female companionship as well as something to dull the pain of backbreaking work, disappointment, and loneliness. If the whiskey ran low, they made do with a home-brew called "tanglefoot," a potent blend of water, sage, tobacco, and cayenne pepper.

The town was surrounded by a crazy quilt of mining claims, the evidence of its *raison d'être*.

Necessarily, the first law was the mining code, based, as was everything, on California practice. The first official was the claims recorder. But gold dust, so valuable and so concealable, invited theft and murder, as well as claim-jumping. At first each miner was too concerned with his own selfish quest to worry about other miners. As the camp became a town, however, men began to think of "other miners" as "fellow citizens." Since law officers were back in civilization, the miners elected their own or, especially in Montana, organized vigilante groups.

Quick justice was not always just, but the vigilantes were successful. They broke the strongest of the outlaw bands, Sheriff Henry Plummer's, which at times controlled the governments of the mining towns of Idaho and Montana. Impromptu justice sometimes worked for the community good without benefit of the hanging tree. One winter when the price of a sack of flour rose from $27 to $100 because certain people were hoarding their supplies, vigilantes took matters into their own hands, commandeered the flour and distributed it to the needy at $27 a sack.

The mining town retained some of its frenzy even after the appearance of duly elected officials. Joaquin Miller (incidentally one of the Northwest's finest poets) said of his term as judge in a mining town, "I had a copy of Blackstone and two six-shooters. My administration was very successful."

Across the border in Canada, the more authoritarian British from the start had a gold commissioner, police, and a judge in every mining camp. One American complained (with some exaggeration) of the tranquility of the Canadian towns: "They told me it was like California in '49; why, you would have seen all those fellows roaring drunk, and pistols and bare knives in every hand. I never saw a mining town anything like this."

The women in the mining regions were a good index of the community's development. The whores came first and stayed, followed by the virtuous but ugly "hurdy-gurdies," or taxi dancers. Then a lady or two braved the profane atmosphere and, aided by merchants and ministers, somewhat tamed the town.

The Chinese, on the other hand, were the harbingers of declining fortunes, because they were permitted to mine only when the whites wanted to sell their claims. Thus, the best measure of the depressed state of mining

When the stream beds played out, miners in Idaho turned to hydraulicking, washing down whole mountains and sluicing the run-off mud for color.

in the Northwest in the 1870s is the fact that more than half the miners in Oregon and Idaho were Chinese. Before and after that depression, the Chinese either paid exorbitant fees for the privilege of mining or became laundrymen and panned the wash water for gold dust left in the miners' pants.

The miner's life was a life of extremes. Fabulous wealth always seemed within his grasp, but starvation was often closer at hand. The moods of the miner and his community ranged equally far. There was in the mining camp a time for brutality and a time for charity, a time for frenzy and a time for reflection—and that time was any given moment.

SUPPLIERS CONVERGED on the Boise Basin from three directions. From Salt Lake City, Mormon teamsters hauled wagonloads of equipment from the Great Plains and produce from their own Deseret; from Chico or Red Bluff, where the Sacramento River steamers from San Francisco stopped, Californians drove wagon teams northeastward. Both routes would increase in importance with the completion of the Central Pacific in 1869. For the time being, however, the third route, by far the longest and most complex, dominated the trade: by ship from San Francisco to Portland, by

steamer to Umatilla, Wallula, or Lewiston (as river conditions permitted), and thence by pack mule to the mines. Before a wagon road was completed in 1864, the final three hundred miles by mule could take nearly a month, but this was merely the norm for wilderness travel. Walla Walla, the trading center nearest the landings at the east end of the steamer run, like Portland, did a booming outfitting business.

Meanwhile, Montana's gold rush had begun. The region in the eastern shadow of the Rockies experienced one year later everything Idaho had gone through. Montana's miners were also "like quicksilver," partly because many of them were on the move from Idaho. In Montana the miners literally went in circles in pursuit of rumor and sometimes gold: camps were erected, abandoned, and occasionally built again.

Bannack, just east of the Continental Divide, was the first gold-rush town. Here in 1862 one could actually "pan gold out of sagebrush" by sifting through the gravel clinging to the roots of bushes on the stream banks. Nevertheless, in 1863 a few miners drifted eastward looking for greener—or yellower—pastures.

In Alder Gulch they found what they wanted. When one of their number returned to Bannack for supplies, three hundred gold-seekers insisted on following him to the new diggings. Soon Alder Gulch was the new mining

Anaconda, Montana, 1887, where copper was king and smoke from the smelter blanketed the town.

center and Bannack was on the brink of giving up the ghost. The gulch was a miserable site for a town, but since the gold was there, so must be the town. By the following year, Alder Gulch was a seventeen-mile-long meandering ribbon of a town with over ten thousand inhabitants.

Western Montana was rugged country. Its mineral wealth lay in parallel ravines or gulches; Confederate Gulch, Emigrant Gulch, and Last Chance Gulch were the big strikes of 1864. If the prospectors had a hard time getting to the diggings, it was harder for the suppliers. Salt Lake City merchants were close enough to reach the mines, but Portland suppliers, who profited immensely by supplying the Idaho diggings, were unable to extend their route to Montana. They tried following the Oregon Trail in reverse as far as Fort Hall, then turning north, but the distance was too great. Even from Lewiston, it was nine hundred miles to the mines. From the upper Sacramento River, the distance was the same. Neither route could meet the new competition for the miners' gold.

The key to the new routes was Mullan's Road, the visionary project (or monomania, according to some) of Lieutenant John Mullan, who first came to the Northwest with Isaac Stevens' railroad survey in 1853. The road traversed 624 miles of uninhabited wilderness from Fort Benton, on the Missouri River, to Walla Walla, near the Columbia, thus fulfilling Lewis and Clark's dream of linking the two great river systems (though not with the ease they had expected).

In the early sixties the western end of Mullan's Road was only a pack trail, but good enough to induce Walla Walla suppliers to by-pass the Boise Basin and cut directly across northern Idaho to the Montana mines. The road's effect was more dramatic at the eastern end. There a genuine wagon road made the 100- to 200-mile trip from Fort Benton to the mines an easy ten- to fifteen-day jaunt. Though the variable Missouri made the steamboat trip to Fort Benton tedious, the route offered midwesterners a reasonable path to the gold country. They flocked to the Montana mines in numbers not seen in the other rushes in the Northwest, and both ends of the route prospered. St. Louis reasserted itself as "the Gateway to the West," a position it had held during the fur trade of the thirties and the migrations of the forties; Last Chance Gulch, the other terminus, deciding it was time to choose a more permanent-sounding name, became Helena.

THE NORTHWEST had experienced the first stage of gold fever. The scars were evident: mining camps spotted the landscape and supply lines streaked across it. But already in the first years of the rushes, the early sixties, symptoms of the next stage of the fever appeared: industrial mining.

After a few seasons of mining in a region, individuals panning gold became a rarity. When all the rich claims were staked out, a new arrival at the diggings had the choice of trying another region or joining a rich miner's labor force. Such organized industry allowed more and more complex forms of placering, or separating gold from gravel by the use of water. Even hydraulicking was being done. Miners blasted away at gold-bearing hillsides with high-pressure hoses that were capable of killing a man and certainly killed the landscape.

But even hydraulicking was a technique to be used at diggings, not mines. To get at the treasure underground, immense capital was required. At this point, the Old Californian stepped in. Frustrated forty-niners had led the way to new diggings all across the Northwest, but it was the Old Californian who, having struck

The Klondike rush of '97, as men clamored for supplies and passage on Northwest docks.
The flood of miners put more gold in merchants' pockets than in miners' pouches.

it rich, sparked the transformation of diggings into mines. George Hearst was one of these, though he had made his greatest fortune in that miners' second heaven, Nevada's Comstock Lode. He set the example for investors by his support of lode mining in the Boise Basin.

In an instant, it seemed, mining was no longer as simple as picking up gold nuggets. Stamp mills began crushing ores for whatever they contained, and miners began to look beyond gold to whatever mineral would be worth processing. The technological know-how acquired in California and the Comstock was put at the service of the Northwest, especially in the Owyhee Basin, near the junction of present-day Oregon, Idaho, and Nevada, where quartz ledges with twice the gold and silver of similar ledges in the Comstock were found. Meanwhile, Montana's miners were naming their camps Virginia City, Nevada City, and the like in the hope

that a little of the magic of the Comstock would rub off on them.

In the decade of the seventies mining in the Northwest was a sleeping giant. While the industries were tooling up—often to extract a mineral that was not there, the glory of the placering days faded, along with many of the prospectors. But in the early 1880s, thanks again to George Hearst's abundant cash, copper, a metal new to Western miners, was discovered in the Anaconda Mine. Cornish miners were brought from England to do the work that was unfamiliar to everyone else, and the new city of Butte prospered as the mines yielded— over $2 billion worth of copper to the present.

Elsewhere in the Northwest the trend was also away from gold. Even the Coeur d'Alene in northern Idaho, billed by the railroads as a gold rush in order to increase passenger traffic, turned quickly to the industrial mining of silver, lead, and zinc. Once again, one gulch after another, with room for a stream at most between its steep slopes, was forced to support a mining town. The most famous example was Milo Gulch, where the Bunker Hill Mine occupied one ridge, the Sullivan Mine the other, and the town of Wardner struggled for breathing room between.

Wardner was a company town, almost the symbol of a company town: the mines where the townsfolk worked loomed over them even when they were at home. And what was home but the company boardinghouse, where the miners were forced to return their wages to the company in the form of exorbitant rent. The store and the hospital were also designed more to profit the company than to serve the workers.

Industrialization had changed the nature of the company town: the relatively benevolent Hudson's Bay Company towns had been replaced by ugly sites for even uglier confrontations between labor and management. Here in the industrial mines of Idaho and Montana the Mine Owners' Protective Association and the Western Federation of Miners were born. And here during the nineties they squared off. It was a running battle of wage cuts, strikes, strikebreakers, and martial law, climaxed in 1899 by the dynamiting of the Bunker Hill and Sullivan smelters. In such a bitter way did civilization reach the mines.

AT A DISTANCE, mining prospects seemed rosy, thanks to a new breed, the public relations men. They made believe that one could step from a train in the Coeur d'Alene and find a fortune at one's feet. One of these dream-spinners—Erastus Brainerd—wrote such glowing prose about the Klondike that the forbidding snowfields barring the way should have melted before the prospectors' steps.

When the steamer *Portland* docked in Seattle in July of 1897, miners staggered off the ship with sacks of gold. At the sight of such phenomenal wealth, the last era of gold rushes in the West began. Ship passage to Alaska soared immediately from $200 to $1,000, and anything that could float, including rafts, embarked on the ocean voyage. There were only two questions in the air: how to get through Alaska to the Yukon Territory, and what city in the Northwest would profit most from the frenzy.

Erastus Brainerd, whose skills had been too esoteric for the Northwest (in desperation, he had even served as Paraguayan consul in Seattle), now found a use for his contacts with eastern journalists. Brainerd took on the task of publicizing Seattle as the only place for the future prospector to outfit himself for the Klondike. He did a remarkable job. Though other towns were equally convenient to the gold rush, Seattle is estimated to have taken from the miners five times as much money as all other ports combined.

Alaska made Seattle swell and strain its natural limits within a cluster of hills holding the town close to Puget Sound; in the first decade of the twentieth century, Alaskan sluicing techniques broke even these natural bounds: the city engineer washed away the hilltops, so that Seattle could expand.

THE MINERS, like other pioneers, saw a multitude of political as well as natural changes in the land they probed. They traveled from California and Nevada through the Northwest to Canada and Alaska and back through the Northwest; and they encouraged others to travel to supply their needs. In short, the miners participated in the revolution of transportation. Where the river steamers stopped, the miners hauled supplies on their backs and those of their mules. Later, when their feverish activity stimulated the industry of the suppliers, wagon roads were built.

Meanwhile, there was a corresponding development in mining technology. In the Northwest surface mining quickly grew too unrewarding for any but the persistent Chinese. The pan, the sluice, and the "long tom" for washing gold from stream gravel soon gave way to the heavy equipment needed for refining silver and base metals like copper, zinc, and lead, which constituted the true gold mine of the Northwest. Eastern capital bought the heavy equipment and the iron horse reached the Northwest just in time to deliver it.

Mining was big business now. Gone were the days when a man with his own two hands could claw at the earth for a fortune. The miner-pioneers of the wilderness had been replaced by a new breed, the wage slaves of the company town. Except for the few diehards who even today perpetuate the image of the loner and his mule, such was the end of the prospector's story.

CHAPTER 18

COURTING THE RAIL BARONS

Imaginary towns and worthless bonds, blind courage and downright chicanery—questionable ties on which the tracks were laid

N 1844 A RETIRED BUSINESSMAN who had made a fortune in the China trade began to pester Congress with his plan for a transcontinental railroad. Asa Whitney suggested—in an almost endless stream of speeches, articles, and letters—that a line be run from Puget Sound to Chicago, the construction to be financed by land sales from a sixty-mile-wide strip along the right-of-way. Initially proposed as the Puget Sound–Chicago link in an American scheme to dominate the Orient trade, the line was a long time growing, and mutating, to fruition. It was thirty-nine years from the time Asa Whitney's first enthusiastic proposals began to bombard Congress until the Northwest was linked to the rest of the nation by rails.

During those years the Northwest was treated to a seemingly endless parade of promises, proposals, dizzying successes, incompleted projects, and dismal disappointments. It was an era of rising expectations, peopled with egocentric empire builders, altruists, charlatans, benefactors, and a good many plain folks, skittering on hot rumors, trying to set themselves down in the path of the future. Countless imaginary towns and paper fortunes would be created, then swept away, in the fervid real-estate speculation that habitually preceded western railroads. The future of existing cities seemed assured or destroyed by the mere promise of a survey; and competition between cities and regions for a railroad's presence created bitter rivalries that, in some cases, persisted for years. Personal fortunes and periodic setbacks notwithstanding, the railroads ultimately proved to be a powerful and positive factor in

the story of the Northwest; because regardless of how the link was achieved, the region needed to end its isolation from the nation.

BY MID-CENTURY the nation wanted a transcontinental railroad, but Congress, splintered by the fears and jealousies of the growing sectional crisis, could accomplish little more than the appropriation of funds to survey five potential routes. The northernmost route represented the Northwest's first hope of strong and close ties to the rest of the nation. Prospects for the northern route were scant, however: recent gold discoveries and the superb port of San Francisco made California a more promising Pacific terminus; and southern senators threatened to block any route which lay too far from the heart of their section and which would develop a region (and a people) not suited or disposed to the extension of slavery.

But pessimism could wait for the future—first a route had to be laid out. The northern survey became the responsibility of Isaac Stevens, a veteran of the Mexican War who had recently been appointed governor for the Washington Territory as a reward for his campaign support of the newly elected Franklin Pierce. The thirty-five-year-old Stevens, plagued by a rupture, gimpy from a foot wound that never healed, and painfully conscious of his short stature, compensated for his handicaps with phenomenal energy. Not only did the governor-designate propose to complete the survey while en route to his new office, he also had himself appointed superin-

Attentive management amid chaos in the Southern Pacific office at Medford, Oregon. Whether boon or boondoggle, railroads were essential to the growth of the Northwest.

Steamboats of the OSN hauled grain and freight up the Columbia to open the interior.

tendent of Indian affairs, that he might negotiate with any natives he encountered.

In the spring of 1853, Stevens grabbed an appropriation for $40,000 and 123 men (the largest yet granted by Congress), sent a crew under George McClellan to Puget Sound to begin surveying eastward, and started west from St. Paul. By September he had reached central Montana, where he slowed the survey and became completely sidetracked in preliminary negotiations for future Indian treaties. Then, with winter approaching, Stevens hurried ahead to assume his office in Olympia before snow blocked his way, leaving his subalterns to complete the mapping.

Despite Stevens' shotgun approach to his responsibilities—and a cavalier attitude toward deadlines and expenses that allowed opponents of the Northern Route to attack his recommendations—a feasible route was laid out through the forbidding terrain of the Rockies and Cascades. But there remained obstacles more formidable than mountains. Jefferson Davis, then secretary of war (his department being responsible for the

surveys), added the political climate to the mountain weather and declared the winter snows too deep for railroads, a finding encouraged by the sloppy work of McClellan's western party. The route was summarily rejected. When time and a bloody conflict invalidated that objection, the railroad to the Northwest faced only the obstacle of money—a hurdle that eventually served to inspire a succession of empire builders.

In 1864 Congress passed the Northern Pacific Act, providing for a railroad to the Pacific along the general route followed by Stevens. As encouragement the act offered a liberal land grant to the builder, eventually amounting to 25,600 acres of land for every mile of track built, but failed to provide for government loans or subsidies to finance construction. Lacking a governmental promise of cash, the idea languished for five years, until a man emerged whose ambition transcended the dismal prospect of laying rails across that many empty miles.

In 1869, Jay Cooke, the Philadelphia banking wizard primarily responsible for financing the Union war effort, was smitten with the prospect of creating an empire in the West and agreed to sell $200 million worth of Northern Pacific stocks and bonds. For his efforts Cooke was to receive $20 million in stock, plus profits from bond sales. Even for a financial giant like Cooke, the commitment was a large one, and he threw himself into the promotion of the Northwest and the lands en route. His widespread advertising in America and Europe praising the bountiful soil and salubrious climate (Cooke was never one to let something as transient as words stand between him and a sale) ultimately led to the line being known derisively as "Cooke's Banana Belt."

While Cooke's crews built west from Minnesota, a western link was being completed from Kalama on the Columbia to a tiny settlement on Puget Sound called Tacoma. This short line, seemingly insignificant compared to the great strides being made by the railroad across the plains, nonetheless introduced the Northwest to the municipal cutthroat and real-estate roulette that attended railroad building. Railroads were a tremendous boost for the economy; property values rose, business flourished, credit and capital were suddenly easy to raise—unless, of course, one did not happen to be near the railroad. Accordingly, every time a railroad came prospecting, cities scrambled for attention—not just to profit, but, they thought, to survive—and everyone became a real-estate speculator.

Seattle, as the largest and most firmly established city on the sound, had strong hopes of being selected as the western terminus of the road, and went so far as to sweeten its appeal with offers of land and cash. Property values and business investments skyrocketed and plummeted with the vagaries of rumor, until Seattle's very size and substance augured against it. Tacoma was selected in 1873 because the financially battered line could not afford the high cost of Seattle real estate, and because Tacoma offered better opportunities for Northern Pacific insiders to make fat profits on real estate. As Seattle's hopes were shattered, Tacoma's were on the rise, and best of all, the future looked good for the Northwest. But even before Tacoma had a chance to boom, Jay Cooke took it all back.

Cooke's empire, built on salesmanship, and badly overextended, collapsed when foreign and domestic credit turned timid in 1873. Construction on the Northern

Where the river was unnavigable, the OSN constructed a "portage railway," as here near Celilo Falls.

Pacific immediately ground to a halt, enthusiasm in the Northwest began to lag, and the region spent almost ten years nursing vagrant hopes that the line would somehow revive.

WHILE THE FUTURE of a national rail link vacillated with the personal fortunes of eastern capitalists and the world economy, and the region alternately exulted and despaired, the Pacific Northwest enjoyed a reliable, growth-inducing, and prosperous system for internal transportation and commerce. The heart of the system was steamboats, its lifeblood the Columbia River, while the brains were a group of men who comprised the Oregon Steam Navigation Company (OSN).

Prior to 1861 steamboating on the Columbia was characterized by a kind of paddle-wheel jungle law, in which simple competition for business was supplanted by a fierce desire to eliminate the opposition. Men like John C. Ainsworth and Robert R. Thompson battled for supremacy with rate-cutting tactics that gradually proved to be self-destructive. But in 1861 the boat owners finally got together, buried the hatchet, and formed the OSN; which, however, left shippers and consumers vulnerable to economic laws like supply and demand—or, more bluntly, "what the traffic will bear."

Almost immediately good fortune shone on the newly formed combine. The Idaho gold discoveries created a phenomenal flow of passengers and freight—all paying uniform (and substantial) rates. As a result the OSN was amassing a tremendous cash reserve, money that inevitably found its way into expansion.

The key to real control of traffic on the Columbia lay in two short stretches of water less than forty miles apart—The Dalles and the Cascades—where the Columbia forces it way through the Cascade Mountains. Both were impassable to river steamers, requiring that goods bound upriver be unloaded at the foot of the Cascades, hauled overland six miles, reloaded aboard another boat for the next forty miles, loaded onto wagons for fourteen miles around The Dalles, and loaded onto yet another boat to continue upriver. Obviously, whoever controlled the portages could exert a powerful influence over shipping on the river.

At The Dalles the OSN began construction on a railroad that would easily dominate transshipment there upon completion. But the Cascades were another matter, calling for the kind of luck and guile that kept the OSN not only solvent, but prosperous, during an era when the sound of collapsing transportation companies beat a rapid tattoo across the entire West.

At the Cascades there were but two feasible sites for a rail line, one on each side of the river, and in each case the right-of-way was controlled by mule-powered tramway operators: on the northside by the Bradford Brothers, and on the south by J. S. Ruckel and Harrison Olmstead. When winter floods of 1861–62 washed out the Bradford brothers, the OSN bought Ruckel and Olmstead a small steam engine and began to build an iron-sheathed wooden rail line. Discouraged by the competition, the Bradfords sold out to the OSN, which began constructing a full-scale railroad on the northside, threatening the inadequate Ruckel-Olmstead line with complete ruin. That line too capitulated, and the OSN held virtually complete control over transportation on the Columbia. In the process the company had built the Northwest's first railroad—the tiny Ruckel-Olmstead puffer—and done it without outside funds.

Success with home-grown railroads was not the exclusive province of the OSN, however. The first railroad in the Inland Empire was a thirty-two-mile stretch of fir stringers crowned with strap iron built by Dr. Dorsey Baker between Walla Walla and Wallula. It was dubbed the "Rawhide Road" because a local yarn had it that Baker bound the strap iron to the wood rails with rawhide (and "wolves ate the railroad" one hard winter). A measure of pride in the line developed, to the extent that on one occasion the citizens of Walla Walla subscribed $25,000 to complete construction on the line. The "Walla Walla and Columbia," as it was officially known, was not only privately financed, but made enough money to encourage the OSN to buy out Baker in 1878 for a third of a million dollars.

As early as 1867, Ainsworth, Thompson, and two Portland capitalists, Simeon G. Reed and William S. Ladd, had gained complete control of the OSN; their company, meanwhile, had grown to enjoy a monopoly on trade with the Inland Empire and the camps of Idaho and Montana. In time the company would be attacked for inhibiting growth through the imposition of prohibitive freight charges. True, rates were high, but so were costs: goods moving the four hundred miles

Brash and unscrupulous, Ben Holladay ran his transportation empire to financial ruin.

between Portland and Lewiston sometimes had to be handled fourteen times; wood to heat the boilers, unavailable upriver, had to be hauled to refueling stations. Expenses notwithstanding, Ainsworth and company probably indulged in some gouging (not the worst of pursuits, given the era); but without the trains and boats of the OSN, little of the interior could have developed as it did, as early as it did.

WHILE THE NORTHERN PACIFIC was rising and falling with Jay Cooke's fortunes, and the OSN was sewing up the interior trade, another attempt at establishing a rail link to the outside was in the making. It took over fifteen years; the people and the route would change dramatically, but another transcontinental line to the Northwest would be the result. It began with a brazen rascal with a penchant for big swindles named Simon Elliot.

In 1866 Congress provided for a rail link from the Central Pacific Railroad in California along the Willamette River to the Columbia River and offered to the builder twenty square miles of land for each mile of railroad built. Simon Elliot saw a fortune in that land, and he was determined to have it, despite two obstacles: he had no money, and another company held the construction rights. Elliot forthrightly proceeded to divide the company by playing on jealousy between Portland and Salem, proposing that perhaps it was not quite fair to run the line up the west, or Portland, side of the Willamette River. Taking over the Salem (or eastside) faction, Elliot declared it the legitimate heir of the grant rights and began peddling a batch of worthless bonds in San Francisco to finance construction. The opposition, chiefly Joseph Gaston, did not simply evaporate, and some of Elliot's chicanery was beginning to catch up with him when Ben Holladay jumped into the fray.

Holladay, the roughhewn entrepreneur who built a fortune on stagecoaching, became interested when he bought some of Elliot's fraudulent bonds. Immediately sensing the huge value of the land grant, Holladay took up Elliot's cause only to shoulder him completely out of the deal. Coarse, blunt, and strong-willed, Holladay secured his grip on the Oregon and California Railroad and the land grant by bribing the necessary legislators and judges. Finally beginning to build the railroad, he found competition from river steamers on the Willamette a nuisance and bought them out. Always seeking to consolidate his hold, he bought out Gaston's vanquished Oregon Central (westside) line and extended its insubstantial beginnings. He now held two railroads, a steamship line, and a stranglehold on transportation in the Willamette Valley. Holladay's whirlwind conquest had taken its toll, however; he needed capital to continue rail construction, and to operate his new Oregon Steamship Company. The solution was to float a batch of bonds, nominally secured by the land grant, to foreign investors.

Most of Holladay's bonds, sold through dummy corporations at badly inflated prices, were picked up by German investors. By 1873 the general decline that accompanied Jay Cooke's collapse began to point up the hollow quality of Holladay's bonds, and the worried Germans cast about for an agent to send to America to

Henry Villard, Holladay's nemesis, finally succeeded in completing the Northern Pacific Railroad.

check up on their investment. They found Henry Villard, who not only spoke English but the language of magnates and empire builders as well.

Henry Villard had emigrated to America from Germany when he was eighteen, and in less than twelve years became one of the nation's leading journalists, reporting on his travels to the gold fields of the Far West and as a combat correspondent during the Civil War. Ill health led to his return to Germany in 1872, but in less than two years he was back in America poking around in Holladay's faltering empire. Villard locked horns immediately with Holladay, ordering changes that would ensure a return to the bondholders—and though Holladay blustered and bullied, the precise German brought him firmly into line.

In 1876, Holladay began to balk, reneging on the agreements, and this time Villard dispensed with polite formalities entirely. He booted Holladay completely out of the transportation empire the stagecoach king

Grading track bed for the Northern Pacific was often difficult and expensive, across hundreds of miles of wilderness that offered no markets. Here near Cabinet, Idaho, in 1881.

had built, took control of the Willamette railroads and the steamship company, and persuaded Holladay's creditors to entrust the rejuvenation of the company to him. Launching an ambitious campaign to encourage emigration and to rebuild all elements of the empire, Villard soon found himself at odds with his German employers, who wanted all energy and money devoted to scooping up the lucrative land grant by extending the Oregon and California Railroad farther south. By 1879 Villard settled the squabbling by buying out the disgruntled investors, and assuming sole control of the companies Holladay had organized.

Villard then began to flex his financial muscles. Organizing his holdings as the Oregon Railway and Navigation Company, he bought out the OSN and by 1882 was building a rail line up the Columbia from Portland to Walla Walla. In less than a year the OR&N was a profitable, stable organization—and Villard had done it all himself.

Villard now controlled commerce in the Northwest, channeling freight and passengers through Portland and along the Columbia. It was an enviable arrangement, since any bulk commodities bound in or out of the interior had to pass through his system. But a flaw existed: Portland, because of the Columbia bar at the mouth of the river, was an unsuitable port. Villard knew that when the Northern Pacific revived and Puget Sound managed to establish rail links with the Inland Empire, traffic through Portland and on the Columbia would reduce sharply.

Rather than risk the competition, Villard set about eliminating the challenge by building the line himself. He gained control of the Northern Pacific in 1881, and to raise capital without tipping his hand and driving stock up in the languishing Northern Pacific, Villard organized his unique "Blind Pool" in 1884. On the strength of his personal reputation he raised $20 million without ever revealing the use to which it would be put. Considering the state of the economy and the financial antics of many of Wall Street's denizens, the faith placed in his character and judgment is nothing short of extraordinary.

Villard pushed construction westward across Montana and over the Rockies, and eastward from the OR&N's end of track at Wallula. From 1881 to 1883 grade was cut and tunnels were bored, Villard balancing the tremendous costs against the economic growth that must surely follow. In September of 1883 the line was completed, and the Northwest finally had its transcontinental link—the future had arrived.

Unfortunately, construction costs had far outdistanced any immediate returns, and although the Northern Pacific would remain reasonably solvent for a time, Henry Villard was sacrificed to stockholders' demands for an accounting shortly after the completion. During that time Villard briefly revitalized the Oregon and California line, pushing it to Ashland where the Southern Pacific could complete the link in 1887—giving the Northwest its second connection to the nation by rail in four years.

When the interests that had originally favored Puget Sound as the terminus for the Northern Pacific regained control of the line from Villard, they pushed tracks through Stampede Pass, thus giving Seattle and Tacoma a direct connection with the Inland Empire and making them more dangerous rivals to Portland.

Villard's legacy was substantial, but within a few years of his departure the empire he restructured and amended would begin to deteriorate. Despite the enormous land grants and a growing prosperity in the Northwest, the Northern Pacific gradually declined again into bankruptcy, the victim of poor management, finally collapsing with the panic of 1893.

W HEN THE NORTHERN PACIFIC was completed in 1883, Puget Sound was tied to the transcontinental system by virtue of the rail line between Kalama and Tacoma. But Seattle, left out of the excitement, fumed and plotted, bent on becoming the paramount city on the sound. True greatness and real prosperity, it was felt, required a railroad—something no one seemed interested in giving Seattle. The only solution, apparently, was to build its own railroad.

A Union Pacific loading transfer on the Snake River in 1883. Before bridges were constructed, whole trains were loaded aboard ferries and hauled to railhead across the river.

A variety of municipally organized or supported ventures were launched between 1874 and 1890, but while Seattle was long on enthusiasm, it was short on capital. The enthusiasm of the city often transcended reason, giving rise to proposals for building a line with volunteer labor or locally subscribed capital. The Lake Shore and Eastern, as another project was known, made tentative starts eastward into the Cascades and north toward Bellingham, but shortly ground to a halt after bilking a group of eastern investors. The solution had to come from the outside, and in 1889 it did, in the form of James J. Hill.

J. J. Hill was a one-eyed Canadian visionary whose intellectual perception, many thought, was also impaired. During the 1880s, when railroads with fat sub-sidies, government loans, and munificent land grants were collapsing routinely, Hill set out to build a railroad without *any* public assistance.

Hill's technique was to take his profits as he went, pushing his line to profitable markets, and developing a population along his right-of-way. Across North Dakota and Montana, Hill offered cheap fares to settlers along his route and gave seed, equipment, livestock, and advice to encourage farming. Planning carefully and building wisely, Hill found shorter routes, gentler grades, and quality construction. Solid business practices characterized Hill's Great Northern, and it paid off; until it was absorbed by J. P. Morgan in 1901, and afterward, the GN remained a profitable enterprise.

In 1889 when Hill determined to complete his line

First eastbound train on the new N.P.R.R. in 1883—which doesn't explain the stuffed cougar.

High in the wintry Cascades, the last spike is driven for the Great Northern Railroad in 1893.

James J. Hill used thrift, planning, and optimism to succeed without government subsidy.

from Helena to Puget Sound, Seattle began to hope for the best and prepare for the worst. Hill had ample excuse to avoid the city, as the approaches were blocked by the old Lake Shore and Eastern, which wanted to extort concessions from Hill in exchange for right-of-way. Hill, never one to tip his hand prematurely, left Seattle on tenterhooks until 1892 when he skirted the problem by looping into the city on the mud flats, laying tracks on earth fill. In January of 1893 the last spike was driven, and Seattle had realized her dream—she was a western terminus.

A RAILROAD FOR THE NORTHWEST had been a long time coming. It had been a questionable proposition from the beginning, required to come long, empty, profitless distances without the federal cash subsidies that helped build the first transcontinental to California. In the process of establishing the link, and as a by-product of the fierce competition between cities, an extensive network of river, rails, and road connections within the region was established. When the feat was finally accomplished, followers came quickly, adding to the success: Northern Pacific in 1883; the Canadian Pacific to Vancouver in 1885; the Southern Pacific in 1887; and the Great Northern in 1893. And while the railroads did not dramatically change patterns of life, they provided the means for continuing growth.

PART FIVE

TWENTIETH-CENTURY CHALLENGES

For those who staked their fortunes and their futures on the Northwest, it was not just a land of extraordinary beauty and diversity, but a land of promise and growth. As the century turned, they settled down to the difficult task of making the promise keep pace with the growth—grappling with the turmoil of colliding dreams, the vagaries of a mercurial economy, and just plain learning to live with their neighbors. But always it was the land in which they placed their faith, changing, shaping, accommodating its face and themselves in order to succeed.

Lake Washington Floating Bridge, Seattle.

CHAPTER 19

HIGH SOCIETY ON THE RAW FRONTIER

The rise of fledgling cities: sensible Portland,
seesawing Tacoma, and ever ebullient Seattle

Until 1900, more than half the population of the Northwest was rural, but as everywhere in America, the cities dominated life. It was in the cities that people found credit to buy land, bought seed to plant and tools for harvest, traded their labor and skills, sought capital to invest, and located transportation to markets. In the cities industries would one day grow to challenge San Francisco and the East, and thereby lift the onerous suspicion that the region suffered a kind of economic colonial status. In cities a man found entertainment to divert him, charlatans to fleece him, a woman to marry him, churches to save him, doctors to mend him, and morticians to bury him. The cities were the focus of attention, the reflection of progress; for it was by the state of his cities—not his farms or pastures—that man measured the relative level and condition of his civilization.

But when the Oregon Country was annexed in 1846, the Northwest lacked anything that could be called a city. Until after the Civil War the villages on the Columbia and in the Willamette Valley were little more than local trading centers; the mining-boom towns of Idaho and Montana, while a tremendous stimulus to agriculture and commerce, promised no permanence beyond the day ores ceased to be profitable; and the timber nomads of Puget Sound, who followed the shoreline cutting San Francisco's lumber, took a long time to congregate around the trading posts and sawmills. But when immigration resumed after the war, the villages and towns began to grow—one even began to assume the proportions and trappings of a major city.

Portland, by virtue of geography—and gravity, which carried past its warehouses and granaries the riverborne produce of the Northwest's two most productive regions—dominated the commerce of the area for more than two decades. Situated at the confluence of the Columbia and Willamette rivers, Portland at one time or another handled everything that passed in or out of the interior: produce from the Willamette Valley, gold and silver from the mines, soldiers to protect or avenge prospectors, household goods, farm implements, immigrants both by sea and overland, and, in time, the wheat of the Inland Empire. It was an enviable position, one that brought tremendous influence and profit to the city, and one that remained unchallenged until the railroads provided Puget Sound with access to the interior in the late 1880s.

The symbol of Portland, certainly the long arm of its influence, was the Oregon Steam Navigation Company. Headquartered in Portland, under the ownership of John C. Ainsworth, Simeon G. Reed, and Robert R. Thompson, the OSN enjoyed a stranglehold on transport on the Columbia [see chapter 17]. Hated by the Puget Sounders (who envied Portland's position and the company's revenues) and the residents of the interior (who conveniently forgot that OSN transport made their very survival possible, and instead unleashed volleys of epithets at the company for its ruthless monopoly and exorbitant rates—both true charges, though somewhat defensible), the OSN was a cautious, conservative, profitable concern. And the city was no different.

Even during Portland's rude beginnings in 1852, some citizens along Front Street managed to sport the genteel mien of a later metropolitan sophistication.

Portland was no boomtown, getting fat on gold or timber, or any other finite resource that might be frittered away, nor was it gilded with a veneer of speculation and inflation, that chipped and flaked when the economy stabilized. Portland made its money in banking and commerce, finding profit in what the rivers carried past its door, and investing the profit for a steady but safe return. This economic philosophy was reflected in the city's social and cultural life. A deep-water port without a market in its earliest years, Portland found its first calling as a supply base for the California gold rush and later enjoyed a secondhand bonanza of gold found in Idaho. Although supplying all manner of needs, Portland never boasted of the rude conditions and primitive social disorders that sprang up alongside the skid roads and docks of the sawmill frontier. Solace was provided for solitary males in Portland, but a strong New England element, which came early to the new community, discouraged discussion of such recreational opportunities. A traveler, conditioned by experience to expect a "new, crude Western town," found instead "a fine old city, a bit . . . of Central New York—a square with the post-office in the center, tree-shaded streets, comfortable homes, and plenty of churches and clubs, the signs of conservatism and solid respectability."

The wealthy commercial class—Ainsworth, Reed, merchant and banker William S. Ladd, freighting mogul Henry W. Corbett, and a score of lesser businessmen—while circumspect and provincial—were no ascetics. They built mansions after the prevailing French and Italian modes, with grounds that covered entire city blocks. They acquired art collections, spared no expense entertaining, traveled abroad, and indulged their wives and children. Occasionally the city was reminded that some patriarch's acquaintance with culture and gentility was rather recent—like Simeon Reed's wretched collection of maudlin canvasses foisted on him by an unscrupulous German art dealer; or some eclectic architectural disaster rising in the neighborhood that melded late Roman, neo-Gothic, Renaissance and brownstone —but for the most part they espoused quiet good taste. They, and their less affluent neighbors, supported churches, maintained schools both public and private, organized a circulating library as early as 1864, sustained theaters from 1858 and a symphony after 1879.

Portland had grown up, right from the beginning, as

Big Three of the OSN: Simeon G. Reed (left), John C. Ainsworth, and Robert R. Thompson (right).

a stable community—the kind men dreamed of building, and so rarely wrought, when they sought a new life in the West. In time it would be transcended by Seattle both in population and economic importance— possibly because it was outhustled, or maybe just as a victim of geographic determinism—but one suspects that Portland, given a choice between placing first or maintaining its dignity, would opt for its dignity.

Portland's steady growth, conservative outlook, and solid economic foundation stand in stark contrast to the experience of other towns in the Northwest. Most grew by lunges, waiting for events that portended greatness, and then plunging into rapid growth and wild speculation. Some waited forever for the big opportunity; others found it only to lose it; some rode an economic seesaw for decades, making and losing fortunes several times over. The sensation was exhilarating, the excitement infectious, the profits incredible to the unscrupulous, and periodic collapses almost inevitable. Such was the case of Tacoma.

Tacoma was just another hopeful hamlet on the southern reach of the sound until July 1873, when the directors of Jay Cooke's Northern Pacific selected it as their western terminus. Rather than build to an existing town, have to buy station sites and right of way, and ultimately raise the land values of early speculators, Cooke and his associates planned to create their own town, wheeling and dealing from the ground floor, and thereby garner *all* the profits. There was some delay, however, in collecting them. Before merchants, settlers, and speculators scrambled in to hack back the forest and make each other rich, the Northern Pacific's financial structure fell apart. Tacoma languished for nearly a

decade, and even the completion of the transcontinental line in 1883 offered threat as well as promise, for Henry Villard presided at the driving of the golden spike, and Villard favored Portland. But Villard, too, had overextended himself. Tacoma's friends regained control of the line, bored the Stampede Pass Tunnel, and gave Tacoma direct access to the Inland Empire. "Tacoma is a town smitten by a boom of the boomiest," Rudyard Kipling reported to his British homefolks in 1889. The city became a worldwide port of call, shipping domestic wheat and lumber, transshipping rail and ocean cargoes, angling to challenge the dominance of San Francisco and Portland.

But the good times were not to last. By the 1890s, Seattle began to emerge as the dynamic center on the sound. Beaten, through no fault of its own, by a better

The bustling city of Tacoma, riding a tide of rising fortune in 1890.

Sloping to the shore, Seattle in 1880 seemed to focus on its waterfront. The sea trade that launched the city's prosperity has continued to keep its fortunes afloat.

combination of harbor and railroad, Tacoma could only wonder at the caprice of fortune, and settle down to the task of maintaining what it had gained.

But in the evolution of Northwest cities, somewhere between the seemingly inert stability of Portland and the artificial beginnings and erratic maturation of Tacoma, stands the phenomenon that was Seattle.

From the very beginning, Seattle was buoyant, enthusiastic, as though convinced that its position as the premier city of the Northwest was a foregone conclusion —and rather than wait complacently, everyone just scurried more to hurry up the inevitable. But despite some

assets—like magnificent deep-water moorages and enormous stands of accessible timber—there was a natural obstacle that should only have served to curb civic optimism. Seattle perched on a narrow shelf at the water's edge, cut off from the interior by the Cascades and isolated from any overland commerce. But for more than forty years, until rails finally provided the inland link, Seattle remained ebullient and exciting, confident in the future.

Puget Sound began to stir with activity at mid-century when a few entrepreneurs began to capitalize on San Francisco's penchant for self-immolation. That city

mill to cut lumber for the California market. Because it was good for the future, Maynard moved his stakes and yielded to Yesler a choice piece of low-bank waterfront needed for the operation of a sawmill, then organized local help to construct a building for the machinery. The mill became a lodestone for activity on the sound, attracting the nucleus of population that would become a city. Maynard would continue his philanthropy to encourage settlement, donating land and material for churches and a blacksmith shop, and selling cheap to any and all who might contribute to the town's growth —until he had little left. He complicated matters for his family—and future titleholders—by giving his second wife the claim he had first filed in the name of his first wife, whom he then divorced. The resultant litigation outlived Maynard by half a century.

Maynard's selfless overoptimism was rare, but others came with ideas and energy that attracted attention and commerce. One of those who attracted considerable attention was John Pennell, who arrived from San Francisco in 1861 and within a month was running a combination bar, dance hall, and bordello. With a little music, some Indian girls he tidied up and anglicized with calico and perfume, Pennell began drawing lonesome loggers from all over Puget Sound. Built on the sawdust from the mills that was dumped in the bay shallows (extremely aromatic when the tide was out), Pennell's "Sawdust Pile" drew good crowds, and only mild approbation from an increasingly civilized community.

While Pennell met an immediate need, the growing city lacked a vital ingredient: for men with respectable aspirations or staid upbringing, there were no women to marry. To meet the challenge rose Asa Mercer, the twenty-two-year-old president and sole lecturer of the recently founded university.* Mercer passed the hat to cover expenses and traveled to Lowell, Massachusetts, where he found eleven young ladies willing to gamble. His journey was an unqualified success; save for one girl who died, all were snatched into holy wedlock in short order. Flush with success, Mercer proposed to go

burned six times in less than two years, and timber cut along the sound's shoreline and hauled south provided the lumber to rebuild each time. At the same time there appeared on the scene a doctor-turned-vagabond-merchant named David Maynard, on the lam from a dull wife and a boring Midwest practice. On the shores of Elliot Bay amid more conventional pioneers he set up a small store, appropriated a large piece of shoreline, and began a lifelong career as Seattle's chief benefactor, civic developer, and one-man chamber of commerce.

Before he was even settled, Maynard met Henry Yesler, a businessman with a plan for erecting a steam

---

*Mercer's efforts probably grew out of his own boredom. When the territorial legislature provided for the university in a fit of public spirit, it failed to recognize the dearth of qualified young scholars. In its early years the university served the community best as a grade school and high school.

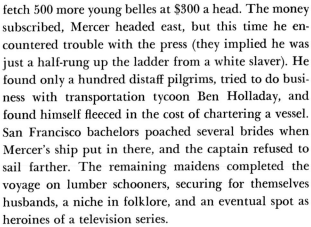

Asa Shinn Mercer, university president and merchant in young ladies of good virtue.

Dr. David Maynard, who practiced more civic development than medicine.

fetch 500 more young belles at $300 a head. The money subscribed, Mercer headed east, but this time he encountered trouble with the press (they implied he was just a half-rung up the ladder from a white slaver). He found only a hundred distaff pilgrims, tried to do business with transportation tycoon Ben Holladay, and found himself fleeced in the cost of chartering a vessel. San Francisco bachelors poached several brides when Mercer's ship put in there, and the captain refused to sail farther. The remaining maidens completed the voyage on lumber schooners, securing for themselves husbands, a niche in folklore, and an eventual spot as heroines of a television series.

By 1865 part of Seattle's population had begun to outgrow the Pennell variety B-girl entertainments. Henry Yesler, whose fortune had grown with the city, built a public hall to accommodate the more conventional entertainments—lecturers, minstrel shows, musi-

cians—that began finding their way to Seattle. In 1871 a touring troupe brought the first professional play *(Uncle Tom's Cabin)*, initiating a succession of dramatic appearances that by the 1890s had ranged from John L. Sullivan (!) to Sarah Bernhardt.

By the last decade of the century, Seattle had grown to a city of 80,000, supported by timber industries and commerce in the harbor. And while everyone hoped fervently for the rail connection that would allow the city to unlimber its fiscal muscle, Seattle had also grown schizophrenic. Part of the town was devoted to legitimate business, the Protestant ethic, and stability; but south of Yesler Way, on what was called Skid Road, the philosophic descendants of John Pennell were keeping alive Seattle's reputation as the openest town in the Northwest.

Emblematic of Skid Road were the "box houses," and the top box house operator was John Considine. Box

With stone edifices and busy streets, Portland realized the aspirations of every western city.

houses were cheap theaters that offered alcohol and women (both of questionable character), with stage entertainment relegated to the bottom of the bill. Regarded as the breeding ground of crime in the city, they were the perennial target of every reform movement. John Considine was viewed in much the same light as his houses; he bribed police, circumvented efforts to close his business, fleeced customers, even killed a man —of course, in self defense. But John Considine was a man caught up in Seattle and its future, and his career of pandering to frontier tastes began to decline and change with the metamorphosis of Seattle.

As the end of the century neared, subtle but powerful changes began to alter the face and life of Seattle: the physical shape of the city had already been altered, as the hills were reduced hydraulically and the waterfront was extended; a great fire in 1889 leveled the entire business district, and from the ashes rose brick and stone edifices that bespoke permanence and stability; the arrival of the Great Northern Railway in 1893 raised Seattle from a boisterously hopeful town crowing for attention to a major center for commerce and industry; the Klondike rush of 1897 generated enormous new revenues and established the city as the mercantile center for Alaska.

Through all this, both sides of Yesler Way struggled for ascendancy, Considine periodically succumbing to the demands of the city fathers for propriety. And finally it was Seattle's new role and its future that beat Considine—he went over to the enemy. He began to traffic in moving pictures, progressing to booking legitimate vaudeville, finally establishing himself as a booking agent on a national scale—a member in good standing of Seattle's establishment.

Seattle's long metamorphosis and final emergence as the hub city of the Northwest, surpassing Portland in population and commerce early in the century, mirrored the aspirations and efforts of a hundred communities in the Fourth Corner. By a variety of behavior, but a similarity of goal, some grew, some died, some lay stagnant, beneficiaries or victims of luck, geography, and persistence.

CHAPTER 20

MAVERICK POLITICS

Vocal farmers and discontent laborers, suffragettes and temperance zealots—all in the vanguard of nineteenth-century reform

URING THE LAST TWO DECADES of the nineteenth century, the Northwest underwent extraordinary changes. The railroads arrived; cities sprouted and grew—some like weeds; commerce and industry thrived. In mines, mills, and forests, on farmland and fishing ground, men pursued a day's wage and hoped for fortune. Prosperity shone in rising wages, land values, and profits. The new industrial age had arrived.

Change meant problems. Government was unresponsive to the people's needs, sometimes because the machinery wasn't there, sometimes because businessmen and entrepreneurs were at the controls and manipulated them to serve themselves. Men who flocked west to make farms found much of the best land locked up in the grants given the railroads. They found themselves forced to compete for industrial jobs. Those who did start farms were at the mercy of marketers and railroads, who set the prices and shipping rates. Increasing numbers of people felt regional prosperity, such as it was, had been wrung from their hides. Change meant problems, problems called for more change.

When change was slow in coming, some sought it in the streets: government by fiat. Others withdrew and tried to live outside the economy in utopias of various design. But, for the most part, northwesterners sought change through politics, and ultimately it was orderly political change that tolled a new era.

The era of political agitation and reform known as Populism had its roots in the agrarian movements that emerged in the latter half of the nineteenth century. In the Northwest, farmers began to organize for self-protection and profit as early as 1853, when a cooperative was formed in Yamhill County, Oregon. In 1860 the Oregon State Agricultural Society was founded, and about that same time chapters of the Farmers' Union or Farmers' Alliances began to appear. In some instances the members of these associations shared equipment and pooled their resources to build cooperative storage elevators and warehouses, but primarily they sought, by their collective strength, to acquire the political influence that would enable them to correct the financial abuses of shippers, marketers, and suppliers. But these groups were largely local, and their effectiveness—if any—was only temporary. In 1873 malcontents in the Northwest achieved a broader alliance with the appearance of the Grange, an agrarian organization of national scope that opposed absentee landlords, trusts, and high freight rates, while often supporting woman suffrage, prohibition, and nativism. In less than two years 140 chapters sprang up, and although the national Grange collapsed in 1876, the local units persisted to provide a foundation for reform agitation.

Although farmers formed the vanguard of the movement, through the decades of the 1880s and 1890s, the mood of discontent with government and business would reach into other elements of society, the demands for reform growing more strident with each addition. The urban workers who retained their aspirations to upward mobility—spiritual counterparts of the small farmers—joined the Knights of Labor to agitate against cheap immigrant labor and legislation which favored

When politics failed, solutions were sometimes found in the streets. During Seattle's anti-Chinese riot of 1886, the army battled a mob and justice took a beating.

A crew of Washington loggers pose stiffly for the camera in their roughly finished bunkhouse. It was common practice to deduct rent for such quarters from a man's pay.

monopolistic business. The Farmers' Alliances, espousing aims similar to those of the Grange, blossomed in the Northwest to challenge what they regarded as the abuses of "corporate tyranny": railroad monopolies that charged ruinous rates; political chicanery that exempted corporate holdings, leaving the burden of taxation on farm land; banking barons who stood above the public good, manipulating credit for their own benefit; and land swindlers who placed the public domain in the hands of speculators.

These various organizations, recognizing that they might have a common goal, met in Salem, Oregon in 1889 to pool their wealth and their resources in the formation of the Union party. Granges, Knights of Labor, Farmers' Alliances, and Prohibitionists (the latter were always good for a sizeable bloc of votes in exchange for a dry plank in the platform) formed the first

regional coalition of any size, and despite a poor showing in the 1890 elections, the example of their cooperation portended the future.

That future coalesced in 1892 when national elements of the agrarian groups and other dissidents met in Omaha, Nebraska to form the Populist party. Advocating the traditional agrarian issues—unlimited coinage of silver at sixteen ounces of silver to one of gold (to ease credit), a graduated income tax, return of the public domain to open settlement, and federal ownership of the railroads—the party lured legislative reformers by promising the Australian (secret) ballot, initiative and referendum, and direct election of U.S. senators.

In the Northwest, the constant agitation by the multitude of small political groups, while not yielding sweeping reforms, nonetheless brought public attention to

A Washington threshing crew pauses with their bagged harvest. Farmers provided the grass-roots support for much of the political reform that swept the Northwest.

the problems the Populists sought to rectify. Assailed by a constant barrage of rhetoric and leaflets, citizens learned of corruption in government, injustice in labor, the evils of drink and of suffrage for men only, the merits of the single tax, the necessity for free silver,* and countless other causes. In an era when Senator John H. Mitchell of Oregon could flaunt his venal failure to serve his constituency by stating that "Ben Holladay's politics are my politics, and what Ben Holladay wants, I want," there was no dearth of scandal to raise righteous indignation. Add to that the fact that the economy was

depressed, that Populist clubs had popped up like toadstools after a summer rain, that the planks in the Populist platform should appeal to a growing region rife with emergent—and expectant—capitalists; the reformers must have waited in giddy anticipation of the election.

It was a strong third-party challenge—the party's presidential candidate, James B. Weaver, polled 30 percent of the popular vote nationwide—but the Populist showing in the Northwest was not convincing. Although Weaver carried Idaho (the state's leading industry was silver mining), the Populists could not make significant inroads into the Republican legislative bastions.

However, prospects for the 1896 election started to improve almost immediately. In 1892 the economy began to slide, and in less than a year it had collapsed completely. Nationwide, banks shut down, homes and

---

*"Free silver" referred to the unlimited issuance of money based on silver. This would result in more money in circulation, easier credit (a Populist goal), inflation (also a Populist aim, in that it made repayment of borrowed money easier), and a market for the silver lying in western mines that was otherwise valueless.

Discontent in the mining industry sometimes boiled over into civil turmoil, as in Wallace, Idaho, where troops turned out in 1892 to cool civilian passions.

farms were foreclosed, unemployment skyrocketed. Now, the Populists could prove that something was drastically wrong with the conduct of government, and there was a ready pool of angry victims eager to join the ranks.

The general depression settled down over the Northwest, but the region disappointed Populist expectations and refused to crash completely. Idaho, heavily dependent on silver, suffered enormously when the mines closed; in the rest of the Northwest agricultural prices dropped by half, some banks and businesses closed, and wages dropped. But the region defied the national pattern: most farms carried only small mortgages, and some estimate foreclosures at less than one percent; the number of commercial failures ran only slightly ahead of normal percentages; and while wages dropped, most of those previously employed remained so. The bene-

ficiaries of a diversified economy and their own sensible investment and growth, the people of the Northwest, for the most part, simply pulled in their heads to wait out the storm.

There was suffering and discontent—enough, in fact, to spawn urban demonstrations in Portland and Seattle. A contingent of "Coxey's Army," a ragged band of unemployed, sought to convince Congress "to do something" about their plight by marching across the nation, hijacking trains where possible. But the depression was not profound enough to create the broad support the Populists needed. Lacking the strength to win independently, they sought, and found, fusion with the Democrats.

In the election of 1896—with Populists and Democrats arrayed behind William Jennings Bryan, reform, and free silver, against William McKinley, the gold

In 1899, discontented miners dynamited the Bunker Hill smelter in the Coeur d'Alene.

standard, and business as usual—the Northwest split fairly evenly. Bryan carried Washington and Idaho, the "Popocrats" a host of state and local offices. Oregon split, but McKinley and the Republicans emerged victorious there. In light of later developments, these results will point up the curious behavior of the Northwest voter.

D URING THE 1880s AND 1890s, while reformers worked for political solutions to the problems of a region learning to cope with the modern industrial era, other segments of society found they could not wait for the millennium and applied their own solutions. The least inhibited answers were to be found in the field of labor relations.

In Washington during the eighties, labor enjoyed an enviable status. Compared to the rest of the nation, wages in mining, lumbering, and agriculture were high. Miners worked only an eight-hour day, while a ten-hour day prevailed in the mills. Unions in both industries offered a measure of security (though a man could still be fired for union activity), and at mid-decade both Seattle and Tacoma boasted prolabor mayors. It was too good to last.

The railroad companies had begun bringing Chinese to America in large numbers after the Civil War when it was discovered that they worked harder, longer, and better for less money than anybody else. This was fine: it made construction cheaper, it relieved the white worker of the dull and difficult tasks, and it gave every bar bum and loafer somebody to feel superior to. But finally the railroads were completed; beginning in the mid-1880s a horde of hardworking, thrifty fellows appeared in Seattle and Tacoma, willing to work twelve-hour days for lousy wages—and that looked like a better deal to the mine and mill owners.

The howl raised by West Coast labor was heard in Congress, and the Chinese were forbidden further immigration. But that did not solve the problem of those already here. When Congress turned a deaf ear to expulsion, labor set out to solve the problem itself. At Issaquah, for instance, some Chinese hop pickers were murdered by a band of whites and Indians, and a jury acquitted the killers. In September of 1885, Dan Cronin, a functionary of the Knights of Labor, called a meeting in Seattle, where it was decided that the only solution was to throw the Chinese out.

Now, where to throw them? Tacoma stole a march on Seattle by pulling hundreds of Chinese from their beds,

loading them in boxcars, and shipping them toward Portland, then burning their homes. When the Seattle Sinophobes tried the same tactic, the city fathers foiled the attempt by having the president declare martial law. In less than three months they tried again, loading the Chinese aboard the *Queen of the Pacific*. The army arrived, snatched the victims back (196 opted to be deported rather than face the mob again), and in an ensuing melee one logger was killed. This, and criminal conspiracy charges against the mob's leaders, served to cool Seattle's nativist ardor.

But laborers did not confine their violence to the Chinese. In 1886 miners belonging to the Knights of Labor struck the Newcastle Mine on Lake Washington; when miners affiliated with the Miner's Union refused to walk out, too, a brawl ensued which killed one man and injured nine others. In 1899 miners striking the Coeur d'Alene district of Idaho over unsafe working conditions and low pay engaged in a bitter, protracted struggle with company-hired detectives and strikebreakers that culminated in the dynamiting of the Bunker Hill concentrator, a declaration of martial law, and the indiscriminate jailing of guilty and innocent alike.

Unfortunately, these were not isolated incidents. All over the Northwest and the entire nation, for that matter, labor disputes were erupting into violence [see chapter 21]—the expression of impatient, even desperate, men caught in a period of economic, technological, and social change.

In the midst of these two decades, which saw cities burgeoning, reformers clamoring for redress in the political arena, the economy rising and falling, and working folks experimenting with solutions to their immediate woes, a quiet counterpoint was being played in the Northwest by groups who also were certain they had the final answer for what ailed society.

The dream of the perfect society, where man can pursue all that is good in life, free from want and fear, in harmony with himself and his fellows, is not a new one. But in nineteenth-century America, men set out to prove it, and during the latter half of the century some experimental utopian communities began to find their way to the Northwest. By a variety of methods, and with a broad range of success, entire planned communities were built to test man's perfectability; significantly, the most durable lasted barely a generation.

The earliest and most successful experiment was Aurora. Philosophically a communist settlement, it was administered by Dr. William Kiel, who forged a thriving community of farms and businesses. Unfortunately, Kiel began to lose his idealism, diverting a large share of Aurora's income to himself, and eventually deteriorating to a drunken autocrat. Upon his death the town abandoned its communal pretensions and joined the mainstream of Oregon life.

Other communities would rise: The Puget Sound Cooperative Colony at Port Angeles—it was dedicated to "free land, free water, free lights, free libraries, exemption from all taxes and rents. All profits paid to the colonists"—disappeared in two years. The community that called itself Equality, at Edison, Washington, asked only that members practice the principles of Christ and complete individuality, neither of which served to eliminate the bickering that brought its downfall. The Freethinkers that moved into Silverton, Oregon, to practice rationalism and atheism, found themselves amiably tolerated by their more conventional neighbors. "Home" was the site on Puget Sound selected by a group of free spirits who built near each other but presumably refused to form a community.

The really extraordinary aspect of all these experimental villages has little to do with their own efforts, but rather with their acceptance and treatment by neighboring towns. With only minor exceptions (notably the intention of some Tacomans to avenge McKinley's assassination by an avowed anarchist with a raid on Home, until cooler heads in Tacoma prevailed), Northwesterners neither meddled with, nor attempted to suppress the private lives and philosophies of their idealistic neighbors.

THE SOCIAL AND POLITICAL REFORMATION that began with the agrarian antecedents of Populism culminated more than a decade into the new century in a program of legislation that came to be known as the Progressive movement. William Allen White claimed that the Progressives "caught the Populists in swimming and stole all their clothing except the frayed undergarments of free silver." Although failing to mention that the Populists had already drowned in the Democratic pond they jumped into in 1896, White

The Noble Experiment, 1900: Members gather in front of the "Equality" colony in Washington.
The sign displayed advertises their newspaper, "Industrial Freedom."

pointed up the similarity in basic objectives: the elimination of corruption in government; reform of the legislative process to permit greater citizen participation; and governmental intervention to correct social and economic problems.

In most respects the Northwest was in the national forefront of progressive legislation, and Oregon to such a degree that the essential reforms in the legislative process became known as the Oregon System. Largely responsible for the traditionally conservative state's position in the vanguard of the Progressive movement was William S. U'ren, a former leader in the Populist party, whose great talents as a practical politician seemed somehow out of character with a persistent advocacy of the single tax. The essential elements of U'ren's reform program, indeed the genesis of the entire Oregon System, were the initiative and referendum. By this means, the voters could create their own legislation,

unhampered by corruptible and self-serving politicians —and, incidentally, because they were good and intelligent people, they would doubtless pass the single tax law he could not get any of his associates to consider.

Support for direct legislation was strong among Oregon's farmers, most reform-minded citizens, and every crackpot who had a proposal the legislature refused to entertain. But even total popular support was of little value; what U'ren needed was an amendment to the state constitution, a measure that lacked support in the legislature—until Jonathan Bourne, a veteran manipulator of pro-business legislation and minion of the railroad interests decided he wanted to be a senator. Bourne needed allies to give him the seat, and U'ren traded his support for passage of the initiative amendment in 1899. The tools of reform were at hand.

Using the initiative and referendum, reformers created the other major elements of the Oregon System:

231

William S. U'ren, Progressive leader who fought for the initiative and referendum.

the Direct Primary Law in 1904, and the recall amendment in 1908. With these laws the public could elect whom it wanted, create and pass legislation in spite of him, and toss him out of office if he continued in his arrogance. Using their new power, the people of Oregon provided for direct election of senators in 1908, granted women the vote in 1912, passed a Workmen's Compensation Act in 1913, and imposed prohibition on themselves in 1914. But they never passed U'ren's single tax.

Between 1902 and 1915, Oregon voters kept progressive men in the governor's chair—George Chamberlain from 1902 to 1909, and Oswald West from 1909 to 1915 —who, between them, rammed through countless pieces of social legislation reforming prison practices, labor laws, business and banking regulations, and social welfare benefits. And all this from the state that roughly a decade earlier had gone for McKinley.

In Idaho the Progressive movement trailed Oregon. Since it lacked the initiative and referendum until 1912, significant reforms like woman suffrage in 1905 and the direct primary in 1907 were the product of legislative, rather than popular, efforts. Probably the most significant contribution Idaho made to the Progressive movement was the election to the U.S. Senate of William E. Borah.

From the time of his election in 1907 until his death in office in 1940, Borah labored on the national level as a Progressive. Besides sponsoring the legislation which created the income tax and the bill which provided for direct election of senators, he was instrumental in the formation of the Department of Labor. But Idaho, despite its dalliance with progressive reforms, was a conservative state; for the electorate at home, Borah wore a conservative mask, only serving, never meddling. Idaho, in its own unpredictable way, seemed to like that.

In Washington State progressive reform met with less immediate enthusiasm than in Oregon or Idaho. Like Idaho, Washington lacked the initiative and referendum until 1912, and although legislation was passed, success was usually the product of hard work and guile rather than enthusiasm. Child labor laws were passed in 1903, a railroad regulatory board was created in 1905, the direct primary provided for in 1907, and woman suffrage was ratified in 1910, largely through the efforts of Abigail Scott Duniway, sister of the editor of the *Portland Oregonian* and the Northwest's leading feminist. But the most important single measure by Washington legislators was the Workmen's Compensation Act of 1911. The most comprehensive program of its day, the bill provided for state control of a central, collective fund, and (following a court test) established the right of the state to regulate industry.

T HE NORTHWEST had faced the challenge of a new era, albeit obliquely at times, and wrought changes in the form and function of government that provided a model for the rest of the nation. The Oregon System of direct government, the creation of legislation to regulate business and protect the individual, and governmental assumption of responsibility for social welfare provide the substance of the Northwest's response to challenge. But the picture would never have been complete, nor even natural, without the violent mavericks and gentle idealists that also sought to contribute to a solution. For it is a country of effervescent vitality, nurturing independence and the primacy of the individual, transcending the ordinary and the self-contented.

Tidy farms checker the fertile valley of the Yakima near Cle Elum, Washington, with 9,470-foot Mount Stuart rising in the distance.

A sea of ripening wheat reaches across the rolling high prairie of eastern Washington, mocking Nathaniel Wyeth's assessment that it offered "little prospect" for the tillers of the soil.

The winter wheat crop and dry-farming methods that opened the Palouse country of Washington continue today to provide the mainstay of that productive agricultural region.

*Purse seiners still ply
Northwest waters, harvesting
the annual salmon run.*

*Engaged in a controversial but essential industry, a logging truck
is loaded in the Northern Cascades, framed by the Monte Cristo Peaks.*

*Dominating the skies, even creating its own mountains, the copper
smelter at Anaconda labors in Montana's leading industry.*

Boeing 747 Superjets being assembled in the facility
at Everett, Washington—an industry of such magnitude
that business fluctuations are felt statewide.

At Port Angeles, Northwest timber is loaded for Japan—an export pattern
that is beginning to have a detrimental effect on American wood supplies.

CHAPTER 21

GREEN TIDE OF TIMBER

*The growth of a prosperous lumber industry, which now faces
the knotty question of how to cut the forests and have them, too*

WHEN DAVID DOUGLAS, the Scottish naturalist, visited Oregon in 1825 and gave his name to the imposing fir trees of the coastal region, he could little imagine the wealth—or the controversy—those firs and the neighboring pines, spruces, and hemlocks would generate in the years to come. Except for sections of the Columbia Plateau, Harney Basin, and Snake River plain, trees are the dominant feature of the Pacific Northwest. Even after nearly 100 years of heavy logging, the Northwest forests (including western Montana) still cover about 93 million acres.

Then, as now, the mainstay of these great forests was the Douglas-fir. Averaging 190 to 300 feet in height, with a girth of 10 to 15 feet after a growth of 150 years, the virgin tree produces a strong, soft, fine-grained, and durable wood that is ideal for building construction. Sometimes called the Oregon pine, Douglas-fir grows from the summit of the Cascades westward to the Pacific Ocean, and through the central mountain ranges of Idaho. The ponderosa, or yellow western pine, grows east of the Cascades at higher elevations, while Sitka spruce grows in the western coastal ranges. Idaho also hosts some of the largest and finest white pine stands in the United States plus extensive forests of yellow pine, western redcedar, larch, and hemlock—all of which can also be found competing with the Douglas-fir in the Cascades.

As the dominant physical feature of the Northwest, the forests also dominated the economy of the region for many years. From pioneer origins at coastal and river ports, the business of cutting and milling timber would grow to boom proportions by the turn of the century. The economic benefits were extraordinary: thousands of men were employed, railroads and ports bustled with the export trade, and cities grew and thrived on the tremendous influx of capital and population. But the bonanza also had a dark side of mindless exploitation that left whole forests ravaged, of illegal acquisition of public forest lands, and labor strife that tore towns apart.

Ultimately the industry, prodded by pressure from without and some instinct for self-preservation, began to make changes in timber management and cutting practices. The evolution was slow, the adjustments difficult, but the Northwest lumbering industry had to transcend the conspicuous consumption of the boom days to survive.

THE FIRST SAWMILL on record in the Northwest was constructed about 1828 on the Columbia at Camas, near present-day Vancouver, Washington, by Dr. John McLoughlin, chief factor of the Hudson's Bay Company. Demands on this waterpowered rig were small, because home consumption was slight, and the export market virtually nil. But the need for boards existed (trees in the Northwest, for the most part, were too big around for the log cabin construction typical of the eastern woodland frontier), and similar ventures followed. In 1844, W. H. H. Hunt tapped the energy of the river to power his mill at Astoria, and in 1847 the first sawmill on Puget Sound was constructed at Tumwater

*Rising from the lush floor of a western Cascade forest, tall sentinels
of the Northwest's most famous industry loom out of a self-created twilight.*

Falls. Henry Yesler acquired a measure of fame in 1852 by erecting the first steam sawmill on Puget Sound, at the anxious settlement called Seattle, while twenty miles to the south, at what became Tacoma, a Swede named Nicholas De Lin was building the mill that would insure him lasting fame—of a sort.

One of Tacoma's first settlers, De Lin was industrious and energetic, cutting a half-million board feet in the first year of his new mill's operation. Much of this lumber was shipped to San Francisco on the brig *George Emory*, which only served to spread the growing notoriety of De Lin's boards. It seems they bore a trademark. As one early settler writing home described it, the De Lin sawmill "had a fault, apparently beyond cure, of turning out boards thicker at one end than the other, and sometimes thicker in the middle than at either end." It is not recorded whether De Lin ever cured his mill of its peculiar habit, but its reputation still survived in 1923, when a Northwest lumberman, Robert Vinnedge, complained that from the demands of some of his eastern customers for reinspection of shipments, it appeared they thought De Lin's sawmill was still cutting boards.

During the 1850s the little mills of the Northwest, especially those on Puget Sound, began to find buyers for their wares beyond the strictly local markets. Despite the disconcerting cargo of the *George Emory,* other ships began hauling to the burgeoning market in California. The *G. W. Kendall,* dispatched in 1851 to get ice to water the drinks of thirsty miners, only to have its skipper report that "water don't freeze in Puget Sound," took on an even more profitable cargo of timber. And while the coastal trade in milled boards grew at a staggering rate, shipments of naval spars to France, England, Spain, and China established at least a limited foreign market. Through the 1860s and 1870s demand grew, and mills proliferated and modernized until by 1880 outfits like the Port Blakely Mill Company could boast a plant of eighty saws, seven engines, and electric lighting. In that year, 160 million board feet of lumber were cut for foreign and domestic sale; the Northwest had found *its* gold mine.

But the real growth in the industry occurred with the arrival of the railroads in the mid-1880s. The federal land grants to the Northern Pacific Railroad, and to a lesser degree the Oregon and California line, formed the basis for some of the largest timber holdings in the country. For the railroads, these lands were doubly valuable: they first could sell the land, and then collect freight charges on the lumber shipped. Competing with a dynamic and profitable pine industry in the South, the Northwest railroads launched a massive advertising campaign to court eastern investment. The railroads played their ace in 1890 by reducing freight rates; to eastern lumbermen and investors, it was too good to believe, and the stampede was on.

For the next three decades the railroads would play to the timber interests the Jekyll-and-Hyde role that they had refined on western farmers. After encouraging purchase and settlement, they began to exact ruinous freight rates, to the point where Washington fir could not compete with wood from St. Paul even in Montana, despite an initial-cost advantage of one-half to two-thirds over the rest of the country. Oregon, the beneficiary of rate juggling on the Union Pacific, could compete in Denver, Salt Lake, and Omaha, but with the exception of cedar shingles, Washington found profits severely eroded by shipping costs.

But the railroads had worked their deceptive magic: by 1890 Northwest timbermen were cutting a billion feet annually—almost a 700 percent increase in only a decade. The temporarily low rates, and the abundance of fine virgin timber standing on the public domain, brought out speculators and investors in droves, and spawned the most corrupt episode in the history of public land acquisition.

Very early the federal government had tried to control cutting on public lands by imposing a "stumpage fee" of $2.50 per 1,000 feet of timber felled, but the loggers just cut and ran. In 1878 the Timber and Stone Act made cutting on public land illegal and sought to close some loopholes in the Homestead Act that were being used for shady acquisitions. The price for a maximum of 160 acres was set at $2.50 per acre, but the act only opened the way to further abuses because it stipulated no residency requirements. Timber interests simply brought in all their employees, shiploads of sailors, and any idlers they could sweep up, had them file on a quarter section (paying with company money), and then sign over title in exchange for a few dollars and a night on the town. By this and other equally blatant evasions, private firms amassed huge domains.

With his stumps cut high and undercut complete, one Washington logger really gets into his work.

Darius Kinsey, photographer of the Northwest woods, caught this logging train about to pull out with a full load—four cars to the train, one log to the car.

It could happen because it was good for everyone immediately concerned: small-time locators sold to speculators, who in turn sold to investors, who cut the timber and then abandoned the ravaged land rather than pay taxes on it. Everybody made a profit, and local merchants, farmers, craftsmen, and laborers never objected because logging operations stimulated a whole town's economy. The only possible victim was something nebulous called "future generations," and that did not stack up to much when there was money to be made right now.

Not all acquisitions were illegal. The largest single purchase of timberlands in the Northwest occurred in 1900, when railroad magnate James J. Hill sold 900,000 acres of land-grant forest in Oregon and Washington to Frederick Weyerhaeuser at $6.00 an acre. Building on this foundation, Weyerhaeuser bought Idaho land grants from the Southern Pacific Railroad to form the Clearwater Timber Company. Additional purchases brought his holdings to 2 million acres, and such a domination of Northwest forest lands that a contemporary was moved to comment that "pretty much everything outside of the government forest reserve is tributary of Weyerhaeuser. He may not own it, his name may not appear on record anywhere, but it is under his domi-

nation. Such is true of Oregon's great forest lands also."

During the first decade of the new century a great deal of the Northwest's forests were being consolidated in the hands of a very few men. By 1913 Weyerhaeuser owned over 26 percent of the privately held timber in Washington, and the Northern Pacific another 20 percent; in Oregon, Weyerhaeuser and the Southern Pacific owned over 22 percent; and the Northern Pacific controlled almost 30 percent of the private timber in Montana. Thus, these three large owners—Weyerhaeuser, Southern Pacific, and Northern Pacific—controlled 237 billion board feet of standing timber, while some 17,000 small owners shared the remaining 205 billion board feet between them. It was the era of the timber barons, and they wielded immense power.

In 1914, about 55 percent of the payrolls in the Northwest derived directly from the lumber industry. This singular dependence of such a large proportion of the populace on one industry, and the goodwill of a few titans in that industry, bred a number of problems. Norman H. Clark, in his book *Milltown*, argues convincingly that bitter class consciousness and rivalries grew out of the arrogant paternalism and contempt shown laborers by the large companies. In logging camps it was not only common practice to deduct from a worker's salary for room, board, and tools (all dispersed by the company at their rates), but there were standing Weyerhaeuser rules against liquor, weapons, conversation at mealtime, and thermometers in camp (what they don't know can't hurt them) which were strictly enforced. The threat of unemployment was used to keep employees obedient and servile; George Long, for instance, a Weyerhaeuser functionary, arbitrarily fired workers in 1908 as a warning to others whom Long thought were becoming "too independent."

Compounding the workingman's humiliation was the economic instability of the entire industry. Timber demand and prices were extremely sensitive to any change in the rest of the country: a minor depression, a drought that slackened demand, and the price of timber would drop, leaving men temporarily out of work; a large fire or flood in a major city would instantly create a demand, and the price would jump, sending every big mill and small "gyppo" outfit into a flurry of overproduction to cash in, and the glutted market would drop again. While employment remained fairly steady, and wages at a decent level, laborers in all branches of the lumber industry always waited on tenterhooks, at the mercy of a mercurial market and the benevolence (which they were never allowed to forget) of their employers.

Life in the camps and mills was hard and dangerous. A logger could fall while topping a tree, be crushed by falling timber, be cut in two by a thrashing cable if a choke slipped, or find himself speared by the jagged end of a tree that "barber-chaired" and kicked back through him as it fell. In the mills, high-speed blades provided another dangerous diversion. Shingle weavers, so called because of the way they stacked the cedar shingles as they cut them from long bolts, were readily identified by their missing fingers. They cut at blurring speed, playing tag with the blades and inevitably missing their timing. The result of such a slip was the loss of a finger, a hand, even an arm.

All of these factors combined to generate strong animosities among the laboring force, and when labor disputes arose, the anger often boiled over into violence. The shingle weavers, under the aegis of the American Federation of Labor, formed the first effective craft

union in the lumber industry, one which led the way toward organizing workers in the mill towns and logging camps. When the organizational efforts faltered in 1914, the more militant Industrial Workers of the World became the spearhead. Big Bill Haywood's "Wobblies" made no bones about where they stood: "The question of 'right' and 'wrong' do not concern us"; workers should "take possession of the earth and machinery of production and abolish the wage system." Obviously trouble was in store.

One of the bloodiest episodes occurred in Everett, Washington, in 1916. The A. F. of L.'s shingle weavers were out on strike when the Wobblies joined in uninvited. After a boatload of forty-one Wobblies were met at the dock by armed deputies, taken out of town and beaten bloody with clubs and ax handles, a fresh batch of about 250 zealots was dispatched from Seattle on the steamer Verona. Again a posse met the ship at the waterfront, but this time shooting erupted. Two deputies and at least five demonstrators were killed, and another fifty persons injured. The IWW claimed that they were unarmed and that the deputies had shot each other in the crossfire, but the state nonetheless charged seventy-four Wobblies with murder. After a prolonged trial, not one was convicted. The incident was typical of confrontations between an insistent union and equally intransigent employers.

Public opinion briefly sided with the IWW but that support vanished when the A. F. of L. joined the Wobblies to shut down Pacific coast mills and logging camps during World War I. Trying to take advantage of the enormous demand for wood to pressure some promises from the companies, the unions succeeded only in antagonizing everyone. Branded as traitors, the unions found themselves challenged by the Loyal Legion of Loggers and Lumbermen, a "patriotic" company union, organized with the government's blessing, that nonetheless managed to get an eight-hour day. The eclipse of the IWW in the Northwest came in 1919 in Centralia, Washington, when an Armistice Day parade erupted into a donnybrook between Wobblies and parading American Legionaires. Two Legion members were killed and later that night one of the Wobblies, himself a veteran, was taken from jail, castrated, shot, and hanged. Other members of the IWW were convicted of murder and given long sentences.

Great log rafts wait their turn in the mills, surrounding the lumber schooners snugged up to the docks of Port Blakely, which in turn wait to fill their holds with Northwest wood.

The hostility and conflict that characterized the early years of unionism within the industry did not disappear with the IWW. Bad feeling between labor and management, as well as shortsighted contention between various factions of labor, prevented anything even approximating lasting settlement and equanimity from being achieved until well into the twentieth century. Even the industry-wide strike of 1935, which won union recognition, failed to achieve a standard contract throughout the industry, due to internal union bickering, and reintroduced militant radicalism because of a nonconciliatory attitude by some levels of management. To quote Vernon Jensen, "The bitterness which developed [out of the 1935 strike], seriously jeopardized worker unity for many years, and gave an unhappy direction to labor-employer relations in the industry."

STEWART HOLBROOK tells the story of Clement Adams Bradbury, who set out in 1847 to cut a tree near Astoria. Making his undercut close to the ground, he found the notch filled with a "copious flow of pitch that would nigh fill a hogshead barrel." Discouraged, he quit the tree, but according to local observers Bradbury soon became "one of the best axmen and loggers along the river"; he learned to cut his stumps high.

Waste, in one form or another, was the overriding habit of the business; and cures, if the necessity was recognized, came only by fits and starts. Every logger in the Northwest "learned to cut his stumps high," and the waste was appalling. Trees were sometimes cut twenty feet from the ground, and a quarter of the good wood from a log was often left on the ground. The mills of the period used wide rotary saws that turned half the log into sawdust, and tons of slab and mill ends were burned as waste. Logs were cut in random lengths, ignoring standards of grade and size demanded in the marketplace. After the turn of the century mechanical improvements like the band saw began to reduce waste; the introduction of the donkey engine, spar pole, and high-line rigging made it possible to swing logs out of the forest with less damage to young growth; and the West Coast Lumberman's Association, formed in 1911, introduced standards in pricing and grading.

But the stumps were still cut high, and nomadic lumbermen still left devastated, cutover areas of bleached slash and dead stumps in their wake. Logged areas continued to be abandoned to avoid taxes, unless they showed promise as mineral or town sites, and no thought was ever given to restoring the land for future harvest.

Reforestation was further discouraged by the likes of Senator Hayburn of Idaho, who dredged up the old adage that "the plow follows the ax," although much logged land in the Northwest was too acid to be arable. He even shrugged off the ravages of forest fires with the same line of reasoning.

Forest fires, started mainly by careless campers, picnickers, and loggers, were generally regarded rather cavalierly by everyone except the victims. In 1903, after losing thousands of acres of timber in the Yacalt burn of 1902, Weyerhaeuser devised legislation providing for cooperative fire controls, and requested Gifford Pinchot's federal Bureau of Forestry to advise him on management of his holdings. The result was that Weyerhaeuser lands not only experienced a reformation in fire prevention methods, but began soil quality and forest growth studies. Thereafter, the concern with fire prevention led the way to a complete overhaul of forest management and conservation methods.

A case in point was the Bitterroot burn of Idaho in 1910. The summer had been hot, the forests dry as popcorn, and fire fighters had handled 3,000 minor blazes and 90 major ones in three months—but on August 20 the humidity dropped, the winds over the Bitterroot rose, and the forest fairly exploded with fire. Flames, sometimes racing at 70 miles per hour, swept across Idaho destroying the towns of Taft, Deborgia, Haugan, and Tuscor, killing 85 men and countless animals, and turning three million acres of white pine to charcoal. Senator Hayburn, who had airily regarded fire as a means for clearing land, saw his hometown of Wallace, Idaho, destroyed by the fire.

Gifford Pinchot, Teddy Roosevelt's evangelistic head of the Bureau of Forestry, had been campaigning for fire prevention and conservation practices since his appointment in 1898. Successful only in convincing Weyerhaeuser before 1910, the lesson of the Bitterroot burn finally prompted a response to his efforts. In 1911 the Weeks Law was enacted, appropriating $200,000 for fire protection of watersheds, and the individual states put up funds for fire patrols and equipment.

Before the end of T.R.'s administration, Pinchot not only increased the national forest reserves by 107 million acres (making it possible to protect the land from wasteful practices), but he managed to convince lumbermen that conservation was in their own best interests.

Port Angeles, Washington: Though the ships have changed with time, the logs abide.

Over the course of three decades, the concern he stirred would augur for change in forest management practices. The practice of clear-cutting came under scrutiny, and modifications were developed; fire protection was greatly increased in 1924 with the passage of the McNary-Clark bill; and the practice of holding lands for regrowth (something Weyerhaeuser had done very early), rather than abandoning them to unpaid taxes, was encouraged by Oregon and Washington. In 1930 the two states designated the land for reforestation and dropped taxes to a minimum.

But the most significant development came in 1941 when Weyerhaeuser, once again leading the way, established the first tree farm on a logged-over section of land on Grays Harbor. The concept of sustained harvest—taking no more than new growth had replenished—was born. By 1967 more than 32,000 tree farms were in operation.

Many ecologists feel that, laudable though the tree-farm program is, the crucial areas are not the small private holdings, but the industrial and government forests. If so, tree farms cannot really be the answer to a conservationist's prayer for the salvation of the great Northwest forest lands—but at least they are an obeisance in the right direction.

CHAPTER 22

THE NORTHWEST CORNUCOPIA

*Agriculture and fishing in a land blessed with rich soil,
abundant moisture, and waters teeming with salmon*

IN THE BEGINNING it was fur that brought men to the Northwest, first by sea and then by land, to skim off fortunes and depart. But there were other riches to be found, less obvious, less transitory, but of even greater value, that would draw and hold a permanent population; it was the land itself which did what otter and beaver could not.

America was a nation of farmers, and when they discovered the fertile soils, ample water, and rich grasses of the region, they came to sow and reap an ample bounty. Agriculture laid the foundations of economic life in the Northwest, and while mining and timber would, by their turns, generate tremendous excitement and wealth, farming endured—providing continuing and stabilizing support. From this quiet husbandry also grew a substantial grazing industry, since it was the cows and sheep of farmers that provided the example, and much of the brood stock, for herds and flocks that spread across the entire Fourth Corner of the continent. The early settlers found the waters of the Northwest as fecund as the soils; when means were found to market the enormous harvest of the annual salmon migrations, another industry was born.

The farming, grazing, and fishing industries that tapped the wealth of the land, though sometimes lacking the adventurous excitement of trapping or mining, were not plodding and predictable. Subject to all the vicissitudes of change in a maturing frontier, they expanded, collapsed, overproduced, alternately courted and battled railroads, advancing technology, the elements, and each other, and made not a few fortunes.

Although never individually achieving the singular dominance over the economy and society that timber did, they all contributed to support growth and to sustain it in times of recession.

THE CRADLE OF CIVILIZATION in the Northwest was the Willamette Valley. Across the Columbia from the mouth of the Willamette, John McLoughlin headquartered operations for the Hudson's Bay Company, encouraging his clerks and *voyageurs* to settle the rich bottomlands of the valley; and it was there that the missionary vanguard of Americans began their assault on British primacy in the territory. To McLoughlin it was merely a convenience that the Willamette Valley had probably the best land in the Northwest for diversified agriculture, providing HBC employees with vegetables and grains almost effortlessly. But to those first American emigrants it looked like home. Unlike the flat, treeless, semiarid prairies and plains of the mid-continent, which confounded and frustrated farmers for three-quarters of a century, the Willamette had regular rains, loam soil, trees and mountains close at hand, and an ample river flowing through. In every respect it was similar to the eastern woodland frontier they had left behind—only better, because it was free.

The familiar ring of enthusiasts' descriptions brought Americans flocking to the region, to reconstruct life as they had known it. It was subsistence agriculture, in which the home and fields produced everything needed for survival, and therefore farms were diversified, grow-

In the Big Bend country of Washington, a twenty-mule team pulls a combine through chest-high wheat. Until irrigation projects were developed, yields were unpredictable.

Under a gridiron of posts and wires to support the plants as they mature, hop pickers
gather the harvest of irrigated land in the Yakima Valley, 1906.

ing wheat, vegetables, potatoes, and pasturage for a milch cow. Small farms spread throughout the Willamette and into the valleys of the Umpqua and the Rogue; and while the land produced in abundance, no outside markets existed to encourage a shift to single cash crops, so the subsistence pattern largely persisted.

While 1837 was a bumper year for the HBC's fur trade, the rapid spread of American farmers through the southern reaches of the Oregon country provided a portent of the future McLoughlin could not ignore. In 1838, he prodded the HBC into organizing the Puget Sound Agricultural Company, staked out 160,000 acres of excellent land at the south tip of Puget Sound, and with £200,000 of company money set about organizing an agrarian community complete with tools, imple-

ments, livestock, mills, and artisans. Intended to counterbalance the growing American presence, the colony provided grains, vegetables, cheeses, butter, and wool for company needs and a marginal Russian market in Alaska for many years, but it was difficult to convince men to work land they didn't own and share the profits realized, when elsewhere a man could have his own land and all the proceeds. Although the Puget Sound Agricultural Company remained a working unit until after the Oregon question was resolved (the HBC finally relinquished title in 1869 for $200,000), the land never realized the potential it promised.

Farming in the valleys of Oregon was diversified further in 1847, when Henderson Lewelling brought by covered wagon from Ohio the first grafted fruit trees to

Since Henderson Lewelling's modest beginnings in 1847, fruit trees have been a thriving part of Northwest agriculture, as the harvest in this turn-of-the-century orchard attests.

Willamette. Apples were particularly successful, and the orchards that developed proved a bonanza when Oregon farmers found their first outside market—feeding the California gold rush. Wheat, vegetables, and potatoes all found a ready market in the mines, but for apples argonauts with more money than amenities were paying $1.50 apiece. Through the decade of the 1850s, Oregon farmers enjoyed high prices and good profits feeding the growing Golden State, but as California developed its own agriculture, the 1860s saw overproduction, a decline in prices, and a retreat to wheat and normalcy.

Similar surges in production and profit would recur with subsequent mining excitements: the Rogue River in the early 1850s; the Fraser River rush in 1859; and

the Idaho gold and silver bonanzas, which not only stimulated production but created whole new farming districts to the east. Not until the arrival of the railroads in the 1880s did Northwest fruits and vegetables find a relatively stable market, but despite fluctuations and setbacks, the Willamette remained the preeminent agricultural region. Even when events conspired to create an enormous new wheat region during the eighties, the genesis valley continued for another decade to produce more wheat.

The Inland Empire gots its name from George Henry Atkinson, an educator, minister, and agricultural enthusiast who had apparently never read Nathaniel Wyeth's evaluation in 1839 that the region offered "little prospect for the tiller of the soil." Atkinson, who

251

A sodbuster turns the dry but fertile soil of eastern Washington — and hopes for rain.

were extraordinary; land was cheap (or free, under the terms of the Homestead Act), the wheat was hard-kerneled (meaning it survived shipment and storage very well), and production seemed unlimited. All of which was very galling to the farmers, considering that the Idaho mines offered a limited market, and that the Oregon Steam Navigation Company's (OSN) stranglehold on river transport to outside markets made shipment prohibitively expensive.

The entire region west of the Cascades, and south of the Big Bend country of the Columbia fumed on top of a bonanza. Although some production continued, without markets no real growth could occur. The arrival of the railroads in the 1880s, opening the burgeoning cities and ports to the west, proved to be the key. Enormous tracts of land—2 million acres in the Columbia Basin and Wallowa district of Oregon, and another 600,000 along the Snake River in Idaho—were turned to the plow with traction engines, gang plows, and combines; mechanized agriculture undertaken with huge capital investment that rivaled the "bonanza farming" techniques of the Dakotas and central California.

To the west the Willamette continued to produce, and intensive specialty farming was growing up around Puget Sound. But the Inland Empire practiced dry land farming at its most expansive and impressive; like the cattle kingdom on the Great Plains, it was not so much a matter of the amount produced as in the manner and scale of producing.

had not raised wheat (and never did), divined that the volcanic soils, ten-inch snowfalls, and warm summers were ideally suited to nurturing winter wheat. Fortunately, he was right; even more fortuitously, the Idaho gold discoveries were bringing a stampede of farmers and stockmen to the vicinity to supply the miners—who really did not care what Atkinson thought but found his optimism encouraging.

In 1862, while Atkinson proselytized, they grazed stock and planted vegetables in protected and well-watered valleys at Walla Walla, Baker, Boise, and along the Umatilla and Colville rivers. Fact followed concept, and soon fields plowed and planted late in the fall were pushing up stalks under the light, protective layer of snow, to be harvested in the early summer. The results

PARALLELING THE EXTRAORDINARY GROWTH of agriculture in the Northwest was the development of a grazing industry. Like agriculture, it began in the ever-accommodating Willamette Valley. The earliest American settlers in the Willamette were loaned milch cows by a benevolent McLoughlin from a small herd he had nurtured since 1824. McLoughlin rarely, if ever, slaughtered a beef, holding the HBC stock for milk and increase, until by 1828 his herd numbered two hundred.

McLoughlin loaned the Americans cows to pasture for milk but demanded that any calves be returned to the company. To get their own livestock the Americans—with encouragement from William Slacum, the secret agent sent west by President Jackson—organized an expedition to California to bring back Spanish cattle.

Less romantically remembered than the cattle industry, the sheep business was more profitable. Here a closely guarded flock grazes near Heppner, Oregon.

During the salmon run on the lower Columbia near Astoria, fishermen by the score wove through the river traffic in tiny sail craft, dragging their gill nets.

Unable to prevent the Americans from bringing in the new livestock, McLoughlin supported the project financially. The Willamette Cattle Company dispatched ex-mountain man Ewing Young to California, where after some weeks of wheedling with suspicious officials, he and eighteen men rounded up a herd of the wildest, leanest, and meanest animals the Oregonians had ever seen. The inexperienced drovers embarked on probably the most difficult cattle drive on record, close herding at night, literally dragging reluctant animals one by one across streams and rivers, chasing strays in the broken country of northern California, until men and horses were exhausted. To compound their problems, they were chased for three days through southern Oregon by a band of Rogue River Indians bent on revenge

(one of Young's men had shot an Indian near camp in retaliation for a massacre two years earlier).

Young's adventure brought 630 cattle to the Northwest, and broke the HBC's monopoly on stock. Animals brought over the Oregon Trail by emigrants would supplement this number—in 1843 probably more than 2,500 came with Jesse Applegate's wagon train alone—to improve the breed and provide the seminal herds for a large industry.

Probably owing to some quirk in the American character, sheep are usually relegated to second status in accounts of grazing in the West, although they often were more profitable and appeared in greater numbers. Such was the case in the Northwest. As early as 1829, McLoughlin brought sheep from California, so did

Jacob Lease in the late 1830s; similarly, Nathaniel Wyeth imported more from the Sandwich Islands, all of which combined to create large flocks in the Willamette and adjacent valleys.

Both sheep and cattle began as an adjunct to farming, but as herds increased, grazing lands had to be found on land less ideally suited to farming. Livestock cannot create the wealth per acre that field crops can, and therefore the grazers constantly moved at the leading fringe of the agricultural frontier. Following the mining excitements in Idaho, stockmen spread into the Inland Empire and eastern Oregon and found the grazing good on the bunch grass not yet turned to the plow. Although they were forced constantly to retreat before the farmers, the herds and flocks increased. Into Idaho, the Harney Basin of southeast Oregon, and Montana they spread through the sixties and seventies, finding some markets in the coastal ports and cities, and the distant mid-West feedlots.

The real boom arrived in the 1880s, when an expanding industry in the Great Plains and Rocky Mountain regions came looking for feeder stock and high quality animals to upgrade the longhorn herds. In 1882 alone, it is estimated that 100,000 cattle and 200,000 sheep headed east to meet the demand. Railroads only improved the marketing situation, and cattle were shipped directly to feedlots and slaughterhouses in Omaha and Chicago. The industry peaked in the last decade of the century—there were more than 4 million sheep in the three states, and probably half as many cattle—as the grazers were pushed into the mountain states and onto marginal lands. But modern methods and range improvement have kept the business solvent, until now more cattle are raised on fewer acres than in the expansive years of the nineteenth century.

For centuries before the white man, fish had been the staple of the Indians' diet. Each year native fishermen gathered at Willamette Falls, Spokane Falls, Kettle Falls, Celilo Falls, and other favored spots, scooping expertly in the spray—often from rickety platforms—for a continuing catch, from the smaller fish of the spring runs to the largest chinook salmon of the

In Northwest canneries before the turn of the century, the onerous task of cleaning salmon usually fell to the Chinese. Curiously, there are none in evidence here.

fall. The scenes of the annual migrations on the Columbia were mirrored to a lesser degree in the other rivers of the Northwest, and probably equaled in magnitude when the sockeyes clogged the channels of the Fraser.

Early settlers found the salmon a cheap and diverting supplement to their diet, although for many years they lacked access to markets which could turn the abundance into cash. At Fort Langley on the Fraser, barrels of salted, dried, and pickled salmon were shipped as early as 1828, but for twenty years the output never exceeded several thousand barrels.

The first cannery on the Columbia was opened in 1867 by the Hume brothers of California; by 1872 they were shipping to Australia, China, South America, and Great Britain. Robert Hume soon shifted his operations to the Rogue River, where he supplemented the established run with the first hatchery-bred salmon and came to control a minor fiefdom in canneries, storage plants, shipping facilities, and most of the local real estate. But despite his defection, the Columbia River industry continued to grow, until by 1880 thirty canneries processing the river's catch were shipping over a half million cases of salmon per year.

To feed the voracious maw of the canneries required techniques which transcended the Indians' baskets and kettles. The standard method was gill netting, which snared a salmon's gills in large weave nets, drowning the fish. Various techniques for setting the nets evolved: "set" nets placed near the mouth of the Columbia before the tide ebbed, then taken up full of fish before the tide turned again; drift nets staked on the shore at one end and pulled through the water at the other; seining with two boats, one stationary, the other swinging in a wide arc around it; and even dragging nets through the shallows with horses. The greatest catches came from fish wheels set in channels near the falls to scoop fish out of the water nonstop, and from fish traps—intricate arrangements of wire netting which guided the migrating fish into an impounding pen from which they could not retreat.

The industry spread during the 1880s to Puget Sound, where railroads, new population, and ready capital combined to create a market. By working on a large scale, canneries packing the harvest of the sound, the Fraser, and other rivers were able to compete with the Columbia River fisheries. Using traps and deep-running seines on the routes to the spawning grounds, the Puget Sound catch surpassed Oregon's by the turn of the century. With trollers trailing as many as twelve lines (with upwards of thirty hooks per line), they fished the deeper waters of the sound and the strait.

Just as the Puget Sound industry transcended the Columbia's, so it was quickly surpassed by the Alaskan canneries. Following consolidation in 1892, the Alaskan salmon fishers and canners coordinated energies and resources to outproduce the Columbia and Puget Sound combined. On three fronts the salmon were being assaulted, and in 1902, when the "Iron Chink" (so named because it replaced the Chinese who cleaned and prepared fish for canning) was developed, production increased even more.

But by its very efficiency, the business was hastening its own decline. Annually the runs decreased, as fewer salmon cleared the gamut of nets, seines, and hooks to reach the spawning ground. The first undeniable evidence of what lay in store occurred in 1913 on the Fraser River, when railroaders blasted rock into the narrow Hell's Gate at the height of the run, blocking the sockeyes seeking their spawning beds. Four years later, when the 1913 spawn should have returned, there were virtually no fish at all; the loss was figured to exceed the then unheard-of figure of one billion dollars. In 1946, the run was partially restored by building fish ladders through Hell's Gate, but the Fraser has never regained its old stature.

Similarly, dams on the Columbia seriously depleted that river's salmon population, although fish ladders around the obstacles have helped to slow the decline. Massive Grand Coulee Dam, too high for fish ladders, cut off the entire upper Columbia spawning grounds, necessitating the transplantation of roe stripped from dying fish to accessible branches of the lower river.

By international agreements regulating catches, by creating new runs of hatchery-bred fish on previously barren streams, breeding salmon for greater size and resistance to disease and pollution, outlawing too highly efficient fishing methods, and circumventing the obstructions raised in the name of progress, men have moved closer to maintaining the salmon in Northwest waters. Even if difficult and expensive, the effort must be continued, for the bounty to be harvested may thus be almost endless.

Its skyline dominated by the futuristic Space Needle and ageless Mount Rainier, Seattle—"Queen City of the Northwest"—sparkles at dusk.

Sailboats on the bay catch the breezes off Vancouver,
Canadian sister city to the American Northwest.

Crowned by the dramatically sculpted Mount Hood, the city of Portland
forms a backdrop for the rose gardens of Washington Park.

Capitol building in Olympia, the seat of government since Washington achieved statehood in 1889.

With the old buildings of Last Chance Gulch in the foreground, the capital city of Helena, Montana, stretches out toward the mountains.

Probing the limits of the Northwest's challenging outdoor playground,
climbers approach the crest of Illumination Rock on Mount Hood.

Hikers in North Cascades National Park look down on the Skagit River from Sourdough Mountain.

Trout fishing on the Sauk River: Ready accessibility to wild areas is the Northwest's proudest heritage.

*Once the bane of explorers, the white water of Northwest rivers
now provides sport for raftsmen, as here on Reese Creek in Idaho.*

*A forest of masts rises from a yacht harbor in Seattle,
a city that now looks to the sea for play as well as work.*

The rusting hulk of the "Peter Iredale," wrecked off an often treacherous coast in 1906, lies at the Fort Stevens State Park in Oregon.

CHAPTER 23

POWER POLITICS AND WATER

*The history of irrigation and hydroelectric power—a boon
in spite of land frauds, bureaucracy, and ecological dilemmas*

THE RAINS OF THE NORTHWEST are legendary. The accounts of early travelers and correspondents were saturated with references to the seemingly endless drizzle and damp fogs, to the point where Oregonians came to be nicknamed "webfoots." But the reputation was properly earned along the coastal and inland regions west of the Cascades; for there is another side to Northwest climate: the dry, often arid plateau country to the east.

Clouds bearing eastward off the Pacific are pushed up by the rising face of the Cascades, cooling and dropping their moisture on the western valleys and the mountains. Largely depleted, the clouds pass over the hot, flat central regions, seldom finding occasion to precipitate until they reach the Rockies, where once again they rise and release their water as rain or snow. Stretching from the Cascades to the Rockies, and south across the Harney Basin and the Snake River plain of Idaho is a land of little rain, but of rivers fed from both east and west that form the Columbia drainage system. The dry lands and relatively abundant rivers combined to create a laboratory for a phenomenon called irrigation in the last agricultural frontier of the Northwest.

From the time of this nation's founding, when Thomas Jefferson envisioned the landowning yeoman tilling his small family farm as the backbone of democracy, the expressed policy of the government was to transform the public domain into a tidy patchwork of individual agrarian enterprise. The dream galloped across the humid eastern woodlands and prairies toward fulfillment until it was abruptly unhorsed by an invisible line stretched tight across the continent near the 100th meridian. Beyond that line, with few exceptions, the land was arid—too dry to support agriculture as pioneering farmers had come to understand it—and the dream faltered.

But the soil was fertile—some of it incredibly rich—and the farmers adapted, developing dry-farming techniques to conserve and make full use of what little rain did fall. They also began to experiment with the rivers and streams, diverting the passing waters onto their land with extraordinary results. The desert could be made to bloom! Irrigation became a universal panacea for western agriculture and development, as indeed it was, for nothing is more fundamentally important in the West than water.

Irrigation transformed the face of the West, nurturing vast agricultural districts on once barren land, sustaining cities that otherwise would wither, and later bringing industries to feed on the energy that dams would generate. But there is nothing simplistic about irrigation. Because water is so very essential, the question of how, when, and where to use it becomes tangled in a welter of conflicting interests; and because projects are more easily conceived than accomplished, all levels of government and private enterprise became involved, finally providing the basis for fundamental changes in the traditional relationships of federal, state, public, and private roles, responsibilities, and functions. In short, who builds the project, who administers it, who benefits, who profits, and is any of it right or fair?

Irrigation has profoundly changed the dry central

*Waters of the Columbia thunder off the spillway of Grand Coulee Dam,
keystone of power generation and irrigation in the Northwest.*

Early irrigation schemes often failed due to high initial cost and delayed returns.
But Idaho — here building canals for the Boise Project — was singularly successful.

areas of the Northwest, bringing immeasurably greater returns from the region than the first visitors ever imagined. Possibly the doubts, distractions, and rivalries raised by the complexity of the task are part of the investment that must be paid for the return.

IRRIGATION BEGAN simply enough in the Northwest. Marcus Whitman grubbed a trench to bring water to his gardens at Waiilatpu, and soon his example was being repeated by settlers throughout the Oregon country. Most of these early efforts involved little more than diverting spring freshets onto crops already sustained by rainfall — the extra water merely increasing the yield. Even in the abundantly moist Willamette Valley, small dams and ditches proliferated because little effort was required and the returns were considerable. But during the early years no really arid land was reclaimed by irrigation; as long as there was land available in the humid regions, no need existed to tackle the labor and expense of a major project.

The development of genuine irrigation agriculture, in which crop success was dependent upon water diverted to the land, began in the waning decades of the nineteenth century after land in the humid valleys was settled and expensive. The cost of constructing and maintaining an irrigation system — often involving large dams, systems for raising water from deeply carved canyons, reservoirs, and miles of transportation canals — quickly grew beyond the resources of individual farmers, giving rise to the appearance of commercial companies.

Although the initial investment might be great, and the risks high, so was the potential for profit, and soon two basic types of companies emerged. The most successful were ventures that dealt in water *and* land; planning a project, buying up all the land to be irrigated, and then beginning construction, these companies could make tremendous profits selling land suddenly worth several hundred times its preirrigation value. Other companies dealt strictly in the sale of water, but they often fell victim to land speculators who bought up all the land and then refused to sell or use the land until the water companies were bankrupt— then moving in on the water rights themselves.

There were notable successes, especially by the Washington Irrigation Company in the Yakima Valley, several projects in the Umatilla Valley; one near Klamath Falls; and the Payette Valley Company and the Boise City Company in Idaho. But in none of the states did commercial companies supply more than 10 percent of the state's irrigation water, nor even approach the demand; and the number of projects that failed was frightening.

As the century came to a close, it became increasingly apparent that the limits of private resources were about to be reached. The easily developed reclamation sites were already being exploited, and the failures had scared investment capital away from projects that seemed either complicated or risky. All over the Northwest, hopeful farmers stood on parched ground, looking on wistfully as millions of gallons of water thundered by in rivers too powerful to tame, or too deep in canyons to lift; but further irrigation would require large capital outlay, a high level of organization and planning, and some substantive guarantee of support. It was this impasse which finally forced the federal government into the fray.

The government was slow to recognize, or admit, that something might be wrong with land disposal policies in the West. Fraud became almost a necessity of survival, since graziers needed vast tracts of marginal land to support even small herds, and irrigation required equally large acreages to justify the enormous initial cost of diverting water. The federal government tried to encourage irrigation with the passage of the Desert Land Act of 1877, offering 640 acres to any settler who would bring water to 80 acres of the claim. The measure made little sense, since individual reclamation was already growing impossible.

To encourage private capital, and to provide some semblance of organization and protection for both investors and farmers, the Carey Act was passed in 1894, permitting the transfer of up to one million acres to the states, provided they would administer the reclamation of the lands. The actual development of the land was turned over to private concerns, but because of poor administration and planning, most of the Carey Act projects were failures. The task was often simply too large and complicated, and throughout the Northwest, companies failed and farmers were left high and dry—literally. By 1913 the *Portland Oregonian* complained, in direct reference to the Carey Act, that "uncompleted projects begun under inadequate laws and [the] imperfect administration of the post" were doing nothing to develop Oregon's arid lands.

Only in Idaho was the Carey Act a success, where 868,000 acres of land were reclaimed on the Snake River

Scrub land above verdant fields in the Columbia Basin Project clearly illustrates irrigation's value.

The skeletal beginnings of a reclamation project:
The Dalles Dam under construction in 1954.

Plain under the Carey provisions—apparently owing to successful administration, planning, and encouragement by the state. The Twin Falls South Side Project was singularly successful in Idaho, eventually covering over 240,000 acres. But in Oregon no projects were ever completed (although almost half a million acres were acquired by the state for irrigation); in Washington no projects were even approved.

The consistent policy of the federal government had been to remain aloof, only disposing of the land, and avoiding any involvement in any venture that might compete with private enterprise. But private endeavor was not only proving unequal to the task, it was creating a tangled mess of incomplete projects, conflicting water-rights claims, and ruined farmers that demanded intervention, planning, and subsidy on a national level.

In response to the need, the Reclamation Act of 1902 (also known as the Newlands Act) was passed. The act provided that receipts from land sales in the arid states would be applied to the construction of irrigation projects, and created a Reclamation Service (soon to become the Bureau of Reclamation) to make surveys and plan projects. The Newlands Act was heralded throughout the Northwest as the dawn of a new era:

not only would it put an end to speculative monopoly and untangle the question of water rights, it would open hundreds of thousands of desolate acres to agrarian industry.

But for a time the act of 1902 fell short of expectations: it provided the much-needed central organization and resources, but rather than pioneering new territory, its projects were limited to upgrading and expanding existing reclamation attempts begun by private enterprise and under the Carey Act. In Oregon the major projects on the Umatilla and Klamath rivers served areas already supplied and developed in some measure by private canals, while in Washington the only large project involved development in the Yakima Valley, where the Washington Irrigation Company had extensive holdings and water rights were tied up by previous claimants. The Reclamation Service muscled in nonetheless, finally forcing Washington Irrigation to sell out its holdings to the government, and construction was begun on an expanded program that eventually brought water to 450,000 acres of south-central Washington.

In Idaho, the pattern continued, as the government moved in to complete earlier unsuccessful attempts to irrigate the land between the Snake and Boise rivers. The keystone of the project was Arrowrock Dam, a 350-foot-high concrete structure completed in 1915. In Idaho the service also entered its first virgin territory, opening the lands of the upper and middle Snake with the construction of dams and canals at Minidoka.

THE LARGEST STRUCTURE built by man in the Western Hemisphere is in the Northwest, tucked down in the Columbia River gorge. Grand Coulee Dam was conceived as another link in the chain of projects to develop the water resources of the region for irrigation, but its completion marked the beginning of a new era of development; for in Grand Coulee and the companion project at Bonneville, the Northwest found that a new resource, fully as valuable as irrigation water, could be tapped from the Columbia River system—hydroelectric power.

The story began simply enough when residents of the Inland Empire revived a long-dormant scheme to bring the waters of the Columbia to the dry but fertile soils of the Big Bend country. The enterprise had its obstacles, not the least of which was the fact that the river ran by in the bottom of a gorge a thousand feet below the proposed fields. In 1918, Rufus Woods, editor of the *Wenatchee World*, began promoting the construction of a dam only high enough to back water up to the Canadian border and then pumping the water the rest of the way to the rim with pumps powered by the electricity the dam would generate.

That this was obviously a harebrained scheme was quickly argued by some concerned residents of Spokane, who proposed instead a reservoir at Albeni Falls in Idaho and a 150-mile system of canals and tunnels to move the water to the Big Bend—which, only incidentally, would pass close enough to their city to be tapped for irrigation and electrical power.

Either scheme was beyond the resources of private enterprise, and therefore most of the arguing took the form of entreaties to the federal government to ignore the lunacies proposed by those other scalawags of uncertain ancestry, and embrace the truth. Congress, after

Chief Joseph Dam, another link in the chain of dams on the Columbia, which drown a mighty river but offer the tantalizing prospect of power and irrigation.

almost ten years, ordered a study instead. The investigation (which evaluated reclamation sites all across the nation) took three years, and when the results were published in 1931, the Army Corps of Engineers had found in favor of the Grand Coulee Dam project, estimating it to cost $400 million. The report also recommended a dam at Cascade Falls, which became Bonneville Dam.

The Depression almost stopped Grand Coulee—Roosevelt hesitated to commit that much money to a project which would create more farmland at a time when the government was buying and destroying surpluses—but the public hue and cry for projects that employed men in large numbers restored the plan. Construction began in 1935, and for five years, eight thousand men poured concrete across the canyon until a lake stretched 150 miles up river. In the meantime, in 1937, the Bonneville project had been completed.

Detractors of the project had often turned their scorn on the tremendous surplus power Grand Coulee would generate, wondering who would ever consume so much electricity. The outbreak of World War II, only seven months after the dynamos began to turn, answered that question. War production in the Northwest quickly began sopping up all the power Grand Coulee and Bonneville could generate, as Henry Kaiser's shipyards and William Boeing's aircraft plant grew to monolithic proportions almost overnight.

Factories shifted production from farm implements to tanks, and everywhere industries expanded in response to war orders. The most extraordinary result was the development of a huge aluminum industry, necessary for aircraft production. Aluminum manufacturing requires enormous amounts of power to reduce the bauxite ore, and while the Northwest lacked bauxite, it had an abundance of cheap electricity—and so the bauxite came to the power.

The consumption of electricity remained high after the war, and with the distractions of the conflict behind them, the people of the Northwest began to question more closely the role and function of this extraordinary resource. The region had grown addicted to an abundant supply of electricity—fully as dependent upon it as the dryland farmer is upon irrigation water—and questions of who should get what amount from whom for what price began to loom very large. The federal government, out of necessity, had trespassed into the domain of private enterprise; it was in the business of creating hydroelectric power, a resource with not only a definite dollar value in the marketplace but the power to make or break individuals, industries, or whole regions—admittedly an awkward role for a government dedicated to protecting individual initiative.

Fundamental questions of the government's functions and responsibilities were at issue, but simple solutions were impossible in the face of the federal government's multiple roles of participant, subsidizer, regulator, and agent for the public good. While the government's philosophical role remains in limbo, the day-to-day administration of power use and distribution has fallen to the Bonneville Power Administration. Originally organized to distribute power from Bonneville Dam, the BPA has fallen heir to distribution of 80 percent of the private, semipublic, and federal power produced in the Columbia basin. Just what the BPA is and does, and how and why it functions are questions open to interpretation*

P LANS FOR THE DEVELOPMENT of the Northwest's water resources did not end with Bonneville and Grand Coulee. Between them, the Army Corps of Engineers and the Bureau of Reclamation had plans for extensive

---

*There have been arguments over proposals to create a Bonneville Power Authority (as opposed to the much less authoritative existing administration), and some argument over the extension of federal generating capacity, but in the Northwest the acceptance of public power as a philosophic concept has not been in question since the war. Much more debated is the question of the degree to which the private sector has quietly come to dominate the BPA policy decisions. At a 1973 meeting of the BPA advisory council, for instance, public members were reminded that BPA's mission is to increase the use of electricity—hence even a discussion of the possibility of limiting demand growth was beyond the policy-discussion authorization of BPA.

Its influence reaches far beyond the Northwest. By virtue of power "interties" with private and public power in California, the Great Basin, and the Southwest, the BPA can influence activity throughout the West. But despite this enormous impact—and the obvious potential for abuse—the BPA has served with remarkable fairness, restraint, and wisdom. In the course of dispensing more than 45 million kilowatt hours of energy per year, and manipulating annual revenues of over $100 million, certain BPA actions have elicited howls of protest; but the record is not bad for an institution that bridges a gap in America's understanding of what government should be.

Newest addition to the AEC's Hanford nuclear power facility at Richland, Washington, is this Fast Flux Test Reactor, now under construction and destined to provide fuel for Fast Breeder reactors. The Hanford project has brought the Northwest to grips with the dilemma of nuclear power: to use it and possibly risk contamination, or to abandon it and continue to dam rivers.

dam development on all the rivers of the Columbia drainage system. Their plans, incorporating irrigation, hydroelectric generating, and flood control projects elicited a collective yawn in the Northwest immediately following the war, until the disastrous floods of 1948—which hit all the major rivers, killed fifty-two people, and left $100 million worth of damage in their wake—created renewed enthusiasm for dam-building.

One hundred fifty dams now dot the rivers of the Columbia drainage system, and many more are planned as the engineers seek "maximum utilization." But many in the Northwest have long questioned whether more dams would help or hurt the region, and the debate continues to grow. The most dramatic example of the damage dams have already done concerns the salmon. Access to the spawning grounds of many fish has been blocked by dams, and many of the shallow breeding streams have been inundated by reservoirs. Despite modest success with fish ladders and artificial transplan-

tation, the spawning runs on many rivers are in decline, others have disappeared completely.

Rising water temperatures, brought on by the multitude of reservoirs and large amounts of industrial effluent dumped into the rivers, have also diminished the salmon runs, since the fish will not breed in waters warmer than 68°F. If present plans were all pursued to fruition, the rivers of the Northwest, including the mighty Columbia and Snake, would be transformed into a series of torpid pools, one above the other.

The question is ultimately one of the priority of values, balancing financial returns against the largely abstract values of conserving the few remaining salmon from extinction or maintaining the grandeur of a wild river. The choice is there, the results are obvious, the time is now.

Oh, yes, that irrigation project for the Big Bend country that began it all in 1918? The people got their water in 1952—and sure enough, the desert bloomed.

CHAPTER 24

PROGRESS, PROSPERITY, AND PROBLEMS

In a Northwest that has enjoyed exuberant growth and an unspoiled environment—but may soon have to choose between the two

THE PACIFIC NORTHWEST grew up on a buoyant wave of optimism that bolstered every aspect of its development. Thomas Emerson Ripley wrote of his years in Tacoma before the turn of the century: "We were no heroes of a western movie. We were just a crew of young men, drawn together in the common purpose to 'grow up with the country' to full stature as independent citizens of a happy town, which itself would grow as we worked." But implicit in "growing up with the country" was the assumption that it would grow rich and fast. With every phase of development, whether it was mining, timber, fishing, railroads, farming, grazing, irrigation, commerce, or manufacturing, the newspapers waxed eloquent on the "bounteous products of this magnificent clime," of cities "arisen as by a stroke of an enchanter's wand," that would "handle the commerce of the world." The *Tacoma Ledger* urged one and all to "let ENERGY! AMBITION! and ENTERPRISE! continue to give lustre to the City of Destiny."

Ripley and Tacoma were typical of thousands of men and hundreds of towns, living with the high expectations and assuredness of success that transcended ordinary typeface and routine punctuation. Their enthusiasm was reinforced at every turn by the abundance of natural resources waiting to be exploited: great forests on the mountains, verdant farmlands in the coastal valleys and plains, abundant rivers flowing through even the driest lands, mineral wealth beyond calculation where the earth's furnaces had created treasure troves beneath regions like the Coeur d'Alene, and natural harbors all along the coast that made the whole world a market place.

The Northwest did grow, the region offering up its natural resources to fuel the hopes of every enthusiast. The process was not entirely painless—expectations not withstanding, the engines of Progress are not capable of perpetual motion or constant acceleration—but the Northwest and its people survived recessions, panics, droughts, rapacious opportunists, political boondoggling, and occasional poor judgment to create a region of remarkable activity and promise.

THE OPTIMISM that characterized the long century of the Northwest's growth has not disappeared with the present, because too much remains of the future. It is easy enough to assay where the region has been and what it has to work with, but the questions of where it is going and what it will do with what it has remain strikingly open-ended. The natural abundance and diversity of the land continue to provide a variety of possibilities for the future, but this very fact leaves many northwesterners wondering what may become of the land they call home.

The most notable phenomenon in the Northwest is the trend towards increasing urbanization. Historically, cities have been regarded favorably—the bigger, the better—for cities meant industries, manufacturing, business, commerce, and large populations that both generated wealth and consumed products; growing cities were the mark of progress, reassuring one and all

On the modern campus of the University of Washington, students find their way to classes— and, hopefully, to a constructive place in the future of the Northwest.

that not only was the region fiscally healthy, but culturally solvent as well. Northwesterners are keenly proud of their cities, quick to recite facts and figures on new industries, growth, and prosperity—and so adamantly proud of their theaters, museums, symphonies, galleries, architecture, artists, and writers that an outsider might begin to wonder whom they are trying to convince.

However, urban growth in the Northwest is beginning to reach a crucial stage. West of the Cascades, in a narrow band running from the north end of Puget Sound, south across the Columbia and down the Willamette, lives over 70 percent of the region's population. One section in particular, the area between Seattle and Portland, shows prospect of growing into a great urban corridor, a surging, pulsating, unbroken mass of humanity. And while this kind of growth looks good on paper, many northwesterners have looked farther south to the spreading urban cancer that is Southern California and have begun to have second thoughts on the felicity of growth.

Longtime residents take their clean air, clean water, and unspoiled land as seriously as they do their cities. A few years back Seattle launched a campaign to attract business executives and white-collar companies that stressed the joys of living in a city only minutes away from quiet wilderness. Although the campaign was marked by a deadpan frivolity—one advertisement featured a gray-flannel-suit executive entering his office clutching a briefcase and an enormous Chinook salmon, the implication being that he had paused on his way to work for a couple of quick casts—it nonetheless pointed up what most residents regard as an important aspect of life in the Northwest: that life in a city need not be a dirty, crowded, harried urban grind, far removed from the amenities of nature.

As early as World War II, a California newspaper, remarking on the necessary proximity of electrical power to population centers for successful manufacturing, noted that "if the Columbia River would only flow through Los Angeles County, you could give Detroit and Pittsburgh back to the Indians." Since the Columbia flows through the Northwest, the question arises whether Los Angeles County might move to the Puget Sound-to-Portland corridor. The Northwest is at the point where it must decide if urban blight follows urban growth and act accordingly. Oregon already, though unofficially, is discouraging immigration, so apparently some residents have already decided.

THE PATTERN OF LIFE IN OREGON is characterized by stability: the timber industry, centered in Eugene, still dominates the economy; the well-balanced agriculture of the Willamette continues to sustain cities like Albany and Salem in the predictable ease to which they are accustomed; in the sparsely settled east irrigation and grazing have evolved to comfortable levels, keeping the population of towns like Pendleton and Baker relatively stable; and in the south placid communities like Ashland offer a haven to retiring veterans of urban life. Even the state's metropolis, Portland, continues to evince the solid permanence that marked its growth. Portland remains a hub of commerce and industry, humming with dockside activity, reshaping its face with high-rise buildings and gigantic shopping centers, but withal its population has remained largely stable through the last decade, its economy steady.

At the opposite extreme stands the swelling, burbling effervescence of Seattle, the largest city of the Northwest and the wheelhorse of economic life for the entire state of Washington. Seattle's influence is especially strong in the interior because of its close ties with Spokane, the distribution and marketing center for much of the Inland Empire. Thus when the city on Puget Sound throbs, the pulse is felt not only in the orchards of the Yakima and Wenatchee, but in rolling wheat fields of the Palouse country and the irrigation ditches of the Big Bend; and lately Seattle has been doing some throbbing.

Ever since the beginning Seattle has shown a penchant for boom-and-bust development, pinning its hopes on, and concentrating its labor force in a single industry, first lumber, then shipbuilding through two world wars, and finally the aircraft industry. It is a situation that makes for a mercurial economy, and the latest bust proved particularly painful.

The business that William Boeing launched during World War I grew enormously—like many Northwest industries—under the stimulus of World War II. Following the war, Boeing continued to expand as its 707s brought the jet age to commercial aviation, until by

*The city of Portland, still strengthened by the commerce that finds its way
to the Willamette River docks, sprawls out toward the horizon and Mount Hood.*

1968, 106,000 people were employed at Boeing facilities building and designing aircraft. The city basked in the midst of its greatest boom: housing was built, businesses and public services proliferated to meet the needs of the numerous and well-heeled employees; then the bottom dropped out. The government canceled orders for cargo planes and bombers, civilian orders declined because airlines found they had reached maximum capacities, and in 1970 the SST project ground to a halt. Between August of 1968 and December of 1971, 68,000 men were let go, a decline of 55 percent.

Seattle did not turn into a ghost town of starving destitutes (although bread lines were formed and Kobe, Japan, was moved to donate a half ton of rice to her beleaguered sister city—a gesture not appreciated), but the city was badly overbuilt and overextended. Construction work held up remarkably well since office-building continued downtown, but business slackened,

and there was a crisis of confidence. The problem was compounded by poor farm prices and/or low yields during 1969–70, and then the bumper wheat crop of 1971 deteriorated in storage elevators because of the longshoremen's strike. The city is already showing signs of recovery—some of the surplus labor left the area, diversified manufacturing has taken up some of the slack, and Boeing has begun hiring again. The wild optimism has disappeared, but unless the recent experience has sunk deeper into the municipal psyche than appears, there is no reason to think Seattle would settle for restrained growth if another bonanza seemed in the offing.

Seattle also provides a microcosm for another decision that faces the population centers of the Northwest: whether to preserve the unique qualities that give it character, or yield to the onslaught of urban reconstruction that has left so many cities with a sterile, amorphous facade. The case in point is the Pike Place Market, one of the last remaining central markets in a major U.S. city. The teeming market near the waterfront provides a montage of vegetable stalls, crab and fish stands, inexpensive restaurants with a view of the Olympics and Puget Sound, hip vendors, skid row bums, and beer parlors—in short, a delightful counterpoint to the slick plastic and concrete of much of downtown Seattle.

The market has its drawbacks, too: the 65-year-old wooden buildings constitute an enormous firetrap, and at night the muggers compete for victims on its shadowy streets. Plans were underway to tear down the old market and replace it with $100 million worth of hotel, high-rise apartments, and parking garage—all of which would provide new jobs, new capital, and new taxes—when the city began to waver. Torn between nostalgia and money, Seattle voters finally opted to save the market, forsaking the desperately needed jobs and taxes in favor of preserving something distinctly theirs that could never really be replaced.

THE FUTURE that demands decisions is not confined to the cities of the Northwest. Because of the increasing tendency of urban dwellers to escape the concrete at every opportunity, unspoiled rural areas and wild lands are becoming increasingly valuable as attractions for tourist dollars. In Idaho, for example, recreation and tourism have grown into a $150 million a year industry, equaling the returns from the timber industry and second only to agriculture as an income producer. With two million acres of designated primitive and wild areas, extensive national forests, numerous lakes and streams, and over twenty winter ski resorts, Idaho's outdoors are a growing asset—one that never need be depleted, provided a decision is made to preserve rather than destroy.

Often the question of development becomes muddled in conflicting priorities and the relative worth of returns —a problem nowhere more clearly apparent than in the case of power projects. Dams create power, a valuable commodity that has lured a great deal of industry to the Northwest, which in turn has been good for the economy; dams also obstruct the spawning runs of fish, and turn often exciting wild rivers into placid, feature-less reservoirs, which is not good for the fishing industry or, in some respects, tourism.

The problem of balancing priorities becomes especially difficult when the region prizes its natural wildness as the Northwest does, but has a crying need for more jobs and income. It is difficult to argue the subjective and emotional worth of a wild river against the measurable returns of a dam. In 1968 alone the aluminum industry, attracted to the area by cheap power from existing hydroelectric projects, employed ten thousand people in Washington and Oregon, and generated $252 million in annual revenues. True, informed observers doubt whether the sites proposed for new dams would permit generation of power at rates low enough to lure industry as before. But that is a question for experts. For most northwesterners, many of whom have personally known unemployment, the choice is simply between a wild river for their grandchildren to see or jobs for themselves today.

While the preservationists and industrial developers battle it out in their all-or-nothing causes, there are innumerable areas in the often-ignored hinterland between pristine wilderness and stampeding development that lack well-financed and vociferous champions or sharply defined issues to guide decision-making. Very often the maintenance of something called "the quality of life" is best served by a combination of development and wilderness. Such is the case of the Skagit River.

From its headwaters in British Columbia the Skagit is a wild torrent until it is joined by the Cascade, after which it runs calmly through broad valleys. The valley of the lower river is dotted with small lumber towns, a few cedar-shake plants, some small canneries, and many small farms. The lower river has had some hydroelectric development, but not enough to radically change the face and character of the region; it is a peaceful, clean, pleasant place where men, small industry, animals, and some great steelhead fishing commingle easily. The mark of man is in evidence, but it dominates neither the valley nor the river.

But the Skagit is facing the prospect of a land boom —second homes and mountain retreats—that threatens to bring subdivisions, developers, billboards, a crowded river, and increased demands for power. Government could protect the flow of the river by classifying the Skagit as a "recreational" river (there is already too much development for a "wild" or "scenic" classification), but since 70 percent of the land bordering the streambed is privately owned, it will be difficult to prevent the banks from becoming wall-to-wall suburbia. The federal government is now seeking easements along the banks to protect the river until final decisions can be made regarding the future of the Skagit.

The choices that face the Skagit, or the state of Idaho, or even the cities and towns of the Northwest are not easy ones—something will be lost whether they opt for unbridled development, severely restricted growth and preservation, or something in between. It is a beautiful country now, with modern cities, rich resources, abundant natural beauty, and a diversity of land and experience that has no rival. For Americans, it is indeed the land of the future.

The enveloping presence of the mountains and the crystal brilliance of the waters of Ross Lake, Washington, alive with sunlight, mirror the timeless quality of the great Northwest.

HISTORICAL CHRONOLOGY

1542–1602 The random probings along the Northwest coast by Ferrelo (1542), Drake (1579), and Aguilar (1602) reveal little substantive information—hardly more, in fact, than the imaginary voyage reported by Juan de Fuca (1592).

c. 1700 The Shoshonis and Nez Perces of the plateau acquire the horse.

1741 Vitus Bering's ill-fated voyage to far Northwest shores ends in disaster, but the survivors' discovery of sea otter herds inaugurates a trans-Pacific era of industry and discovery for Russia.

1774 Spain responds to the Russian presence by sending expeditions north to consolidate her claims: first Juan Perez, and later Hecata and Bodega y Quadra, whose discoveries and charts were concealed by Spain as state secrets.

1778 Captain James Cook's third voyage takes him to Nootka Sound, where the English blunder onto the possibilities of the maritime fur trade.

1788 The first American vessels, commanded by John Kendrick and Robert Gray, trade along the coast.

1789 Spain's Jose Martinez seizes John Meares's trading vessels at Nootka Sound, nearly inciting a war between Spain and England.

1792 Capt. George Vancouver systematically maps Puget Sound and points north, but misses the Columbia and the Fraser rivers. Shortly thereafter Robert Gray (on a second voyage) enters the Columbia to establish an American claim to the river. Vancouver returns and sends his subaltern, Lieut. W. R. Broughton, up the Columbia one hundred miles.

1793 Alexander Mackenzie, after descending the Mackenzie River to the Arctic in 1789, follows the Peace, Fraser, and Bella Coola rivers to the Pacific, becoming the first white man to cross the continent north of Spanish America.

1804 Lewis and Clark launch their three-year exploration of the land between the Mississippi and the Pacific.

1811 American fur traders dispatched by John Jacob Astor reach the mouth of the Columbia aboard the *Tonquin* and establish a fur post to contest British domination of the beaver trade. The land party under Wilson Price Hunt reaches Astoria the following year.

1813 The North West Company buys Astoria from the Americans during the War of 1812 and renames it Fort George.

1814 The Treaty of Ghent ends the War of 1812. It makes no mention of the Oregon country but says property which changed hands as a result of the war must be restored. The American flag is raised over Astoria, but the North West Company retains possession of the post.

1818 The Convention of 1818 agrees that the country west of the Rockies, south of Russian America, and north of Spanish America is open for use by both American and British subjects.

1821 The Hudson's Bay Company absorbs the North West Company and assumes control of all British commercial activity west of the Rockies.

1824 Dr. John McLoughlin is appointed chief factor of the Columbia District of the Hudson's Bay Company. He builds a new headquarters on the north shore of the Columbia: Fort Vancouver.

1834 Jason Lee establishes his mission on the Willamette, followed two years later by Marcus Whitman at Waiilatpu.

1837 Ewing Young brings 630 California cattle to the Willamette, breaking the HBC's monopoly on brood stock.

1843–1846 The tide of American migration to Oregon reaches flood stage.

1843 A provisional government is organized among the settlers of the Oregon country.

1846 The Oregon boundary is established along the 49th parallel to the Strait of Georgia. Two years later the United States organizes a territorial government for Oregon.

1847 The Whitman Massacre puts a temporary end to missionary efforts among the Indians.

1852 Henry Yesler erects the first steam sawmill on Puget Sound.

1853 After petitioning to become the Territory of Columbia, the citizens north of the river are recognized as Washington Territory.

1854 Isaac Stevens begins arranging treaties with the Indians, touching off four years of conflict.

1858 The Fraser River gold rush exceeds the Rogue River excitement of 1851.

1859 Oregon is granted statehood seven months after the state government begins to function.

1860 Idaho's mining era begins with the rush to Oro Fino, followed two years later by an exodus to the Boise Basin.

1860 The Oregon Steam Navigation Company is formed to facilitate river transport on the Columbia.

1863 Idaho Territory is separated from Washington Territory, encompassing Montana and much of Wyoming.

1864 Asa Mercer returns to Seattle with eleven "mail-order brides."

1870 Jay Cooke begins construction on the Northern Pacific, but the effort collapses with the Panic of 1873.

1876 Henry Villard takes over Ben Holladay's steamship and rail empire in the Willamette, and begins expanding—ultimately buying and completing the Northern Pacific.

1883 The Northern Pacific rails reach Puget Sound.

1885 Silver strikes in Idaho's Coeur d'Alene rejuvenate the territory's mining industry.

1889 In November, Washington is granted statehood.

1890 Idaho becomes a state.

1893 James J. Hill completes his Great Northern Railway to Seattle.

1894 The federal government passes the Carey Act, leading to the irrigation of 860,000 acres in Idaho.

1897 The Klondike gold rush boosts Seattle and the Northwest into a major supply depot.

1899 The "Oregon System" of political reform begins with the initiative and referendum, followed in 1904 with the direct primary, and in 1908 with the recall. Washington and Idaho quickly follow suit.

1900 Frederick Weyerhaeuser lays the foundations of a timber empire by buying 900,000 acres from J. J. Hill.

1902 The Newlands Act brings federal irrigation projects to the inland plateau and basins.

1911 Spurred by the Bitterroot burn of 1910, government and industry band together behind the Weeks law to fight and prevent forest fires.

1936 Bonneville Dam is completed, followed four years later by Grand Coulee, the wheelhorse of Northwest power and irrigation.

SCENIC AREA GUIDE

THE COAST

Olympic National Park

Enclosing within its boundaries the glacier-clad Olympic Mountains of northwestern Washington, a scenic Pacific coastline fifty miles long, conifer rain forests, swift ice-fed streams, and abundant wildlife, Olympic is one of the West's most diverse national parks.
History: Attracted by the virgin Olympic rain forest, the lumber industry long coveted the region and the land became embroiled in political controversy. But early proponents of conservation were able to win their point, as Olympic became first a forest preserve (1897–1909), then a national monument (1909–1933), and finally a national park (1938).
Key features: Galleries with stalactites, limestone canopies, and only from the north side, where Hurricane Ridge has spectacular views of Mount Olympus and the Bailey Range. Roads lead to Lake Crescent, Sol Duc Hot Springs, and the Seven Lakes Basin Trail. Nearer the coast are the incomparable rain forest valleys; the Hoh Valley is the most accessible and has two self-guiding nature trails. Though the park is open all year, the high country is usually closed by snow from early fall until July.

Oregon Caves National Monument

Forty-five miles from the Pacific Ocean and 4,000 feet above sea level, the Oregon Caves are nonetheless products of the sea.
History: The rock layer in which caves have formed was once limestone, a marine sedimentary rock that collected and compacted on the ocean floor millions of years ago. Later it was uplifted, and as mountains were formed, the limestone turned to marble. The great voids were created by water seeping through cracks and dissolving away the marble. Once within the great chambers, water evaporated, leaving behind carbonate deposits called dripstone, which form the draperies and pillars of cavernous rooms.
Key features: Galleries with stalactites, limestone canopies, and flowstone are the major attractions; the monument is open and guided cave tours are conducted throughout the year.

THE PUGET-WILLAMETTE LOWLANDS

Fort Vancouver National Historic Site

Located at the head of deepwater navigation on the Columbia River, Fort Vancouver was Washington's first city.

History: Founded by the Hudson's Bay Company, this hub of a fur-trading empire (1824–1846) became the United States' first Pacific Northwest military post in 1849.
Key features: The stockade and buildings of the old fort are outlined in their original positions, and the fort's north wall and gate have been restored. A museum displays artifacts, trade goods, and china from the fort's early days and relates the history of the Hudson's Bay Company in the nineteenth century.

THE CASCADE RANGE

Crater Lake National Park

The indigo waters of Crater Lake sink to depths of 1,932 feet, deeper than any other lake in the United States and second in the western hemisphere only to Great Slave Lake, Canada.
History: The rim of Crater Lake and the rocky wall that rises above lake level are remnants of Mount Mazama, a Cascade volcano that virtually disappeared seven thousand years ago by a volcanic eruption and the collapse of its summit. Initially dry, the basin gradually filled with rain and melting snow to its present stable level.
Key features: A scenic, thirty-five-mile rim drive passes Discovery Point (where John Wesley Hillman, a prospector, first saw the lake in 1853), Union Peak, the Watchman, Pumice Point, Cleetwood Cove (Cleetwood Trail is the only access to the water and is the point of origin for launch trips), Cloudcap (highest point on the drive), Kerr Notch, and other vista points. The southwest road to Rim Village is plowed in winter for cross-country skiers and tobogganers.

Lassen Volcanic National Park

Lassen Peak now sleeps at the southern tip of the Cascades, but from 1914 to 1921 there were 298 outbursts from the volcano. In 1915, Lassen's volcanic terrain and coniferous forest became a national park.
History: The Lassen volcano was formed as stiff, pasty lava squeezed up from a vent of a larger, extinct volcano, Mount Tehama. The thick lava cooled to a rough, dome-shaped peak and plugged the vent from which it came. Volcanic fires re-kindled in 1914. Evidence of this recent volcanism may be viewed at the Devastated Area, north of the peak.
Key features: A thirty-mile park road winds around three sides of

Lassen Peak, affording views of the volcano and its destructive action. The park also has more than 150 miles of trail. Thermal areas are the Sulphur Works and Bumpass Hell. In the Butte Lake (eastern) section of the park is Cinder Cone, a 700-foot volcanic cone formed with almost perfect symmetry.

Mount Rainier National Park

The park is dominated by Mount Rainier, highest of Cascade volcanoes. John Muir said, "Of all the fire mountains which, like beacons, once blazed along the Pacific Coast, Mount Rainier is the noblest."

History: The time of Mount Rainier's first eruption is unknown—it may have occurred tens or hundreds of thousands of years ago. It was followed by eruptions of fragmental lava, steam explosions, and massive lava flows, which formed Rainier's composite cone. Later, glacial activity removed much of the mountain's height, and the modern summit is several thousand feet lower than the original.

Key features: Rainier's vibrant living community can be sampled along the ninety-mile Wonderland Trail, which completely encircles the mountain and provides views of the peaks, glaciers, forest, lakes, streams, waterfalls, wildflowers, and wild animals. There are sight-seeing roads to Sunrise Ridge, Reflection Lakes, Stevens Canyon, Paradise, and Chinook Pass. Climbing the mountain is a two-day round trip. The park is open all year, as is Sunshine Camp near the Nisqually Entrance.

North Cascades National Park

Established in 1968 in north central Washington and nicknamed the "American Alps," the park has two units, separated by the canyon of the Skagit River.

History: Mountains of the North Cascades are made of granite and metamorphic rock that has been uplifted by forces acting through the past 10 million years. High peaks spawned alpine glaciers in the Pleistocene; and over 315 glaciers are active today.

Key features: Because a front range masks the mountainous interior from the road, trail travel is imperative. On the north are Mount Shuksan, Glacier Peak, and the glacier-streaked peaks of the Pickett Range. By climbing Sourdough Mountain, one can view some of the peaks that tower at the heart of the range. Cascade Pass is popular with tourists, and there is a trail which leads down from the pass to Lake Chelan. In the southern section, the Eldorado Wilderness is replete with spectacular vistas.

THE LAVA PLATEAUS

Lava Beds National Monument

Midway between Crater Lake National Park and Lassen Volcanic National Park, the Lava Beds also contain many features formed from molten rock, including lava flows of both pahoehoe and aa types, cinder cones, spatter cones, buttes, and lava tubes.

History: Some of these lava flows and volcanic features are only five thousand years old. This rough volcanic terrain was the site of the Modoc Indian War, 1872 to 1873. Lava Beds Monument was established in 1925.

Key features: Schonchin Butte is a central landmark in the monument and was the source of a lava flow which has been traced for three and a half miles. Lava tubes number in the hundreds; some have lava stalactites and stalagmites, the walls of others are ribbed or rippled. Just outside the northeastern entrance, Indian rock carvings may be viewed on Petroglyph Cliff.

Whitman Mission National Historic Site

Seven miles west of Walla Walla is the Indian mission established in 1836 by Dr. Marcus Whitman and his wife.

History: Called Waiilatpu, "place of rye grass," the Whitman Mission was one of the first of its kind in the Northwest. It was originally dedicated to Indian welfare, but it became the refuge of emigrants weary with the Oregon Trail. Indians watched the influx of white men with growing alarm, until in 1847 a misunderstanding between Dr. Whitman and some Cayuse Indians ended in the death of the Whitmans and twelve others. As settlers called for American troops they helped end British influence.

Key features: Though burned after the massacre, the early buildings have been excavated and outlined. The mission millpond, part of an apple orchard, and part of the Oregon Trail have been restored. Exhibits in the Visitor Center chronicle regional history, the Northwest missionary era, and the life of the Whitmans.

Craters of the Moon National Monument

Covering eighty-three square miles in south central Idaho, the monument's cinder cones, lava flows, and other features are products of geologically recent volcanic activity.

History: Quiet fissure eruptions on the Snake River Plain 5 to 10 million years ago continued throughout the Ice Age and brought outbursts of volcanic activity within historical time. One of the latest lava flows is 461 years old.

Key features: Lava comes in many forms—jagged chunks, ropy flows, cinder fields, and cones. Among many interest points are North Crater, Devil's Orchard, Inferno Cone, Big Cinder Butte, Indian Tunnel, Great Owl Cavern, and Spatter Cone; some lie along the monument road, others lie on trails. The craters are most striking early or late in the day when lighting is oblique.

THE NORTHERN ROCKIES

Big Hole Battlefield National Monument

Ten miles west of Wisdom in western Montana, a major battle was fought on August 9 and 10, 1877, between a nomadic group of Nez Perce Indians, led by Chief Joseph, and U. S. troops, aided by civilian volunteers.

History: Government forces staged a surprise attack against the Indians. Having refused reservation life, the Nez Perce were fleeing to Canada. Chief Joseph surrendered near Chinook in north central Montana.

Key features: The monument covers 536 acres. Firearms and frontier relics may be seen in the Visitor Center, where an audiovisual program depicts and describes the battle.

Glacier National Park

Beautiful escarpments of rock, huge ice-carved amphitheaters, and more than 200 shimmering lakes attract tourists to what an early French explorer called "the land of shining mountains."

History: Glacier peaks are made of sand, silt, clay, and lime that was deposited on the bottom of an inland sea, compacted to stone, and folded and faulted by mountain-building forces. The knife-like shape of these mountains resulted from renewed uplift, erosion, and alpine glaciation.

Key features: Although this is primarily a wilderness park with one thousand miles of trail, the Going-to-the-Sun Highway also ties Lake McDonald and St. Mary Lake by 50 miles of scenic road. There are naturalist-conducted tours to Grinnell Glacier, launch trips on Lake McDonald and Swiftcurrent Lake, and many other activities. Waterton Lakes National Park, Alberta, may be reached by the Chief Mountain International Road, on the eastern flank of Glacier.

SOURCES AND SUGGESTED READING

General

Empire of the Columbia (2nd Ed.) by Dorothy O. Johansen and C. M. Gates; Harper & Row, 1967.
Idaho by the Federal Writers' Project of the Works Progress Administration; Oxford University Press, 1968.
Land of Giants by David Lavender; Doubleday, 1958.
Montana by the Federal Writers' Project of the Works Progress Administration for the State of Montana; Viking, 1939.
Oregon by the Federal Writers' Project of the Works Progress Administration; Binfords & Mort, 1951.
Pacific Slope by Earl Pomeroy; Knopf, 1965.
Westward Tilt by Neil Morgan; Random House, 1963.

Geology

Cascadia by Bates McKee; McGraw-Hill, 1972.
Geology of Mount Rainer National Park by Richard S Fiske et al.; Geological Survey Professional Paper 444, U.S. Government Printing Office, 1963.
Geology of Olympic National Park by Wilbert R. Danner; University of Washington Press, 1955.
Landforms of Washington by Don Easterbrook and David Rahm; Western Washington State College Press, 1970.
Our Changing Coastlines by Francis P. Shepard and Harold R. Wanless; McGraw-Hill, 1971.
Physiography of the United States by Charles B. Hunt; W. H. Freeman, 1967.
Regional Geomorphology of the United States by Wiliam D. Thornbury; John Wiley & Sons, 1965.
The Restless Earth by Nigel Calder; Viking, 1972.
Volcanoes: In History, in Theory, in Eruption by Fred M. Bullard; University of Texas Press, 1962.
Waves and Beaches by Willard Bascom; Doubleday, 1964.

Geography

Beaches: Their Lives, Legends, and Lore by Seon and Robert Manley; Chilton Book Co., 1968.
Edge of a Continent by Don Greame Kelley; American West Publishing Co., 1971.
Exploring the Olympic Peninsula by Ruth Kirk; University of Washington Press, 1964.
Glacier National Park edited by Robert Scharff; David McKay, 1967.
The Great Columbia Plain: A Historical Geography, 1805–1910 by D. W. Meinig; University of Washington Press, 1968.
"Many-Splendored Glacierland" by George W. Long; *National Georgraphic*, May, 1956.
Moods of the Columbia by Archie Satterfield; Superior, 1968.
My Wilderness: The Pacific West by William O. Douglas; Doubleday, 1960.
National Parks of the West by the Editors of Sunset; Lane, 1968.
The Oregon Desert by E. R. Jackman and R. A. Long; Caxton, Caldwell, 1964.
Sixty Unbeaten Paths by Bob and Ira Spring and Byron Fish; Superior, 1972.
Snake River Country by Bill Gulick; Caxton, Caldwell, 1971.
Trail Country by Robert L. Wood; The Mountaineers, 1968.

Indians

Cultures of the North Pacific Coast by Philip Drucker; Chandler, 1965, paper.
Indians of the North Pacific Coast edited by Tom McFeat; University of Washington Press, 1967.

The Jesuits and the Indian Wars of the Northwest by Robert I. Burns; Yale University Press, 1966.
The Nez Perce Indians and the Opening of the Northwest by Alvin M. Josephy; Yale University Press, 1971.
The Totem Pole Indians by Joseph Wherry; W. Funk, 1964.

Exploration and Fur Trade

The California Sea Otter Trade by Adele Ogden; University of California Press, 1941.
The Columbia River by Ross Cox, edited by Edgar and Jane Stewart; University of Oklahoma Press, 1957.
Cook and the Opening of the Pacific by James A. Williamson; Macmillan, 1948.
Exploration and Empire by William Goetzmann; Knopf, 1966.
Fur Trade and Empire: George Simpson's Journal, 1824–1825 (Rev. Ed.) edited by Frederick Merk; Belknap Press of Harvard University, 1968.
The Journals of Lewis and Clark edited by Bernard DeVoto; Houghton Mifflin, 1953.

History

Borah of Idaho by Claudius O. Johnson; Longmans, Green, 1936.
East of the Cascades by Phil F. Brozan; Caxton, 1964.
Farthest Frontier: The Pacific Northwest by Sidney Warren; Macmillan, 1949.
Francis Norbert Blanchet and the Founding of the Oregon Missions, 1838–1848 by Sister Letitia Mary Lyons; Catholic University of America Press, 1940.
The Great Northwest by Oscar O. Winther; Knopf, 1950.
Heritage of Conflict by Vernon H. Jensen; Cornell University Press, 1950.
History and Government of the State of Washington by Mary W. Avery; University of Washington Press, 1961.
The Populist Revolt by John D. Hicks; University of Minnesota Press, 1931.
Skid Road: An Informal Portrait of Seattle by Murray Morgan; Viking, 1960.
Western Politics edited by Frank Jonas; University of Utah Press, 1962.

Mining

The Ballyhoo Bonanza: Charles Sweeny and the Idaho Mines by John Fahey; University of Washington Press, 1971.
The Bonanza West by William S. Greever; University of Oklahoma, 1963.
Gold and Silver in the West by T. H. Watkins; American West Publishing Co., 1971.
Mining Frontiers of the Far West, 1848–1880 by Rodman Paul; Holt, Rinehart and Winston, 1963.

Transportation

Henry Villard and the Railways of the Northwest by James B. Hedges; Yale University Press, 1930.
James J. Hill by Stewart Holbrook; Knopf, 1955.
Sternwheelers up the Columbia by Randall V. Mills; Pacific Books, 1947.
The Story of the Western Railroads by Robert Riegel; Macmillan, 1926.
They Built the West: An Epic of Rails and Cities by Glenn C. Quiett; D. Appleton-Century, 1934.

Timber

The Great Forest by Richard Lillard; Knopf, 1947.

Lumber and Labor by Vernon H. Jensen; Farrar & Rinehart, 1945.
Mill Town by Norman H. Clark; University of Washington Press, 1970.

Water Industries and Management

The Columbia by Stewart Holbrook; Rinehart, 1956.
The Dam by Murray Morgan; Viking, 1954.
Hail Columbia: The Thirty-Year Struggle for Grand Coulee Dam by George Sundberg; Macmillan, 1954.
Uncle Sam in the Northwest: Federal Management of Natural Resources in the Columbia River Valley by Charles McKinley; University of California Press, 1952.

The Salmon King of Oregon: R. D. Hume and the Pacific Fisheries by Gordon B. Dodds; University of North Carolina Press, 1963.

Probably the most outstanding aids to research on the Northwest are the journals published and sustained by regional historical associations. In these journals are to be found informative, readable articles on virtually every incident, personality, and question related to the history of the Northwest. Rather than enumerate the hundreds of articles consulted, the authors direct the reader's attention to the indexes of the following journals: **The Oregon Historical Quarterly; The Pacific Northwest Quarterly; The Washington Historical Quarterly;** and **The Pacific Historical Review.** The return more than justifies the effort.

ACKNOWLEDGMENTS

The writers and editors of this book wish to acknowledge their great debt to historian Murray Morgan, who not only shared his historical expertise and close personal acquaintance with the Northwest, but contributed his time, interest, and enthusiasm far beyond any reasonable expectation.

The librarians of the United States Geological Survey, Pacific Coast Center, Menlo Park, California, were invaluable in suggesting sources on the geological past and present of the region; and Dr. Jack Hyde critiqued the chapters on geology with thoroughness and candor.

For special assistance in procuring graphics, thanks are due to Richard H. Engeman, photograph and map librarian, the Oregon Historical Society, Portland; Archibald Hanna, curator, Beinecke Rare Book and Manuscript Library, Yale University, New Haven; Bruce Le Roy, director, and Frank L. Green, librarian, Washington State Historical Society, Tacoma; Robert Monroe, Special Collections, University of Washington Libraries, Seattle; Donna Rankin, Travel Information Services, Oregon State Highway Division, Salem; and Marsha Rodney, photo editor, Royal Ontario Museum, Toronto.

PICTURE CREDITS

The American Museum of Natural History: Page 111. Amon Carter Museum, Fort Worth, Texas: Pages 122-123. Bancroft Library, University of California, Berkeley: Pages 136, 140 (right). Beinecke Rare Book and Manuscript Library, Yale University: Pages 106, 178 (bottom), 186. Boeing Photo: 239. Burlington Northern Railroad: Page 213 (top). California State University, Humboldt Library: Page 112. Peter Carni: Page 103 (third row, right). William Carter: Page 182 (bottom, left & right). Columbia River Maritime Museum: Pages 130, 174. Ed Cooper: Pages 16-17, 24, 43 (bottom), 48, 50-51, 53, 62, 64-65, 75, 84-85, 87, 91, 100 (top, left; middle, left; bottom, right), 101 (top, middle, & bottom, left), 234-235, 240, 257, 259 (top), 260, 264. Corcoran Gallery of Art, Washington: Pages 180-181. Culver Pictures: Page 159. Forestry Library, University of California, Berkeley: Pages 243, 244. Thomas Gilcrease Institute of American History & Art, Tulsa, Oklahoma: Pages 179 (bottom), 182 (top), 184, 190. Keith Gunnar: Pages 18, 54, 59-61, 101 (top, right), 102 (top, left), 214-215, 277. Bob Gunning: Pages 32, 92-93. Warren Hamilton: Page 262 (top). The Haynes Foundation, Bozeman, Mont.: Pages 196, 198, 219. Idaho Department of Commerce and Development: Pages 81, 86. Idaho State Historical Society: Pages 228, 229, 266. Independence Hall Collection, Philadelphia: Page 135. Don Greame Kelley: Pages 74, 95 (bottom). Ruth Kirk: Page 30. Larry C. Lack: Page 103 (top, right). Jerry Larson: Page 44 (top). Barry Lopez: Pages 95 (top), 181 (bottom). William D. McKinney: Pages 90, 94-95, 100 (bottom, left), 238. Missouri Historical Society: Page 139. Montana Historical Society: Pages 165 (top), 176-177, 201. Murray Morgan: Page 226. David Muench: Pages 2-3, 4-5, 6-7, 8, 22, 26, 28-29, 31, 41, 42, 43 (top), 52, 58, 63, 66, 70, 72, 73, 76, 79, 82, 89, 97, 98-99, 100 (top, right), 237, 258 (bottom), 259 (bottom). Museum of Fine Arts, Boston: Page 145. Tom Myers: Pages 101 (middle, right), 102 (second row, third row, left), 103 (middle & bottom, left), 172 (top), 183, 258 (top), 263. The National Gallery of Canada, Ottawa: Page 134. National Maritime Museum, London: Page 124. The New York Public Library, American History Division: Pages 141, 147. New York Historical Society: Page 116. Northwest Photographic Services, Portland: Pages 223, 255. Ontario Department of Public Records & Archives, Toronto: Page 144. Oregon Historical Society: Pages 114, 128, 129 (top, right), 132, 148 (top), 150, 151, 155, 165 (bottom), 168, 170 (top), 178 (top), 200, 204, 207, 208-212, 213 (bottom), 216, 218, 232, 251, 253. Oregon State Highway Department, Salem: Pages 39, 71, 131, 138, 152, 160-161, 162. Portland Chamber of Commerce: Page 275. Provincial Archives, Victoria, B. C.: Pages 129 (top, left; bottom), 140 (left). Public Archives of Canada, Ottawa: Pages 127, 148 (bottom). Betty Randall: Page 102 (bottom, left). Mary Randlett: Pages 20, 23, 37, 69, 167, 247. Merg Ross: Page 272. Richard Rowan: Page 262 (bottom). Royal Ontario Museum, Toronto, Canada: Pages 104-105, 118-121, 169, 171, 172 (bottom), 179 (top). San Francisco Maritime Museum: Page 246. Smithsonian Institution, National Anthropological Archives: Pages 188, 189. Bob & Ira Spring: Pages 36, 38, 44 (bottom), 45-47, 101 (bottom, right), 173, 175, 233, 236 (bottom), 261. Stanford University Library: Pages 108, 110, 113, 115, 142, 164, 166 (bottom), 193, 194, 195, 224, 254. Stark Foundation, Orange, Texas: Page 158. Robert Strindberg: Page 235. David Sumner: Page 96. Collection of The University of Michigan Museum of Art: Page 170 (bottom). University of Oregon Library: Page 154. University of Washington Libraries, Special Collections: Pages 202, 220-221, 222 (left), 227, 231, 250. U.S. Army Corps of Engineers, Portland District: Page 268. U.S. Army Corps of Engineers, Seattle District: Page 269. U.S. Atomic Energy Commission: Page 271. U.S. Bureau of Reclamation: Page 267. Washington State Historical Society: Pages 146, 157, 187, 206, 222 (right), 248, 252. Ralph H. Williams: Pages 102 (top, right), 103 (top, left; second row, right; third row, middle). Steven C. Wilson: Pages 102 (middle, right; bottom, right), 103 (bottom, right), 236 (top).

INDEX

Map on following two pages © Jeppesen & Co., Denver, Colo. Reprinted by permission of the H. M. Gousha Co., proprietors, San Jose, Calif.

VANCOUVER I.

Strait of Georgia

Sumas

Lynden

Nooksack R.

BELLINGHAM

SAN JUAN IS.

STRAIT OF JUAN DE FUCA

VICTORIA

Admiralty Inlet

Coupeville

FIDALGO I.

WHIDBEY I.

Skagit R.

Mount Olympus

OLYMPIC NATIONAL PARK

Hoh R.

Kalaloch

Queets R.

Quinault R.

OLYMPIC MOUNTAINS

Hood Canal

PUGET SOUND

Snohomish R.

EVERETT

Skykomish R.

SEATTLE

L. Sammamish

Snoqualmie R.

TACOMA

Grays Harbor

Chehalis R.

OLYMPIA

Tenino

Grand Mound

Nisqually R.

MOUNT RAINIER NATIONAL PARK

Mount Rainier

Chinook Pass

Willapa R.

WILLAPA HILLS

Cowlitz R.

Astoria

Longview

Mount St. Helens

Lewis R.

Mount Adams

Beacon Rock

The Dalles Dam

Bonneville Dam

Vancouver

Columbia River Gorge

The Dalles

PORTLAND

PACIFIC OCEAN

COAST RANGE

WILLAMETTE VALLEY

Willamette R.

SALEM

Mount Hood

Barlow Pass

Mount Jefferson

Santiam Pass

McKenzie Pass

McKenzie R.

EUGENE

Siuslaw R.

Deschutes R.

Bend

Lava Butte

Three Sisters

Oakridge

Willamette Pass

Umpqua R.

Coos Bay

East L.

Paulina L.

OREGON

Fort Rock

Christmas L.

Mount Thielsen

Crater L.

CRATER LAKE NATIONAL PARK

Rogue R.

Summer L.

Paisley

L. Abert

Mount McLoughlin

Upper Klamath L.

MEDFORD

ABERT RIM

Plush

Oregon Caves National Monument

Lakeview

Klamath R.

MODOC PLATEAU

Goose L.

CALIFORNIA

KLAMATH MOUNTAINS

Mount Shasta

BRITISH COLUMBIA

Mount Shuksan

Harts Pass

PICKETT RANGE

NORTH CASCADES NATIONAL PARK

MONASHE

Mount Baker

L. Chelan

METHOW VALLEY

Okanogan R.

OKANOGAN HIGHLANDS

MONASHE

Arlington

Bonanza Peak

Pateros

Brewster

Grand Coulee D.

Coulee City

WASHINGTON

Stevens Pass

Mount Stuart

Snoqualmie Pass

Wenatchee

CHANNELED SCA

WENATCHEE MOUNTAINS

Easton

Ellensburg

Moses L.

SADDLE MOUNTAINS

Priest Rapids Dam

Yakima

YAKIMA RIDGE

RATTLESNAKE HILLS

SNA

LOST HORSE PLATEAU

Yakima R.

Richland

TOPPENISH RIDGE

Kennewick

Pasco

Ice Harbor Dam

HORSE HEAVEN HILLS

McNary Dam

John Day Dam

Wallula Gap

Laurel

COLUMBIA R.

Umatilla R.

Wal

Pendleton

CASCADE RANGE

Condon

BLUE MOUNT

COLUMBIA PLATEAU

John Day Fossil Beds

John Day

Unity

Malheur R.

Silvies R.

Malheur L.

Harney L.

OREGON DESERT

Donner and Blitzen R.

WARNER VALLEY

Frenchglen

STEENS MOUNTAIN

Hart Mountain National Antelope Refuge

HART MOUNTAIN

NEVADA

Owyhee

Arrow L.
Brilliant

SELKIRK MOUNTAINS

Pend Oreille R.

Priest L.

Kootenai R.

Pend Oreille L.

Coeur d'Alene R.

• Coeur d'Alene

Coeur d'Alene L.

St. Joe R.

LEWISTON

Clearwater R.

HS

Hells Canyon

SEVEN DEVILS MOUNTAINS

Weiser R.

Salmon R.

He Devil Peak

Hells Canyon Dam

SALMON RIVER MOUNTAINS

BITTERROOT MOUNTAINS

SAWTOOTH MOUNTAINS

IDAHO

• Stanley

Borah Peak

Hyndman Peak

PIONEER
MOUNTAINS

Payette R.

Boise R.

★ BOISE

Craters of the Moon
National Monument

rio •

SNAKE R.

• Hagerman

Thousand Springs

• TWIN FALLS

Milner Dam

ALBERTA

WATERTON LAKES NATIONAL PARK

GLACIER NATIONAL PARK

LEWIS RANGE

CONTINENTAL DIVIDE

ROCKY

Hungry Horse Res.

Flathead L.

MISSOURI R.

MONTANA

MISSOULA •

Lolo Pass

Clark Fork R.

HELENA ★

ANACONDA •

• BUTTE

• Bozeman

M
O
U
N
T
A
I
N
S

LOST RIVER RANGE

Little Lost R.

Big Lost R.

Birch Cr.

Arco •

SNAKE RIVER PLAIN

• IDAHO FALLS

Jackson L.

WYOMING

American Falls Res.

• POCATELLO

THE NORTHWEST
Physical Features

Scale in Miles

0   50   100   150

The body type for this book is Baskerville, set by Hazeltine Typesetting, Oakland, California. The display faces are Melior, set by Atherton's of Palo Alto, California. Lithography and color separations are by Graphic Arts Center of Portland, Oregon; binding by Lincoln and Allen of Portland.

Design by Dannelle Lazarus.